World Yearbook of Education 1982/83
COMPUTERS AND EDUCATION

Edited by Jacquetta Megarry, David R F Walker,
Stanley Nisbet and Eric Hoyle

Preface by Roy Jenkins

This now well-established series is published annually with contributions
on particular themes from distinguished international authors.

The World Yearbook of Education 1982/83 is concerned with computers
and education. It argues that today's generation needs information-
processing skills and computer literacy, and shows that computers will
affect not only the methodology of education but also the curriculum, the
distribution of opportunities and the nature of its institutions.

The first part of the book introduces general issues and problems,
including the evaluation of computer-assisted learning, and the impact of
the computer-based technology on teachers' unions.

'Computers in action' is the subject of Part 2. Among the topics discussed
are computer-managed learning, the handling of information by
computers, and the computer as a medium for distance education.

Five international studies form the third part. The cases deal with subjects
as varied as educational computing in Quebec, and software in geography
teaching in New Zealand.

Part 4 examines how computers contribute to subjects across the
curriculum. A final chapter describes an approach to computer literacy for
adults. There is a classified and annotated bibliography, glossary and
index.

Kogan Page Ltd
120 Pentonville Road
London N1

Published in the USA by
Nichols Publishing Company
PO Box 96, New York, NY 10024

WORLD YEARBOOK
OF EDUCATION 1982/83

World Yearbook of Education 1982/83
Computers and Education

Edited by **Jacquetta Megarry** *(Series Editor)*
David R F Walker *(Associate Editor)*
Stanley Nisbet *(Associate Editor)*
and **Eric Hoyle** *(Consultant Editor)*

 **NP**
Kogan Page, London/Nichols Publishing
Company, New York

Previous titles in this series:

World Yearbook of Education 1980
Professional Development of Teachers
Edited by Eric Hoyle and Jacquetta Megarry
US Consultant Editor: Myron Atkin

World Yearbook of Education 1981
Education of Minorities
Edited by Jacquetta Megarry, Stanley Nisbet
and Eric Hoyle
Subject Adviser: Ken Eltis

First published 1983 by Kogan Page Ltd,
120 Pentonville Road, London N1 9JN

British Library Cataloguing in Publication Data

World Yearbook of Education. – 1982/83
  1. Education – Periodicals
  370'.5 L16

ISBN 0-85038-565-2
ISSN 0084-2508

First published in the USA 1983
by Nichols Publishing Company,
PO Box 96, New York, NY 10024

Library of Congress Cataloging in Publication Data
Main entry under title:

Computers and education.

  (World yearbook of education; 1982/83)
  Bibliography: p.
  1. Computer-assisted instruction – Addresses,
essays, lectures. 2. Educational technology –
Addresses, essays, lectures. I. Series.
LB1028.W67 1982   371.3'9445   82-12414
ISBN 0-89397-138-3

Printed in Great Britain by T J Press (Padstow) Ltd

Contents

List of contributors

Preface

Roy Jenkins

This *World Yearbook of Education* addresses an important theme. The impact of computers and microtechnology on our society is of pressing concern. Pundits and serious thinkers offer an endless variety of conflicting visions of the future. The education system has to do more than this; it must help to shape that future now, and provide for needs as yet unknown.

To the politician and to the interested citizen, concern must be two-fold. How can the education system best assist the nation as a whole to take advantage of the new technology to create greater prosperity and a more thriving economy? What should it offer young people (and adults) so that they may understand, rather than fear, the tools at their disposal, using them and the wealth they generate to organize a humane community? These questions have implications for the purposes, the content and the methodology of education. Some of them are of particular concern to professional educators, some to computer experts. They are discussed later in this book.

The prosperity of an individual country decreasingly depends upon natural resources and geographical situation. This is not to dismiss fortunate windfalls such as North Sea oil which, if carefully exploited, can bring substantial benefits. However, the growth industries of the future, perhaps especially those heavily dependent on microtechnology, will not be tied to coalfields, oil-wells or good harbours. They will be mobile, drawn to reservoirs of skilled labour and scientific expertise rather than to any natural commodity. It is the task of the education service to ensure that those human resources are developed and fruitfully applied.

The cultivation of such human resources is the most obvious of the services which education can yield to economic development. It has received much attention; in most developed countries, programmes of study designed to produce computer scientists and technologists are being mounted in universities, colleges and schools. There are, however, other types of study which must be promoted with equal urgency if the full economic gains are to be realized.

Automation through microtechnology increasingly becomes the key to efficient manufacturing. Such is the scale of the manpower savings involved that not even the most massive imaginable expansion of trade nor of the scale of production can hope to maintain the manufacturing labour force. A successful search for new markets and an improvement in everyday clothing ensured that the Spinning Jenny and the Mule would ultimately expand and not reduce the textile work-force. No available new market and no further saturation of the world in consumer goods can similarly compensate for the effects of wholesale automation. The coming of the new manufacturing technology will surely destroy industrial employment – and those countries which fail to adapt will lose more through the extinction of whole industrial sectors than will those which succeed.

This is not to argue that automation must reduce overall job opportunities. The new jobs, however, will be in service industries, both public and private. The new technology can indeed create employment, but only at some remove from itself. This increasing separation of the wealth production from the points of employment of the great bulk of the labour force demands new and radical policies for the circulation of resources through the economic and social fabric. It also requires the assent of an electorate 'literate' both in economics and in computer science.

Even in the most advanced societies of the first industrial revolution, the connections between wealth creation and employment, between agriculture or manufacturing and the few simple services were clear and obvious. As the lines of communication become longer, the interdependence of the whole economic structure needs to be more fully and widely understood. The shares of the national wealth enjoyed by different interest groups – both those in employment and those dependent upon them – will become less a matter to be settled by relationship to the point of production of wealth and more a question of conscious social decision. The advance of microtechnology must be accompanied by the development of a new form of liberal education which can provide the consensus for a well-balanced modern society.

This need is further emphasized by the centralizing characteristics of advanced technology. A society where the extent of the economic interdependence is as apparent as is envisaged above is not necessarily a highly centralized one but there is a real danger that it might become so. Many people are rightly concerned that the growth of huge data banks will lead to the invasion of privacy and the concentration of decision-making in undesirably few hands.

Education has a vital role to play in bringing home the liberating and beneficial possibilities of information technology. If knowledge is power, then the computers, data banks and terminals which can allow the contents of all the world's great libraries to flow through every living room in the land must be potentially the most massive influence for personal development. This applies not only to the participation of the individual in government but also to small local units in large companies and trade unions.

Change always presents threat; continuing change permeating every aspect of life can appear so intimidating as to produce mass Luddism or resigned alienation. The only antidote to either is the self-confidence born of knowledge and familiarity. Schools, colleges and universities must produce qualified people able to design, organize and operate the new technology. They will be relatively few in number. The education system must also disseminate computer literacy in its widest sense and accord it as high a priority as to the older forms of literacy. This is inevitably a complex task. It cannot be simply a matter of devoting a couple of hours a week to an arid study of 'the social implications of computers'; neither can it be simple programming for the uninitiated or playing 'Space Invaders' at public expense. No doubt the appropriate provision will vary very widely from place to place and person to person; sufficient practical experience to create familiarity and allay fear is an essential ingredient. To tackle such difficult and important tasks, it is wise to draw on international expertise. By reporting pioneering work from four continents, this book makes a significant contribution.

Rt Hon Roy Jenkins, PC, is a politician and statesman. He has been Chancellor of the Exchequer and Home Secretary. He was President of the European Commission from 1977 until 1981, when he co-founded Britain's Social Democratic Party. In 1982 he became Member of Parliament for Glasgow Hillhead and was elected Leader of the SDP.

Part 1:
Issues and problems

1. Thinking, learning and educating: the role of the computer

Jacquetta Megarry

Summary: The pace of technological change has outstripped the capacity of the educational system to react to it, let alone to influence it. Computers are powerful processors of information and rapidly becoming smaller, cheaper, and more 'intelligent'. None can yet pass the Turing test for machine intelligence, but this may be only a matter of time. The application of computers to aid human learning has so far made little use of the computer's ever-expanding capabilities and much so-called 'educational' software is of lamentable quality. It is a poor basis on which to judge the medium's long-term potential.

There is a debate about how far educational applications require teachers and their pupils to learn to program computers. The package approach makes computer use accessible to the majority, especially if the program is 'user-friendly' and well documented. Critics say that children should learn to program the computer, not vice versa. Large-scale production of 'black box' packages is uneconomic, over-centralized and tends to reinforce the spurious authority of the computer. The use of high-level languages like LOGO is helpful to promote rapid appreciation of the power of the computer, how to program it and how to debug those programs.

Computers will not merely affect methodology, however, but also the curriculum, possibly the distribution of educational facilities, and perhaps also the nature of its institutions. Knowledge is becoming rapidly obsolescent; today's generation needs information-processing skills and computer literacy. Evaluation studies which concentrate on futile comparative experiments have neglected important questions like the interaction between computers and values.

The reaction of the teaching profession is a key factor. Society must decide to will the means to help and support teachers to incorporate computer-based approaches. The cost of hardware is insignificant compared with the real costs of software development and teacher education. The convergence of technology has opened up such tremendous possibilities for education at a distance that the role and very existence of schools and colleges will be open to question. Teachers should concentrate on performing those tasks where they cannot easily be replaced by microcomputers.

Introduction

Only a hundred years ago, the very idea that a machine could be built to execute calculations was treated with ridicule and scorn. Charles Babbage – whose designs for the Analytical Engine and the Difference Engine were hopelessly ahead of their time – died in obscurity after a life of financial struggle. Once the technology became available, progress in calculating machines was rapid and the computer* – as it came to be known – went from strength to strength as vacuum tubes gave way to transistors, only to be displaced in their turn by the ubiquitous silicon chip*. With *fifth* generation computers on the way before many people have come to terms with the capabilities of the first generation, the sheer pace and profundity of a truly revolutionary development is difficult to grasp or convey. Exponential increases are always harder to accommodate than linear ones. An analogy with motor cars may help, for the developed world is already familiar with the radical changes which motorized transport has wrought in the environment, the economy, town planning, methods of communication and even on patterns of life and work. But if the internal combustion engine had developed as rapidly as the central processing unit of the modern computer since 1945, a Rolls Royce would now have 45,000 brake horse power, cost £2 to buy, do three million miles to the gallon, and six could be parked on this full stop.

It is not surprising, then, that these developments have overtaken the capacity of the education system to react. Nor is there any sign of fall-off in the rate of change. Bubble memory, the £50 microcomputer*, flat-screen televisions, videodisc* linked to microcomputers, telesoftware* by telephone and broadcasting, combined microcomputer, screen, printer* and power supply in a briefcase – all these are already here, on the drawing board, or in the high street computer shop. There is no reason to suppose that a plateau has been reached in design progress as happened for the motor car in the 1920s.

It is already estimated that there are more video shops than book shops in Britain – how long before there are also more computer shops? The recent convergence of technologies means that equipment already common in homes in the developed world (or becoming so), like the domestic telephone, television, cassette player and video recorder can all easily be linked to a microcomputer and thus amplify its capacity to capture and process information – in Roy Jenkins' phrase to bring 'the contents of all the world's great libraries to flow through every living room in the land'.

Computers and thought

The term 'computer' is, of course, a misnomer. The average citizen has little use for the complex calculations which can be performed so quickly and accurately – helpful though they may be to those who have to land planes in fog, calculate stresses and strains in bridges or monitor production processes in chemical engineering. What makes the general-purpose electronic digital* computer such a significant development is its capacity to store, process and compress large bodies of information. *Whatever* the original form of the information – whether words, pictures, logical statements, music or even

---

* Explanation of this and other words will be found in the Glossary which starts on page 265.

(though this is much more recent) speech and handwriting – so long as it is capable of being *consistently* coded into digital form, it can be fed into the computer, processed and transferred into meaningful output* in some convenient form. Furthermore, the processing can be logically very complex, involving many stages, loops within loops and even the capacity to 'learn' from experience.

The earliest computers tended to be specialized. The immediate impetus for developing the COLOSSUS machine was the urgent wartime need for efficient code-breaking, and the computer's limitless patience, large memory* and round-the-clock accuracy were obvious assets (despite the high proportion of 'down-time' due to valve failures!). Initially programs* were written to test specific hypotheses, just as the early attempts at programming computers to play chess tried to specify in advance what strategies were to be followed. As programmers became wiser and more experienced, they began to see the necessity of thinking recursively (Hofstadter, 1979). Since a computer has a larger and more dependable memory than a human being, it obviously makes sense to get it to store the strategies attempted together with the results, so that the computer can determine which approaches are likely to be successful in code-breaking, chess-playing or whatever. This marked the evolution of programs which 'learn' from 'experience' – anthropomorphism is unavoidable in the interests of clarity and economy. Thus a programmer can write a program which can beat him at chess, solve problems he cannot solve, crack codes which defeat him. From this arises a certain uneasiness, crystallized by the idea of artificial intelligence* (AI) which evokes an odd mixture of fear, excitement and cynicism in most of us. The notion of programs which learn how to learn, or which 'know what they are doing' (Knapman, 1974) is even more disconcerting. In what sense *can* a machine think? Can intelligence be artificial? If a baby is 'programmed' at birth to learn *whatever* language it encounters, why not a computer program to do likewise? How would you assess whether a machine is behaving intelligently anyway?

Alan Turing – a brilliant but ill-fated mathematician – proposed an operational test for machine intelligence which is helpful in thinking about these questions (Turing, 1950). He suggested a scenario in which the interrogator was alone in a room with two teleprinters*. One would be connected to a computer, the other to a human being of average intelligence, each in a separate room, but the interrogator would not know which was which. He can put any question to each teleprinter, and if he is unable to tell which is connected to the computer, then it can be concluded that the machine is displaying intelligence. Sophisticated though some current software* is, it could only deceive an interrogator who confined his questions to a restricted topic and vocabulary. Programs can already outshine most or all of us (programmers included) at interpreting space photographs, at diagnosing diseases, at detecting and interpreting foreign bodies on a radar screen, at landing a space craft on the moon; but none can do all of these, however. Few can interpret the meaning of ordinary English from its context, and none can maintain really plausible small talk for more than an instant. At present, then, no computer system could pass the Turing Test. However, computer science is young, and *sophisticated* programs relatively undeveloped; the *logical* complexity of the average word processing*, simulation* or calculation program is not great, although efficient and error-free implementation needs a surprising amount of endeavour. So a machine that passes the Turing test – or at least, one which requires the interrogator to display a degree of ingenuity and native cunning to expose it – is no longer inconceivable. Artificial intelligence – even if we dislike the handle – is already here in some limited senses and may in a general way be just around the corner. Who can say whether Jack Good's vision of an Ultra Intelligent Machine is not just behind it?

All this is so far removed from the nineteenth-century scepticism about calculating machines that we have to ponder what *naïveté* the twenty-first century *World Yearbook* writers will attribute to our present doubts and concerns (if, indeed, this publication has not by then been superseded by an electronic publishing network (Chapter 4)). Whatever the future holds, it does seem certain that there is no longer an easy negative to the question which many find disturbing: 'Can a machine think?' Simple though the internal processes of a computer are, the fact that they are performed with breathtaking speed, accuracy and reliability is of greater importance than the fact that they are ultimately reducible to a series of simple devices – on or off, 1 or 0; the binary* language of computer 'thought' may be no more serious a limitation than the firing or not firing of a human neurone. Now that the number of components in a computer of manageable size approximates to the estimated number of neurones in the brain, the functional analogy no longer seems fanciful, though it raises challenging philosophical and psychological questions.

Computers and learning

The previous section sought to establish the credentials of computers as rapidly developing thinking machines. Their capabilities have hardly begun to be exploited by the very simple (if useful) drill and practice software which most people with any experience of the subject associate with the idea of computer-assisted instruction*, nor by the mechanized programmed learning which is sometimes called the 'tutorial' mode of computer-assisted instruction. Of course, there is already a wide range of 'educational' software – and much of it is of dismal quality, poorly documented, gimmicky and unimaginative, some of it actually dangerous in the sense that prolonged inexperienced use could lead to the perpetuation of maladaptive strategies, and the learning of errors. Given the youth of the field, this is hardly surprising. It would be as wrong-headed and shortsighted to base forecasts of the future potential of computers to assist learning on the present offerings as to have predicted the likely future of books in education 25 years after the development of the first mass printing press.

Imagine the scenario: Mainz in 1482 and Johann Gutenberg confronts a collection of scribes, monks and professors with the first educational textbooks. Typographical conventions have yet to be evolved and modern ideas of layout and design are undreamed of. The ill-assorted display includes books which require a variety of different and expensive special lighting arrangements to read them, and use a variety of different scripts, dialects and languages (a disadvantage handsomely offset by the publishers' offer of a free dictionary or set of translation tips). Furthermore the teachers (unless they have been on special crash-reading courses) are partly or wholly illiterate because many of them left school before the printing press had been widely talked about or even invented. Worse still, the advocates of the newfangled book lobby allowed themselves to get carried away by the possibilities of mass production and mass markets, and wild and tactless claims about books replacing teachers have been bandied about in a way the teachers understandably find threatening – especially as this invention seems to be a bit more revolutionary than the last fad which was supposed to revolutionize their teaching methods . . . . Coming back to the present day, it may be obvious to many that technological progress has outstripped the education system's capacity to apply it calmly and creatively, but it is only clear to the minority of insiders that the sales overkill has been counter-productive and inimical to the industry's best interests.

There are various schools of thought about how computers should and could assist learning. Some argue that it is a specialist job to produce good quality educational software, and much effort and thought has gone into good design and the development of 'house style' by various notable centres in North America and Europe, most of which have been based on universities or government-sponsored projects. Centres of excellence like the pioneering Huntington Project at the State University of New York and Chelsea College, London, developed 'packages' for mainframe* computers in the 1960s and 1970s which were subsequently adapted to the microcomputers which began to spread widely in the latter 1970s. Many of these were simulations of experiments which would be too difficult, dangerous, expensive or time-consuming for students to perform personally, or mathematical models of systems which the student could explore operationally, for example by varying one parameter and observing its effect upon other variables. Such packages often made good use of the computer's power and flexibility, and later ones made good use of graphics* and animation*. Some even had excellent documentation* which helped the student and teacher to extract maximum benefit from them. The skills required to produce such a package are specialized, as they need elegant programming, good educational design, excellent screen layout, good dialogue, convincing graphics, and 'crash-proofing' to combat accidental and deliberate sabotage by users who know little or nothing of the computer's functioning, still less of the programming language* in which the package is written. It takes anything from 50 to 500 skilled man-hours to produce and document a single hour of student-contact time this way and such packages are thus extremely expensive to develop if the manpower input is properly costed.

Critics of this approach have not only pointed to the impossibly high cost of developing and updating significant proportions of each student's learning time in each subject by these means. They also argue that the 'package' mentality gives users the wrong approach to the uses of the computer. Programs should not be perceived as a black box whose workings are mysterious, but should be transparent to enquiry and questioning. The authority of the computer risks being even more spurious and even less open to question than the printed word, and is the more dangerous when concealed in the workings of a program. To combat this, Dwyer (whose pioneering Project Solo began in 1969) developed ways of helping students to take charge of the computer; drawing his analogy from learning to pilot an aeroplane, he argued that successful experience under dual control is a necessary preparation for flying solo (Dwyer and Critchfield, 1981).

By contrast, the assumption of those who have sought to produce user-friendly* packages is that computer expertise will continue to be the province of a few. Most people, they might argue, are content to fly as passengers; only a few have the dedication and perhaps capability to train as pilots. Thus the average teacher – and, at a further remove, the average and not-so-average student – is cast in the role of consumer, or vicarious consumer, of goods produced centrally by experts. Because so much specialized manpower is needed to produce the package, the economic imperative dictates a mass market for the product. The consumers need not go to the trouble of learning or trying to learn the language in which the program is written – and some package designers do not try particularly hard to raise questions in their minds about the model which may be buried deeply within.

It may be tempting to throw at the proponents of this view various critical accusations, such as intellectual authoritarianism, *élitism*, and centralization. However, the issue is not so simple. To return to the example of the motor car, it would be wholly unjustifiable to restrict driving licences to such would-be drivers as can explain the principles of the four-stroke combustion cycle, and just as irrational to prevent students from discussing the environmental impact of motorized transport unless they could first pass a Heavy Goods Vehicle proficiency test. Indeed, the effect of such an insistence would be far more *élitist* than the policy of those who seek to distinguish the different levels of computer comprehension. Far Eastern culture may be appreciated by many more people than those who can read Mandarin, let alone speak it, to say nothing of the other Chinese languages.

Furthermore, the tendency to centralize production of software packages stems from the specialist needs of a design team and the hard economic fact that a development overhead of, say £10,000 would pose an intolerable obstacle to small-volume sales but can be spread out at £2 per package on a sale of 5000. We accept that the publishing of school textbooks is centralized, it is argued, and do not insist that all teachers should produce their own textbooks. Why then should we baulk at the same principle for computer software?

This argument can be rebutted at a number of levels. The most conservative response is to focus on the need for teachers to have genuine freedom of choice in how they integrate computer software into their teaching. This requires that they are able to make an active choice among a variety of possible approaches, not be dictated to passively by the hardware* they possess or the language their machine supports. As Gray notes in Chapter 2, the introduction of computers can, if mishandled, result in the undermining of the professional skills of teachers. Teachers should be encouraged to adapt packages locally to suit their pupils and their curriculum, especially in subjects like geography, as Forer notes in Chapter 16. This requires not only enlightened design by the software houses but also sufficient confidence and familiarity with the workings of the package and the language in which it is written. Even if every teacher does not write his/her own textbook, most at least believe that they could do so if sufficiently motivated, and many suspect deep down that they would produce far better results than the publishers.

Thus 'textbook literacy' allows teachers to be discriminating consumers, to pick and choose, to use selected passages or chapters, to devise follow-up work cards, to use audio-visual enrichment and to adapt the textbook authors to local circumstance. A high level of computer literacy* is required among teachers if they are to feel similarly in control of computer software, though in Chapter 7 Lewis explains an interesting 'keyword' technique for giving users easy control over software which also helps teachers to adapt software to their pupils' needs without having to master a programming language. As we have already noted, a computer program is not like a book. It cannot be browsed through, though good documentation can partly remedy this as Tagg has demonstrated (Chapter 10); the attempt to use sections of a program is likely to lead to quite unexpected difficulties elsewhere, its language and structure may be quite inaccessible; and so on. Returning to the apparently inviting driving analogy, there are circumstances (eg high Alpine roads or a breakdown in the Sahara) in which some understanding of the principles behind the internal combustion engine can be a life-saver.

Thus even if the rapid spread of computers leaves the traditional classroom dynamics of teacher, student and educational resource material unchanged, difficulties inherent in the concept of 'teacher-proof' packages are not only economic ones. More fundamental problems abound. It was argued in the first section that the intellectual power of computers is increasing rapidly. It seems conspicuously wasteful, therefore, to persist in using them either as elaborate teaching machines, turning pages of pre-designed text and graphics according to predetermined rules, or as super slide rules, to save pupils the trouble and distraction of elaborate calculations irrelevant to the purpose in hand, or even (more recently) as all-singing, all-dancing, audio-visual jack-in-the-boxes. Their capacity to shine in any of these roles should not distract, the argument goes, from their manifest failure to capitalize on the immense power of the modern computer.

Since Turing proposed his test, a number of key academics have developed a discipline under the somewhat Orwellian label of artificial intelligence. They have devoted their energies to a variety of tasks in robotics, machine perception and computer interfacing*. One area of research which is of especial importance to the use of computers for learning has been the development of high-level languages* radically more accessible to the non-specialist than programming languages such as BASIC*. In so doing, they have opened up new possible ways for the computer to assist the process of learning.

Powerful author languages* like LOGO* allow easily-learned and quasi-natural communication between human and computer. Quite young children and handicapped learners can learn to control the computer by these means. Howe in Chapter 6 and Geoffrion in Chapter 21 document exciting successes achieved by work in this tradition. The availability of languages like LOGO on microcomputers offers a radically different perspective on the relationship between teacher, student and micro. As Papert (1980:5) remarks, instead of the computer being used at the teacher's behest to program the child, the child programs the computer and in so doing extends his own understanding.

Papert and Howe (Chapter 6) have demonstrated the value of a robot-like toy called a Turtle as concrete 'object-to-think-with'. In building a program to make the Turtle execute a chosen manoeuvre, the child learns how to recognize bugs* and learns the very process of debugging*. (Although the original Boston Turtles were expensive experimental prototypes, it is interesting to see the arrival of toys like Big Trak which, though much more limited in their capabilities than Turtles, can be used similarly in the learning of dynamic computational geometry. They run on batteries and can be bought in toy shops for the price of a good paddling pool.) Crucial to Papert's thinking (which can only be hinted at here) is the notion of computers helping children to develop and debug their own conceptual structure naturally, as a baby learns to speak, by trial and error, practice and immersion in a cultural climate which is conducive to learning. This is greatly removed from the attempt to impose received wisdom and alien conceptual structures on the child through the medium of computer-assisted instruction.

The role of the computer in centralizing learning is a major theme in the literature of computer-managed learning*. Many CML workers, as McMahon explains in Chapter 8, have assumed a tidily structured learning cycle* into which fits neatly the computer's capacity to test, assess answers and prescribe routes and remedies. The technology easily lends itself to student profiles*, routing* instructions and comprehensive performance reports, both of individuals and of cohorts of students. This facility produces dangers. Too many CML workers have developed systems which force a rigid and over-simplified model of knowledge on the teacher and a linear, modularized method of learning upon the student.

Computers and education

It is clear, then, that computers can be helpmates and catalysts in the process of human learning, and also that their arrival raises major questions and poses certain dangers. Their educational significance is not confined to *how* teaching is done; they will profoundly affect *what* is taught, in a much more fundamental way than the addition of computer studies (Chapter 18) as another slot in the timetable. Such curriculum change will demand different skills and perhaps a new role for the teaching profession. In the longer term the microelectronics* revolution places a question mark over the very existence of schools and colleges as educational institutions.

The 'information generation' became a catch phrase in the UK during 1982, the Year of Information Technology. The explosive growth of knowledge and the spectacular advances in microtechnology have underlined the importance of teaching students *how* to learn and *how* to retrieve information, rather than facts and even skills which may become rapidly obsolescent. The education system has yet to catch up with the speed of change in the world outside; as witnessed by the omission in a 1982 Advanced Level physics paper of any reference to microelectronics. The curriculum is in danger of becoming increasingly dated and irrelevant.

Nor does this concern about curriculum merely affect the educational needs of the specialist manpower required by a post-industrial society. Computer literacy is now the birthright of every citizen. During the nineteenth century, the industrial revolution gradually led to a reassessment of the marginal status of science – once an extracurricular option – so that it took its place as a permanent and mainstream feature of the formal curriculum. Similarly, what Toffler (1980) calls the Third Wave must surely bring computers and their implications into the school curriculum if tomorrow's citizens are to have any tools for understanding what is happening (and about to happen) to their jobs, their lifestyle and their leisure pursuits. The age of the personal computer* should deprofessionalize computer science much faster than the advent of mass printing challenged the monopoly of the literate *élite*.

Awareness of the huge gap between what the average citizen knows and what he needs to know has led to various initiatives in computer literacy. Art Luehrmann pioneered cheap public hands-on* experience at the Lawrence Hall of Science in California in the 1970s, and the 'Computertown USA' movement spawned imitations elsewhere. More recently in the UK, the British Broadcasting Corporation has just launched a major initiative (Chapter 22). It is an example which combines high-quality central provision with flexible local tutorial support and self-help groups. This model could well be exported or imitated.

Given the world-wide recession and the decline in recruitment to the teaching profession, a major question for its survival and development is how it will respond to the challenge of microelectronics. One possibility is the 'head-in-the-sand' posture which takes support from the weary 'we've heard it all before' response to an apocalyptic or Utopian forecast for the future. It is quite true, of course, that the advent of teaching machines/television/tape recorders did not – as some predicted – revolutionize teaching methods overnight. Hoyle recalls the fate of recent innovations in Chapter 5. Indeed, cynics might observe that the arrival of the printing press has barely changed methods of teaching in some university arts faculties since the Middle Ages. In schools generally, the basic armoury of exposition, question-and-answer and written exercises has proved extremely resistant to change; there are powerful conservative forces at work in the education of teachers as well as of children. This is not to 'blame' teachers; conservatism seems to be a natural tendency for human organizations, even in recent groupings like the computer industry.

The QWERTY keyboard – designed to avert the danger of mechanical type-writer keys jamming – has been perpetuated in electronic keyboards and has become a modern-day equivalent of the Sabre-Tooth Curriculum (Benjamin, 1939).

The attitude of scepticism of the claims made for computers has derived support from the results of evaluation studies which purport to find 'no significant difference' between the results of computer-assisted learning* and traditional methods. Alas, some evaluators are still wedded to the notion of such comparative experiments, though there are abundant reasons why attempts to assess educational innovations this way are futile, as Walker demonstrates (Chapter 3). The comparative experiment is particularly self-defeating in the case of a new medium like computing which is exciting precisely because it can change the nature of education. Of course, if the computer's role is artificially restricted to that of an electronic blackboard or super calculator, the experiment will probably demonstrate that it has no more effect on the quality of learning as measured by pre- and post-tests than you would expect of a blackboard or calculator. But the crudeness of evaluation methods and the intellectual poverty of its paradigms cannot disguise the fact that schools cannot fail to be affected by microelectronics, and if they try to turn their backs, it will be they, not the electronic developments, who stand to be bypassed.

Instead, evaluation should concern itself with issues about the nature and implications of computer-based learning. Let me suggest two examples. We know surprisingly little about the nature of students' experience when using CAL*. What is the effect of an open-ended exploratory approach compared with that of a closely structured tutorial? Are misconceptions easily acquired, and if so, how can they be rectified? How can the computer program help the student to acquire a new concept meaningfully and avoid imposing it just because it leads to right answers? Laurillard explores some of these issues in Chapter 20, but there is plenty of scope for further research of this kind.

A second fertile topic for evaluators is that of computers and values. There is no such thing as a value-free methodology. A professor who maintains a monologue is teaching many hidden messages in addition to his words – that received wisdom is transmitted in ancient universities, that lecturers are entitled to 100 per cent of the airspace, that lecturers are quite often white-haired and bearded, that you pay to learn but are paid to teach . . . . and so on. What do computers teach? Some programs paint a false picture of simplified certitude and bogus binary choice. Others – especially many games – purvey uncritical acceptance of violence and militarism: shoot or be shot, intergalactic genocide, capital punishment for spelling mistakes! Others again show a lack of prejudice and stereotype which human beings could not emulate – not since the Garden of Eden, at least. For example, a computer-assisted careers guidance system is truly indifferent to sex and race and agnostic about supposed 'language deficiencies' of working-class children unless it is actually programmed to be sexist, racist, or whatever. So much of what is loosely called discrimination is actually the unconscious operation of subliminal or ill-informed stereotypes of race, sex, religion or class – but no computer can project a self-fulfilling prophecy of underachievement by accident. Nor can it unintentionally betray impatience with stupidity or slowness, nor provide a different treatment according to age or ability *unless* its program so specifies and the data* for discrimination is provided. So whether the moral overtones of education with computers are positive or negative depends entirely on how they are used. But in the meantime we need more evidence to explode the myth that they are morally neutral, and more evaluation of their ethical implications and the hidden curriculum of using them and, indeed, of not using them. By the end of the century, if the education system decides to turn its back on computers, the message will be perfectly clear, even if not stated out loud: schools are out-of-date, out-of-touch, on the way out . . . .

So the teaching profession has a major task of retraining to do and readjustment to make. While examining authorities are still debating whether or not to permit the use of electronic calculators, some children are already beginning to use home computers, hand-held spelling aids and talking calculators with *speech synthesizers*. If schools fail to recognize the value of such devices or, worse still, try to ban them, they risk a serious loss of credibility with the generation of pupils who are growing up into a world of commonplace computers, liquid crystal displays, animated computer graphics, communication satellites, lasers and videodiscs.

It seems likely that teachers of younger children adapt more easily. Primary schools are in many ways less rigid and departmentalized than secondary schools; computers are less likely to be automatically perceived as the property of the maths and science departments. Primary teachers have less strong vested interests in their subject as a discipline, more openness to eclecticism and projects. But they also have considerable insecurities about their mathematical ability and technological competence; in many cases their diffidence is justified. To breed the confidence in handling computers which is essential if they are to use them inventively and to encourage children to experiment, a large-scale campaign of in-service education is essential. The leader of a British teachers' union has already called for a massive programme with a year's crash course of in-service training for primary teachers in the use of microcomputers (Times Educational Supplement (Scotland) 23.7.82). He points out that unless the management side make available the money to employ 4000 unemployed young teachers to replace those on the course, the government 50 per cent subsidy for microcomputer purchase will seem an irrelevance. Politicians and taxpayers must be willing to finance computer literacy for teachers with hard cash, not merely bemoan its absence with cheap lamentation. Some at least of the teachers' methodological conservatism stems from the fact that innovations have always cost more, taken longer and needed more skills to handle.

The decision is clearly a political one. Whether the motivation is to get qualified potential teachers off the unemployment register (and incidentally thus turn them into potential union members) or an idealistic belief in the importance of in-service education in computers does not affect the issue. The manpower costs are considerable – around £20 million for the scheme suggested, which is more than double the budget of the four-year programme described in Chapter 13. It would be *much* cheaper to supply a free computer to every school. Actually, the surprising fact is that most developed nations could probably already afford to give a microcomputer to *each pupil*. At 1981 prices, a child entering primary school will cost about £10,000 to educate to secondary school leaving age and as much again if he or she goes on to university. The cost of supplying, maintaining and replacing a sophisticated personal computer throughout that time could hardly be more than £500 in total even if prices do not fall further.[1] In fact, taking account of technological advance, the probability is that hardware costs will continue to fall both because of the economics of mass production – especially as demand rises – and also because labour-intensive activities such as education will become more expensive as salary costs continue to rise. Thus, even on the least favourable assumptions, personal computing for all pupils would account for a mere 5 per cent of the education budget – which could, if it were thought desirable, be recovered by an increase in class size of a pupil or two, or a slight reduction in the length of the period of compulsory schooling. (See also Papert (1980:17) for an American equivalent of this calculation which reaches a similar conclusion.)

Technological advance has not been confined to the production of cheap personal computing power, however. The implication of the recent convergence of telecommunications technology with microelectronics has been much more profound. New and exciting possibilities have opened up for instantaneous education at a distance as Hooper demonstrates in Chapter 9. Correspondence education began to outgrow its Cinderella image in Britain with such developments as the Open University which showed what an effective combination of well-designed print and broadcasting could achieve. More recently, major developments in computer-managed learning, teleconferencing, electronic blackboards, private and public viewdata*, telesoftware, videodisc and interactive video have all combined to bring distance education into the vanguard of the twentieth century. Perhaps institutions of distance learning have been especially willing to innovate, or perhaps technology is especially necessary to help overcome the loneliness of the long distance learner. Either way, these developments offer, at the very least, new hope to learners who are housebound and handicapped, like the student cited by Allen at the end of Chapter 22, and to the inmates of a 'total institution' like a hospital, ship or prison. They must also, surely, raise pertinent questions for the rest of society. If exciting and powerful means of education are available in the comfort of one's home, at the touch of a button whenever it seems convenient, why go out to school or college? It is easy to call up dark images of an introverted society, with dehumanizing or remote

---

[1] According to Hansard the average *per capita* cost of public sector education in Scotland in 1981 was £636 for primary school and £1016 for secondary school. Thus, for seven years of primary and five years of secondary the total cost at 1981 prices would be £9032. A BBC Microcomputer model A currently costs £299, a Sinclair Spectrum £125 and Binatone are about to produce a micro at under £50.

control of thought processes. It is also important to remember that a computer-literate electorate will insist that the channels are all two-way and this facilitates direct communication learner-to-learner voter-to voter, without central intervention or monitoring.

For many purposes, teleconferencing or video-conferencing may suffice and may even be preferable to physical proximity. It will certainly save energy and time and perhaps even lead to a higher quality of learning. Just as records have not yet killed off live concerts, the video screen is no substitute for sitting at the feet of a great teacher. Nor is a computer-linked teleconference a substitute for a good debate or seminar. Young children need physical supervision and contact with other children, with sand, water and musical instruments. Yet the arrival of such potent techniques of distance education should at least concentrate our minds on what purposes do and what purposes do not require physical proximity of the learner. This is an issue which the unquestioned hegemony of schools over the last few centuries has led us not to question.

Certain prophets have already predicted the demise of schooling. Evans (1979:228) anticipated 'a complete shift from group to personalized teaching, much of which could be done satisfactorily – more satisfactorily for all we know – in the pupil's home environment'. Wilson (1979:49-50) asked 'might not schools and colleges be up for sale by the end of the century as plentifully as churches are today?' Papert clearly hopes that he is right:

> Schools generally do an effective and terribly damaging job of teaching children to be infantile, dependent, intellectually dishonest, passive and disrespectful to their own developmental capacity. (Papert, 1982:41)

Against these apocalyptic forecasts must be set the powerful political pressure which will be exerted by the teaching work-force to preserve their jobs and institutions. They will argue (as Hoyle does) that significant sociological and psychological processes can only take place where teachers and pupils are gathered in a social unit. However, given the extent to which secondary education is already under pressure, with serious criticism from employers, taxpayers and the consumers themselves, these quotations cannot lightly be shrugged off. There *is*, I believe, an important future for schools as places which encourage inventive learning, social mixing and physical opportunities which no home is likely to emulate. However, to maintain any appeal they will have to adapt themselves to the twenty-first century, to the needs of the information generation and to the demand for greater flexibility in their curriculum, methodology and organization. If the teaching profession is to survive, it must develop and capitalize on those skills which are *not* easily replaced by microelectronic devices. To this end, the teacher education sector requires a massive increase in its level of microelectronic awareness and skills. 'Otherwise tomorrow's teachers will be as handicapped as yesterday's illiterates' (Megarry 1980:265).

The challenge is to provide a large-scale effort of sufficient quality. The world is critically short of people who can face without fear and grasp in full the implications of what has already begun to happen. To spread enlightenment and informed debate we need thinkers of vision and humanity, people of all-round intellect and a liberal education, not computer hobbyists or uncritical enthusiasts for gadgetry. There are real dangers to guard against of miseducation by computer, of excessive centralization, of dehumanizing monotony, of instantaneous and comprehensive searches through data bases* of garbage, of excessive reliance on rationality and algorithmic* thought, of technocratic *élitism*, of a new and sinister oligarchy. Boyd and Hoyle explore many of these in Chapters 4 and 5; it is crucial to avoid vacuous optimism. The dangers must be recognized and discussed openly in classrooms and colleges, within teachers' organizations and political parties, by local government officials and elected members – and in every living room in the land. They do not constitute a reason to try to turn the clock back. That is neither possible nor desirable.

References

Benjamin, H (1939) Foreword in *The Sabre-tooth Curriculum* McGraw-Hill Inc: New York

Dwyer, T A and Critchfield, M (1981) Multi-computer systems for the support of innovative learning pp7-12 in *Computer Assisted Learning* edited by P R Smith. Pergamon: Oxford

Evans, C (1979) *The Mighty Micro* Hodder and Stoughton: Sevenoaks, Kent (Coronet edition)

Hofstadter, D R (1979) *Godel, Escher, Bach: an Eternal Golden Braid* Penguin: Harmondsworth

Knapman, J (1974) Programs that write programs and know what they are doing *Bionics Research Reports No 18* School of Artificial Intelligence: Edinburgh

Megarry, J (1980) Selected innovations in methods of education pp 241-269 *in World Yearbook of Education 1980: Professional Development of Teachers* edited by Megarry and Hoyle. Kogan Page: London

Papert, S (1972) Teaching children thinking *Mathematics Teaching* **58** Spring

Papert, S (1980) *Mindstorms: Children, Computers and Powerful Ideas* Harvester . Press: Brighton

Papert, S (1982) Tomorrow's classrooms? *Times Educational Supplement* 5.3.82: 31-41

Toffler, A (1980) *The Third Wave* Collins: London

Turing, A M (1950) Computing machinery and intelligence *Mind* **59**: 433-60

Wilson, R (1979) Looking towards the 1990s *British Journal of Educational Technology* **10** 1: 45-91

2. Teachers' unions and the impact of computer-based technologies

Lyn Gray

Summary: Trade union responses to new technologies are usually marked by suspicion, merging into outright hostility, whether in factories, railways, mines or offices. In education there has been little evidence of this as yet, mainly because teaching has remained a labour-intensive, low-technology industry. But there are signs of change. Concern has led to industrial action by the clerical and administrative staff unions in response to the introduction of word processors in higher education. Some evidence from US applications of new computer-based technologies in schools and colleges suggests that the teachers' unions might be drawn into similar reactions.

A case study from a Utah school district suggests that the impact of a centralized computer-based curriculum management system gives cause for concern. It led to a significant restructuring of the working activities of teachers, with a consequent reduction in the amount of student-teacher, learning-oriented interaction and an increase in the testing, administration and application of 'teacher-proof' learning resources developed by central office staff. For at least some teachers this seems to have led to loss of motivation and deskilling – a reduction in role from teacher toward that of technician.

The current policies of the major teachers' unions in Britain are summarized, and some current and future areas of contention are considered. These include the development of new computer-based control mechanisms, which could markedly reduce the flexibility and autonomy of teaching staff, particularly in higher education; and distance learning technologies which, while increasing the productivity of some staff, might do so at the expense of the job security of others.

More positively, some possible safeguards are considered, which, if agreed by employers and unions, might enable teaching staffs to co-operate in the development of computer-based initiatives which could develop staff capabilities, increase productivity and facilitate staff involvement in institutional decision-making and forward planning.

Responses to the new computer-based technologies tend to be characterized by extremes either of uncritical enthusiasm for their revolutionary benefits (Reynaud, 1982) or apocalyptic warnings of the dire consequences brought in their wake (Harman, 1979). Not surprisingly, as in the examples cited, the former tend to derive from a management perspective, and the latter from the viewpoint of organized labour. This is not merely a late twentieth century reiteration of the Luddism of the early nineteenth century. Rather, it recognizes that labour organizations exist to defend their members' jobs and working conditions, and that, in the economic climate prevailing in the closing decades of this century, innovation and change is likely to be paid for by job displacement and the radical alteration of working conditions for a significant proportion of those workers affected. Hence, proposals for the introduction of new technologies on the railways, in mines, docks and offices in recent years have been met with vociferous opposition and organized resistance from labour organizations representing the work-forces in those industries.

In the education industry the impact of the new technologies has been relatively slight to date. Debate has focussed upon the strategies for introducing technological innovations to the education service, rather than on the quest for management-union agreements which would protect workers' interests while permitting such innovation. The exception to this has been the activity of the unions representing clerical and administrative staff, which in Britain have used their experience in negotiating the conditions upon which new technology might be introduced to offices in industry and commerce to initiate discussions of the possible impact of new computer-based technology in educational organizations, including schools, colleges, and local authority education departments.

However, in spite of the promise or threat of radical technological change for at least a decade, teaching staffs have remained relatively unaffected by new technology. While the world of commerce comes to terms with the automated office, and the industrial world with the robotized assembly line, education remains a low-technology, labour-intensive industry. The promises held out in the 1960s by the proponents of teaching machines and programmed learning (eg Kay, Dodd and Sime, 1968) remain unfulfilled. The products of the first educational technology 'revolution' can still occasionally be found dust-covered in the storerooms of schools and colleges. The overhead projector has invaded most classrooms by now, but the technological innovation which has probably had the most powerful impact upon teaching and learning over the past decade has been the electronic photocopier – a source of concern for authors and publishers. The resultant rather cavalier approach to reprographic activity and some aspects of the copyright legislation have at least facilitated the spread of resource-based approaches to teaching and learning. However, the combined impact of the overhead projector and the electronic copier has been relatively slight; the greater part of educational practice has yet to be affected significantly by technological innovation.

The new computer-based technologies seem likely to bring to an end this age of innocence in the education industry. As computers (mainframe*, mini-* and micro-* and word processors*) are both acquired in ever-increasing numbers by schools, colleges and education departments, and are deployed by increasing proportions of the education personnel in those organizations, the mystique surrounding them is beginning to be dispelled, and the concerns about the employment and industrial relations aspects of their penetration are becoming increasingly apparent. Evidence from recent studies in the United States and in England and Wales suggests that teachers, both individually and collectively through their labour organizations, are progressing from an initial wonderment at the promises held out by new technology to a more hard-headed assessment of the potential and actual implications for job security, working conditions and working practices. Careful analysis of potential career benefits may give way to the beginnings of collective action to check the unrestricted adoption of such innovation. This chapter attempts to identify ways in which teachers, through their unions and professional organizations, are responding, and might respond, to new technology. As professional associations they are considering the educational and academic requirements and implications of technological development. As trade unions they are considering aspects whose implications affect teachers' job security, working conditions and labour relations.

Two examples

Before examining the views of British teachers' unions, two examples will illustrate how the introduction of new technology into the education industry might affect teachers and their work. One is a case study from the USA, the other from an English polytechnic. The American example is drawn from the state of Utah, where one of the largest school districts has introduced a comprehensive, computer-based curriculum management system. A centrally developed sequential curriculum covers the areas of English, mathematics, reading, art, music, science, social studies, home economics and guidance, from kindergarten through to twelfth grade (18-year olds), although it is not as yet developed in all of these areas throughout the full age range. Based on concepts of skill mastery learning, the system comprises specified goals, with criterion-based, pre- and post-tests together with the appropriate learning strategies and materials. The tests are sent by teachers to the central office, where the school district computer processes them, and indicates the necessary remedial strategies required for the teaching group and for individuals, and/or the next goals, pre-tests and learning strategies to which the class should progress. The program* also provides comparative data* on the performance of a class over a period of time, and in relation to the other classes at the same grade level in schools across the district.

The centralized curriculum has been produced by dedicated teams of teachers and curriculum specialists. Those who have been involved in this development process speak with considerable enthusiasm about the learning benefits deriving from a coherent, sequential curriculum programme with detailed materials for class and individual use which are precisely related through the curriculum management programme to goals and tests. However, teachers who have not been so involved in the development of these materials hold rather different attitudes. They are required to teach a programme whose goals they do not necessarily adhere to, in which learning materials are dictated by the computer program, and whose staged development is not necessarily either understood or accepted by them. Furthermore, a substantial part of their working week is spent administering tests, whose results can be used to reflect upon their competence in comparison with colleagues in the same school or teaching comparable classes across the school district. As a result, the scheme has been resisted by many teachers. Those who have implemented it complain of being 'deskilled', and regret the loss of the traditional teacher's autonomy to decide learning materials and teaching strategies. In consequence, although there is no tradition of teacher union militancy in Utah, teachers collectively seem to have been able to obtain a partial dismantling of the control mechanisms, and the adoption of a more voluntarist strategy by the district administration.

In the British example the issue has not been curriculum management but staff management. The introduction of new auditing procedures in an English polytechnic has been accompanied by an attempt to develop a comprehensive personnel management system, which would include details of staff expertise, projected and actual timetables and availability. This could then be used to monitor the accuracy of timetabled information, and to provide more precise data concerning the distribution of teaching activities, student group attendance and teachers' work-loads. Requests for the relevant information have been ignored by the majority of teachers, rendering the proposed management system ineffective.

New technology and the unions

In both examples, the availability of new information technology* has encouraged educational administrators to develop comprehensive computer-based management systems, which (they expected) would enhance the efficiency of their organizations. However, in both cases the innovations have met with opposition from teachers, whose traditional working practices and professional autonomy have been perceived as being under threat. It is a pattern already familiar in many occupational areas, where the initial opposition is then formalized into union-management confrontation, leading to negotiations and possibly industrial action and/or arbitration. In Britain the trade union movement has recognized the potential of new technology for bringing about technological change, job dislocation and consequential industrial relations problems. The impact of new technology was a main subject of debate at the 1978 Trades Union Congress, and its official report from the following year's conference on employment and technology dealt comprehensively with the impact of microelectronics* technology on job prospects and trade union negotiations (Trades Union Congress, 1979). The report also accepted that the introduction of new technology should not automatically be opposed, but that negotiators should seek to enhance the resultant benefits for workers, by giving high priority to the achievement of a 35-hour week, a reduction in systematic overtime, longer holidays, better provision for public and trade union duties, and better early retirement conditions for older workers, along with improved pensions.

The teachers' unions in Britain have not as yet had to cope with and negotiate about the introduction of new technology, either nationally or locally, to any great extent. In neither example above was teacher resistance organized or formalized; this is in keeping with the historic informality of labour relations in the education industry, which has been related to professionalism and the relatively high degree of autonomy held by teachers in schools and colleges (Stenning, 1979).

In consequence, the major British teachers' unions have considered the impact of new technology from their perspectives as professional associations. The prime concerns to date have been professional and educational. These concerns are discussed below, but it is argued that the unions are likely to have to concentrate more upon the service conditions and labour relations aspects of new technology in the near future, as existing local and informal approaches prove ineffective in coping with the dislocations threatened by technological innovation. Four educational and professional issues are considered first, with reference both to existing policies and potential areas of contention. Then three labour relations issues are discussed, before the final section suggests some safeguards which might facilitate the introduction of computer-based technologies in the education industry.

Educational and professional issues

The educational and professional issues can be categorized under the headings of resources, training, curriculum and access. A basic concern of the teachers' unions is that sufficient resources should be made available from central and local government to ensure that schools and colleges are able to equip their students with the skills and capabilities needed to cope effectively in working and domestic life with the developments resulting from technological innovation. The major national initiative in the United Kingdom is described by Richard Fothergill, its director, in Chapter 13. While the objective of introducing microcomputers into all schools by the end of 1984 has been generally welcomed by the teachers' unions, some aspects of the government's proposals have been severely criticized. The major criticisms have focussed upon resource issues. The government's Microelectronics Education Programme (MEP) was reduced in scale by some 25 per cent from an already meagre base of £12 million, with a reduced time-scale and a requirement that the Department of Industry grant for hardware* purchase must be matched by an equivalent contribution from the school, local education authority or some other source.

The proliferation of central government funding sources for computing hardware, software* and training support has drawn adverse trade comment. In place of a coherent and unified governmental policy, a variety of central government agencies, including the Departments of Education and Science and of Industry, the Manpower Services Commission, the Industrial Training Boards and the Council for Educational Technology, have pursued what would appear to be unrelated policies.

Other criticisms of governmental resource allocation policies have been focussed upon the directions chosen. Thus the National Association for Teachers in Further and Higher Education (NATFHE) has been very concerned at the apparent omission of further and higher education from the areas selected to benefit from MEP resources (NATFHE, 1982). MEP has also drawn a rather arbitrary distinction between the applications of microelectronics technology and its 'science', excluding the latter; it has given highest priority to those areas in schools where staffing shortages and training needs have provided the most intractable problems over recent years – science, mathematics, craft design and technology, business studies and special education. It has been argued that these problems might be better tackled in other ways.

The provision of training is an issue for which Britain's MEP has also drawn union criticism, because of the low priority given to training in its initial stages. It is ironic that it was the Department of Industry rather than the Department of Education and Science which should emphasize training. The Department of Industry has required schools in receipt of its 50 per cent computer purchase grant to ensure that two teachers from each school attend appropriate training courses. The unions have argued strongly for the extension of computer education throughout teacher education. In a policy statement the World Confederation of Organizations of the Teaching Profession (WCOTP) asked that all teachers 'regardless of their particular subject or specialization . . . must receive suitably adapted theoretical and practical technological training' (WCOTP, 1981). WCOTP expanded upon the nature of the initial training sought, asking that it should make teachers conscious of the dangers as well as the benefits of new technology.

However, British unions recognize that, with the low recruitment levels likely in most sectors of the education service in the next few years, the major training tasks lie with existing rather than potential teachers in the immediate future. They have pressed, therefore, for a comprehensive range of training provision, with the necessary resource support. These include induction courses for incoming staff, at the very least to familiarize themselves with the equipment and software available in their new schools and colleges; and for developmental, refresher and retraining programmes, which would update and reinforce the capabilities of existing staff, and enable teachers to develop new competences in the application of computer-based technology, both as users within their own subjects and specialisms, and as teachers in the new curriculum areas which are likely to emerge in response to new technology. The National Union of Teachers (NUT) has put this philosophy into practice, and has organized a series of residential courses at its training centre, Stoke Rochford, for teachers to consider curricular applications, develop personal computing skills and discuss the social implications of the new technology.

The unions have been conscious of the impact of new technology on the curriculum. Thus WCOTP, in re-emphasizing its policy that school curricula should prepare students for adult life, looks to the necessary revision of curricula as new technology contributes to economic and societal change, and presses for the central involvement of teachers in curricular revision and design (WCOTP, 1981). NATFHE has explored in greater depth some curricular implications for further and higher education. The impact of microelectronic technology on the classroom experiences of students through computers linked to visual display units*, sophisticated simulations* and new forms of individualized learning are all noted, as is the need for examining bodies to include technological awareness in their curricula (NATFHE, 1982). The Assistant Masters and Mistresses Association (AMMA) has stressed the integration of information technology as an additional and very powerful learning resource, and has emphasized the need to develop curricula which prepare pupils for individualized computer-assisted learning*, and then provide the appropriate teacher-selected materials (AMMA, 1981). The NUT, more cautiously, is concerned that rote learning should not be promoted by computer use, and is aware of the dangers of the curriculum becoming distorted to fit the computer's capabilities.

More generally, teachers' unions are anticipating that new technology will transform many aspects of working life and leisure. Such changes imply significant curriculum change – both in the content of established subjects and through the recognition of new subjects which must compete for timetable space. However, curricular changes are seen as extending much further than changes of content. The greater individualization of learning, and the need for new methods provide opportunities both for the development of greater student control over the learning process and the development of a more diverse variety of learning modes, including home-based and distance learning, with the proviso that 'microprocessors* will never be able to substitute for the trained professional in the classroom' (TUC, 1979).

These changes relate closely to the fourth educational issue raised by the teachers' unions – that of access. The major unions have long been concerned about inequalities of access to education, and as such were pioneers in the struggles for comprehensive education in England and Wales (Fenwick, 1976).

NATFHE has drawn attention to the disadvantaged position of women and girls in education, and seeks positive education and manpower policies to remedy it. The problem is not only one of how to avoid further disadvantage – which is all too likely because of the vulnerability to job displacement of the major employment areas in which women predominate (finance, office work and service industries); it is also a problem of how to provide women with the experience and qualifications to find work in the new employment areas created by new technology (NATFHE, 1982). AMMA focusses attention upon the needs of handicapped pupils, and looks to the provision of resources which will develop the immense potential of new technology to facilitate the learning of pupils with special needs (AMMA, 1981). The unions have recognized, however, that new technology might well increase inequality. Schools in remote and sparsely populated locations with impoverished catchment areas could well be less successful in acquiring the necessary equipment and software than schools in suburban and affluent areas, thereby accentuating existing qualitative differences of educational experience. Similarly, within schools and colleges, students already familiar with many manifestations of new technology at home could well derive more benefit from school facilities than those without such home support.

Labour relations and working conditions of teachers

To date the concerns of the teachers' unions have been primarily for the educational and professional issues discussed above. Labour relations issues are referred to only briefly in conference discussions and policy documents. Thus the recent NATFHE draft policy statement on microelectronics and further education devoted only four of its 55 paragraphs to conditions of service issues (NATFHE, 1982). These issues can be categorized under three headings – control, working conditions and job security.

The issues of information control are probably the most contentious of the many aspects of new technology under consideration by managements and unions. Grave concern is expressed almost daily at the new problems of data management and control which arise from the vast information storage and retrieval facilities now available. The information held in this way by the government, the police, the security services, financial organizations and industrial management is the subject of continuing public debate, focussing not only on the increasing amount of such information collected and stored by computer, but also on its security and availability, its accuracy and obsolescence, and the issue of who controls access to it.

In the education industry, concerns about the confidentiality or other-wise of information concerning staff and students/pupils have long been expressed, as, like other professional groups, teachers have attempted to restrict access to their records and associated documentation. It is only very recently, however, that educational organizations have begun to acquire the equipment which would enable them to transfer these paper records to computer. Indeed, in recent years, faced with the increasing computerization of local government information, teachers have been more concerned about the inefficiency of computerized payroll and purchasing systems than about control issues (Gray, 1982).

However, with the elimination of the early difficulties which beset such systems, it is their potential efficiency which is beginning to attract attention. The example cited earlier is just one of many such attempts, particularly in higher education, to utilize the recently acquired computer-based capacity to develop more efficient staff management systems. Such developments have been hastened by pressures on institutions for both greater administrative efficiency and firmer central control and standardization of information. The changing role of the University Grants Committee, the emergence of a National Advisory Body for public sector higher education, and the shift in emphasis of the national financial auditing system to a closer monitoring of educational policies and their efficiency (Gray, 1980) are all combining with the straitened resources available for higher education to create demands for the intensification of control systems for the deployment of manpower resources in higher education.

As yet, union concerns are emerging at local, rather than at national level. The availability of equipment and expertise which can relate individual staff timetables, student timetables, course timetables, staff expertise and attendance registers, enables manpower planning and deployment to take place in ways which run counter to traditional teacher autonomy and flexibility in higher education. Contentious issues are beginning to emerge – for example, the more detailed monitoring of time spent by staff in teaching and related activities, as employers attempt to increase perceived productivity by increasing both class sizes and the number of hours actually spent teaching. The computerization of such information could provide a very powerful management tool, relating forecast and actual hours taught, group sizes and resources utilized. This becomes contentious when related to the institutional and national resource allocation system. Controversial too is the deployment of 'non-teaching' time, whether this is currently unspecified or subject to a conditions of service agreement. A third contentious control issue is the location and availability of teaching staff, particularly as the distinctions between further and higher education and the school sector become more blurred. Computerized staff management systems can locate staff, and record the utilization of the working week. At local education authority level, computerized staff management systems can facilitate the implementation of policies developed to cope with contraction, including redeployment, retirement and redundancy schemes. The insensitive application of such information could become a significant source of conflict at local levels.

Most current discussions in the education industry concerning the impact of new technology upon working conditions have concerned the unions for non-teaching clerical and administrative staff, particularly NALGO (National and Local Government Officers' Association) and ASTMS (Association for Scientific, Technical and Managerial Staff). These have centred upon the introduction of word processors, electronic copiers and related equipment. Automated offices have been blamed for a variety of actual and potential ailments, including eye-strain from prolonged use of visual display units, back ache, headaches and depression. While the teachers' unions, through their health and safety representatives are closely monitoring the health, safety and ergonomic aspects of the installation of such technology for use by teaching staffs, they are also concerned that teachers are not thus being required to undertake work previously performed by displaced non-teaching staff. The introduction of new technology at a time when staffing establishments are being reduced may require clear and more formalized demarcation between the work of teaching and non-teaching staff.

It is the *indirect* effects of the installation of new technology which seem likely to be of major concern to the teachers' unions at both local and national levels. The unions are emphatic that information technology should not be used to increase teacher/student ratios, but argue rather for the need for reduced ratios to facilitate individualized computer-assisted learning. Nor should there be any deterioration in the amount of time spent at work. The efficient use of computers is optimized by 24-hour operation for seven days a week. Some teachers take advantage of this by working overnight and at weekends. However, attempts to formalize such arrangements could lead to conflict, particularly if work-loads are increased while ancillary staff support and appropriate forms of compensation such as overtime payments are not available.

The impact of new technology upon individualized and distance learning methods has already been referred to, but there are obvious implications for teachers' working conditions in such developments. The shift in emphasis from traditional teacher to facilitator and information manager was marked in several parts of the education system before the impact of computer-based technologies was felt, but is very likely to be accentuated by new technology. Already Britain has one of the first, largest and most successful examples of computer-based distance learning in the world in its Open University, where the service conditions of the teachers are very different from those in other higher education organizations. As new technology enables teachers in other institutions to develop distance learning approaches, working conditions need to be negotiated which take full account of developmental and evaluative activities, and which may also need to make allowance for radical modifications of some cherished concepts both of what constitutes 'teaching activities' and of the working week and the working year. As part of their recognition of the potential benefits of these developments the teachers' unions would also be concerned to ensure that adequate staff development opportunities were made available, and that staff were able to meet with groups of colleagues, locally and nationally in the preparation and evaluation of such approaches. Employers are, therefore, being asked to take note of the resource requirements if teachers are to undertake more diversified roles.

The third area of potential labour relations conflict over new technology is that of job protection and security. As in other industries, technological innovations are likely to disrupt existing relationships and organizational structures. While there need not be any reduction in the numbers of teachers required as a result of new technology, the unions are concerned that adequate support staff be provided, so that teachers are not required to undertake either clerical or technical tasks because of new equipment. Rather, many of the routine tasks required of teachers should be undertaken by new information systems, although there is general agreement that the new technology should be used for educational rather than administrative applications. This indeed has been the primary concern of the NUT. But the jobs and status of staff whose current positions are related to their administrative work-loads need to be protected, where threatened, by negotiated local agreements. Areas of particular sensitivity include the relationships between libraries, computing departments (both teaching and service), educational technology services, the teaching departments and institutional administrations.

Safeguarding teacher interests and promoting educational benefits

The major British teachers' unions have taken positive attitudes to the introduction of new technology, but the major impact has yet to be felt in schools and colleges. The time is, therefore, opportune to consider means by which the interests of teachers and students might most effectively be met in preparing for technological innovation. At both local and national levels, in schools and colleges, three interrelated themes would seem likely to dominate discussions concerning computer-based technologies – those of teaching/ learning methods, staff development and consultative processes.

The impact of computers on teaching and learning methods is considered in detail in the first chapter of this book. It is ironic that potentially radical changes in the nature of a teacher's work and of pupil learning are occurring at a time when the specification of the former – and thus by implication the latter – is becoming increasingly formalized through the development of conditions of service agreements. These already exist in further and higher education in the UK and also in the Scottish school system; the issue is under discussion for schools in England and Wales. Such agreements can provide a basis from which different and more flexible working conditions for substantial groups of teachers can be negotiated, to facilitate the effective utilization of new technology. It seems likely that for many teachers the traditional five-day week and three-term year will become increasingly irrelevant, and the experience of teaching a class of 20 or 30 students by traditional methods increasingly uncommon. If such teachers are to work effectively without being exploited, a firm and clear conditions of service agreement would seem essential. This would need to define carefully the working week and year, covering such issues as the length and timing of vacations and sabbaticals, the provision of allowances for working 'unsocial hours' and methods for taking proper account of time spent in research, development, administration and evaluation activities. Agreement would also be required about the provision of resources, both human and material. A far-sighted agreement would give protection against unforeseen changes in working conditions, organizational structures and technology which could rapidly make courses, skills, teaching materials and jobs obsolete.

With the support of such an agreement, although the teacher will remain irreplaceable, the nature of his/her work can alter radically, to take full advantage of the opportunities presented by new technology to increase the effectiveness of teaching and learning processes. Staff development is a necessary concomitant. Employers must realize that investment in a comprehensive and career-long range of training and associated activities is an essential accompaniment to investment in new technology. They need also to appreciate that the teachers' unions can themselves contribute effectively to meeting some of these needs. However, staff development involves far more than course attendance. It can include the creation of new organizational structures, and the encouragement of extra-institutional networks. The development of such networks in special education as part of the MEP is a useful, if under-resourced model here. Even more fundamentally, staff development policies cannot be applied top-down by managements and employers. A collaborative model of staff development, in which teachers are represented by their professional associations and unions, is far more likely to achieve the necessary combination of teacher expertise and teacher motivation.

In turn, this relates to the final issue, that of consultation and institutional management. New technology will create a host of new pressures and demands upon those with management and administrative responsibilities, both within and outside schools and colleges. The managers have their own staff development needs, especially in personnel management fields, and it seems unlikely that existing management systems and structures will be able to cope with the resultant strains. Resources for the development of new, more effective systems and management processes can be drawn from the new technology itself, and from both within and outside the educational institutions. But if these resources are to be mobilized and deployed effectively, consultative processes are needed which take full advantage of the experience and expertise of the professional associations and unions. Co-operative rather than adversarial models of management-union relations are far more likely to release the energies and expertise of teachers, and promote the discovery of new and more effective ways whereby technological innovation can be used to the benefit of students and the local community. Such developments contain risks for management and unions.

New technology is but one of a densely interrelated range of issues, which is unlikely to be perceived as of prime importance by either side for most of the time when faced with more urgent issues. However, if new technology is to fulfil its potential for producing a better informed and more democratic society, this must be demonstrated at the point where students first are taught to recognize this potential. The open availability of computer-stored information, and its use in the operation of more informed consultative and management processes will require very different attitudes and responses from both management and unions. For schools and colleges to become better models of the democratic society for which they aspire to prepare their members, changes in both management and union practices will be necessary. This will depend as much upon the quality of union leadership at local levels as upon management capabilities. Effective trade unionism requires a democratic context, and educational institutions have not normally been renowned for their internal democracy. The effective adoption of new technology in education seems likely both to require and to produce major changes in the management of educational institutions and the roles played by the teachers' unions. Appropriate changes are urgent if the new technology is to realize its potential to extend staff capabilities, to increase productivity, and above all to produce more effective teaching and learning in an informed and democratic setting.

References

Assistant Masters and Mistresses Association (1981) *New Information and Communication Technologies and Secondary Education* AMMA: London

Fenwick, I (1976) *The Comprehensive School 1944-1970* Methuen: London

Gray, L (1982) *The Management of Resources in Primary Schools* Sheffield Papers in Education Management: Sheffield

Forester, T (1980) *The Microelectronics Revolution* Basil Blackwell: Oxford

Harman, G (1980) How to fight the new technology *in* Forester (1980)

Kay, H, Dodd, B and Sime, M (1968) *Teaching Machines and Programmed Instruction* Penguin Books: Harmondsworth

National Association of Teachers in Further and Higher Education (1982) *Draft Association Policy Statement on Microelectronics and Further Education* NATFHE: London

Reynaud, B (1982) No cause for people concern *Management Today* April 1982 37-40

Stenning, R (1979) The changing nature of employment relations in secondary schools *Educational Administration* 7 2:99-121

Trades Union Congress (1979) *Employment and Technology* TUC: London

Waitt, E *ed* (1980) *College Administration* NATFHE: London

World Confederation of Organizations of the Teaching Profession (1981) *Implications of New Technology for Society and the Impact on Educational Policy and Provision* WCOTP: Morges, Switzerland

3. The evaluation of computer-assisted learning

David Walker

Summary: Educational computing is moving from a phase of pioneering towards widespread institutionalization. As it does so, the need for systematic and rigorous evaluation of available materials will increase. During the pioneering phase there has been relatively little evaluation and much has been misdirected. Most early work was experimental, comparing the effectiveness of conventional teaching with the use of the computer to achieve the same objectives. This is now recognized to be inappropriate and there is much more interest in the 'trials' types of formative evaluation.

There is scope for a framework for developmental and formative evaluation of materials, especially as more teachers become involved in the process of writing. The major current need is for evaluation to take the form of reviews in journals that are widely available to teachers and which can guide them in the purchase and use of computer-assisted learning materials. The chapter outlines potential areas of weakness in the design of packages and suggests a critical set of features for which new packages should be examined.

Introduction

Like most things to do with computers, computer-assisted learning* materials are difficult to define and impossible to generalize about. Although they share the computer as a common element, that is in many ways the least important aspect of CAL* materials. The exciting and interesting part is the software* or courseware*, which is limited more by the imagination of the designer than by the limitations of the medium. So the problems of evaluating computer-assisted learning materials are potentially as wide-ranging as those of evaluating learning materials in general. In practice this overstates the case somewhat, since at any moment there is a degree of consensus as to what computer-assisted learning material is like and some agreement as to what is good and what is bad. The difference from other forms of educational technology is that the educational options made available by the computer keep changing as a result of rapid technological advance, and this makes the task of evaluation, never very easy, considerably more complex and difficult.

Computer-aided instruction and comparative evaluation

The conclusion of the five-year National Development Programme in Computer-Assisted Learning (NDPCAL) in 1977 marked the end of what might be called the first phase of educational computing in Britain. In their contribution to the NDPCAL final report Macdonald *et al* (1977) summarized the main features of computer-assisted learning as it was then manifested. At that stage the potential of the computer was just beginning to unfold and, rather than attempt to evaluate the whole of the Programme, they outlined the roles that they saw the computer playing within education. They gave evaluation relatively little attention, noting only that, because it made different demands on its evaluators, NDPCAL marked a significant departure from the stereotype of computerized programmed instruction, and that it therefore had different requirements for its evaluation. In the traditional CAI* prevalent in North America, evaluation of the teaching units is considered essential, both at the program* development stage (formative evaluation) and subsequently when the computer-based approach is compared with teacher-based methods which it is supposed to supplant (summative evaluation). The Carnegie Commission on Higher Education had suggested that CAL offered limited advantages. The computer, it said, had been overemphasized as a sole medium of instruction; its true role should be the enrichment of learning, complementing rather than replacing current learning methods (Rockhart and Scott Morton, 1975).

In any event the comparative method of evaluation has come under increasing criticism in educational circles over the last ten years. A series of critics have followed Parlett and Hamilton (1972) in questioning educational researchers' unthinking adherence to a model of evaluation which owed more to agricultural botany than to the study of human learning, let alone of learning in complex social institutions like a classroom or a school. The whole rhetoric of pre-tests and post-tests, gain ratios and significant differences depended on an illusory and fictitious scientific determinism. The assumption that significant variables could be isolated, that teachers' attitudes could be controlled, that the effect of novelty or the arrival of a researcher could be discounted – all these have been seriously called into question and evaluators have turned to more eclectic and appropriate techniques of evaluation taken from the disciplines of history, anthropology and clinical medicine. It is ten years since Seymour Papert parodied the special folly of trying to apply the agricultural botany model of evaluation to computer-assisted learning. He likened the failure to find significant differences in favour of CAL to the failure of a nineteenth century engineer to show that engines were better than horses.

> This he did by hitching a 1/8 horse power motor in parallel with his four strong stallions. After a year's statistical research he announced a significant difference. However, it was thought that there was a Hawthorne[1] effect on the horses . . . the purring of the motor made them pull harder. (Papert 1972)

---

[1] The way in which the behaviour of the subjects of an experiment is affected by the very presence of an investigating team is often referred to as the Hawthorne effect, after the electrical plant where Elton Mayo discovered in the 1930s that workers' productivity was affected more significantly by the act of investigation than by the level of illumination.

Overall dearth of evaluative studies

In spite of the enormous scale of experimentation in computer-based education, the flood of new journals on the subject and the continuing predictions of a sensational revolution in learning and teaching, the actual quantity of evaluative data – trustworthy and accessible – is small. To a certain extent this is inevitable, given the very recent and rapid development of CAL as a teaching medium. Not only is there much more excitement and adventure in development than in evaluation, but the technical advances in both hardware* and software are proceeding so fast that evaluators suspect that the product will be obsolete before they have written their evaluation. Even if the whole concept has not been rendered obsolete, there is a tendency for authors to produce new versions at frequent intervals. It is so easy to make modifications and to produce a new set of copies – much easier than it is with print materials. Equally significant in deterring the potential evaluators is the lack of standardization of the product; of necessity there have to be versions of each program for most of the common microcomputers* and perhaps for mainframe* computers as well. Each of these versions will differ; for instance some may offer graphic output*, while other versions produce lines of text. The evaluator is unlikely to have access to examples of all the machines, and is certainly likely to lack the skills to operate more than a few. The situation will undoubtedly change when the market is bigger. None of these problems occur in the field of books, which can be read by everyone, and which do not tend to go into their second edition before anyone has had time to evaluate the first.

Feedback evaluation

The tradition of evaluation studies is stronger in the USA where it has become linked to the accountability movement and the 'back to basics' drive. The danger is that a preoccupation with evaluation leads to a narrowing of the computer's role to those applications in which it is possible to undertake comparative evaluation. For CAL – a medium which is exciting precisely because it opens up new possibilities and makes different techniques attractive – the comparative experiment is particularly inappropriate. In the UK little work has been done using comparative evaluation procedures, partly as a reaction against the type of computer use that developed in the USA, and partly because of a determination to develop new styles of computer-based learning*, many of which are not susceptible to comparative testing exactly because they open up new learning experiences.

Two approaches can be adopted. One is to specify the educational objectives of the unit and then develop test procedures to assess to what extent they are being met; the other is to develop a package and try it out in a learning situation with emphasis on 'feedback' from teachers who send in suggestions for removing ambiguities or errors, improving layout and design and perhaps adding additional options.

This style of formative evaluation has been characteristic of the prolific

Schools Council Computer in the Curriculum Project (eg, the Geography collection of eight programs and associated documentation* – Watson, 1979). It is an approach which ensures that most of the potentially infuriating problems of poor design are eliminated, and it produces the type of software that teachers like to use, and which they will assess in much the same way that they assess a text book. The approach does not consider the aims of the teaching material except in the broadest terms, nor does it provide any criteria against which it can be judged, but then nor do teachers expect these of a text book or a set of slides.

There is, after all, little enthusiasm among teachers for the comparative experimental approach to the school text book; what should the book be compared with? However, there is a considerable body of literature researching into the process of learning with reference to specific media, and this more theoretical approach to evaluation is now developing in the field of computer-assisted learning. Kent (1982) argues that the weakest element of recent CAL developments across the curriculum has been the paucity of related educational research. He suggests that the reason for this lack has been the pressure on developers to develop, and that in times of financial stringency the evaluation of developments must take second place. Kent goes on to suggest that surveys of current use of CAL and of teacher training are needed, together with detailed studies of the way in which pupils, teacher and microcomputer interact. He proposes to investigate this by making video recordings of students and teachers, by interview, and by interaction analysis.

The need for evaluative reviews

Within the last three years there has been a dramatic shift in the availability of computers and computer software for education. An entirely new situation has been created by falling hardware prices, government initiatives to encourage the use of computers in education (see Chapters 12 and 13), and by the entry of the major educational publishers into the market for computer-based educational software in North America and the UK. Only a few years ago, computers were used only by enthusiastic teachers who were prepared to use whatever software was available or to write their own programs. But in a very short space of time the scenario in these countries has changed from a small band of enthusiasts clustered round a single computer or terminal* to a situation where pressure is being put on all teaching staff to make use of the two or more computers which have already been purchased and are in danger of becoming an embarrassment. Professional organizations such as the Geographical Association frequently receive requests for help from teachers in schools where several computers have been bought before much thought was given to the acquisition of software or the exploitation of the facility. Teachers need guidance and help in deciding which software to obtain; they need the software to be evaluated. There is a real danger of schools wasting money on software that is unsuitable to their needs or just plain bad. Provision of previewing facilities can be no more than a partial answer because it is so time-consuming. In addition to time spent travelling to use the program wherever a suitable facility is available, it may take several hours to become sufficiently familiar with a program to decide if it can be incorporated into a teaching unit.

Although it is no substitute for classroom evaluation, teachers can be helped by the descriptive material put out by the publishers, which should tell them what hardware the materials require, for what age range the software is suitable and what subject matter it covers. Of course most publishers also say that it is easy to use and effective. In addition, there are growing numbers of lists of educational software such as those produced by Computers in Education as a Resource (CEDAR) based at Imperial College in London, and by Wang (1976).

A teacher thinking of making use of a newly published book will usually be able to find reviews of it in the usual subject journals. This desirable expectation is only just beginning to develop for computer software in education. There are several reasons why it is more difficult to obtain review copies of programs than of books: production runs are shorter so review copies would be a larger proportion of the budget – indeed they might absorb a significant proportion of the profits. Rights protection is another problem area; publishers are naturally concerned about violation of copyright. For books at least it costs the would-be pirate a considerable sum to photocopy the contents, and the photocopy is self-evidently inferior to the printed version. Not so for software. A specialized program might have cost a great deal to develop and an unscrupulous reviewer can fairly easily produce copies indistinguishable from the original at a fraction of the cost. Small wonder, then, that publishers are cautious about even lending review copies of programs. Again, there is no established tradition of publishing software reviews and surprisingly few competent reviewers. The editor of *Computers in Schools* recently lamented the difficulty of getting material for a software review section. After two years of trying, the first review covered only five games with educational applications and the reviewer hedged his bets with the caution 'Whether they have any great educational value is a matter of judgement'. By contrast, the following section contained detailed reviews of 14 books on topics relevant to educational computing.

Unfortunately such reviews as these tend to appear in journals that are read by computer enthusiasts rather than the classroom teachers who should be assessing how suitable the materials are for teaching purposes. The need is for reviews of a high standard and for them to be published in the *same* journals which carry reviews of other educational materials in that subject or for that age group. Meanwhile there is a growing network – formal and informal – of views about the limited quantity of software that is of high quality and worth obtaining. The network operates most effectively through the in-service teacher education activities such as those carried out in the UK under the Microelectronics Education Programme (MEP) (Chapter 13), and through educational advisory services, teachers' centres, colleges and universities. It will be greatly extended when each of the MEP Regional Information Centres has established a software library which is available for teachers to browse through. This latter facility is growing rapidly. During the summer of 1982 one of these Regional Information Centres was able to accumulate 300 packages (Blunt, 1982), though the process of assessing their quality will take considerable time and resources.

Educationists with an interest in CAL and those responsible for making software available to teachers may be able to make use of specialist evaluation services. A North American initiative in this area is MicroSIFT, established with sponsorship from the National Institute of Education within the Computer Technology Program of the Northwest Regional Educational Laboratory in Portland, Oregon. MicroSIFT aims to produce quarterly evaluations of new educational software and courseware and is working towards a standardized form of evaluation (Edwards-Allen, 1981). If this style of evaluation could be extended it might provide a comparable service to that which was provided for test users by the Mental Measurements Yearbooks in the heyday of mental testing.

Criteria for evaluative reviews

If and when evaluative reviews do appear in published form, it is important that they should cover all the main features that a teacher will be interested in. First, it is necessary to convey the style of learning for which the unit has been designed. Howe and du Boulay (1979) warn of the dangers of the misuse of inappropriate packages and are particularly worried about the prevalence of drill and practice programs which are relatively easy to write but 'turn the clock back to an earlier era in education'. Linked with this, it is essential that the teacher should be able to tell immediately if the program is for demonstration to the class, for private study by a pupil, or if it can be used in either way.

Second, the program should be user-friendly*. This does not necessarily mean chatty dialogue. Although it can be frustrating if the dialogue is *too* terse, this can be remedied by reference to good documentation. It is a worse fault if the program always goes through the same wordy dialogue each time and allows no short cuts. A good program gives clear and simple instructions to the user. It is neither too concise nor too 'friendly'. There are disadvantages if the student fails to appreciate that the computer is a programmable electronic machine and is unable to think rationally about its behaviour. Furthermore it can become extremely tiresome for the student to have to read the same feeble jokes repeatedly, or to have the computer constantly use the student's name. A more desirable aspect of user-friendliness is 'crash-proofing' – a robust resistance to program failure or inappropriate responses in the event of a wrong or unexpected entry being keyed in. (This can only be tested really effectively in classroom use because the acid test is provided by inputs* which – by definition – the developer cannot anticipate.) It is also important to avoid the need for repetitive typing in of standard information, especially of lengthy or difficult words, and it is helpful if the program is not intolerant of unconventional spelling.

The aims of the unit should be clear from the program description and documentation. The description should make clear statements about the nature of the learning that is likely to take place with the unit. For instance, if the unit is a simulation* to allow the students to analyse the relationship between temperature and the rate of a chemical reaction, this should be stated explicitly in the description.

Underlying this relatively superficial evaluation there must be a critical examination of the educational process that the package is supposed to promote. In the early stages it is easy to develop and circulate packages that reflect the author's enthusiasm for programming rather than concern for the educational development of the potential users of the program.

Equally important is the need to examine critically the model that is encapsulated in the package. I once asked a program designer about the source of his data in some published packages and discovered that they consisted of random numbers. Although he had intended to replace them with genuine data, somehow this crucial step was overlooked. It is all too easy to concentrate on the mechanics of the program when it is running and to forget to check that the underlying model is correct and realistic.

There are very few computer-based learning units that do not need some written documentation. Indeed there are very few computer programs of any type that are not improved by such support. Paper still has the great advantage that it can be taken home and skimmed through much faster and more conveniently than text on a computer screen. This documentation should be clear and well-illustrated.

The value of the program is related to how widely and how flexibly it can be used. A simple drill and practice program dealing with only a very small part of the syllabus is much more restricted and hence less valuable than an applications program or a model that can be used with different ages of pupil and even for different subject areas.

Any evaluative review should give the teacher information about the form in which the program is supplied. Some programs are distributed as a list of program statements which have to be typed in by the purchaser. This is apparently cheap, though it is a false economy if account is taken of the time needed to type the statements in line by line and to correct the errors which inevitably have crept in. Other programs are supplied on discs* that are protected from copying; this has serious disadvantages in that discs are vulnerable to dust, moisture, fingerprints, and magnetic fields. Back-up copies of programs in classroom use are essential if the teacher is to be able to count on them for serious educational use.

In order to help readers to select suitable software for practical use, the evaluative review should at least give some subjective comments from teachers who have used the program, and statements on the extent to which the students found it interesting or boring, easy or difficult to follow, and how long it took to complete a session of use. It should also make clear what the teacher will have to do when the unit is in use, and whether it can be used by individuals entirely on their own, or is intended as an adjunct to class work.

We are just entering a period of rapid development and diffusion of educational computer packages. There is a great need for evaluative studies, both to help teachers in the process of integrating CAL into their teaching and to help those involved in development work to improve the quality of the product.

References

Blunt, L (1982) *Report on the Establishment of a Software Library for the East Midlands MEP Region* Unpublished

Edwards-Allen, J (1981) *Evaluator's Guide for Microcomputer-based Instructional Packages* available from Computer Technology Program, NWREL, 300 S W Sixth Avenue, Portland, Oregon 97204, USA

Hooper, R (1977) *The National Development Programme in Computer Assisted Learning: the Final Report of the Director* Council for Educational Technology: London

Howe, J A M and du Boulay, B (1979) Microprocessor assisted learning: turning the clock back? *Programmed Learning and Educational Technology* 16 3:240-6

Kent, W A (1982) Geography and CAL: research directions *CALNews* 20:3-4

Macdonald, B, Atkin, R, Jenkins, D and Kemmis, S (1977) Computer assisted learning: its educational potential *in* Hooper, R (1977)

Papert, S (1972) Teaching children thinking *Mathematics Teaching* 58 Spring

Parlett, M R and Hamilton, D (1972) *Evaluation as Illumination: a New Approach to the Study of Innovatory Programs* (Occasional Paper 9). Centre for Research in the Educational Sciences: University of Edinburgh

Rockhart, J F and Scott Morton, M S (1975) *Computers and the Learning Process in Higher Education* A report prepared for the Carnegie Commission on Higher Education. McGraw Hill: New York

Wang, A (1976 and annually) *Index to Computer Based Learning* Instructional Media Laboratory, University of Wisconsin at Milwaukee

Watson, D (1979) *Computers in the Curriculum Project: Geography* Edward Arnold: London

4. Education and miseducation by computer

Gary Boyd

Summary: Pervasive technologies have unintended effects, often ones which we do not wish to notice. Aside from the obvious educational benefits and obvious time-wasting addictive characteristics of computers there are other serious effects:

1. incomprehensible and unrepairable everyday machines lead to apathy;
2. pervasive planning for and with machines encourages us to treat each other as things;
3. performance-giving machines rob people of the needed opportunities to give performances to their pupils, and friends;
4. the global computer-communications network could support open educational networking. What it does support is dominative financial capital transfer.

Introduction

Education is concerned with helping people to be *both* more autonomous and more responsible to society in their choices. Computers*, and especially computers linked through telecommunications, can be an effective means of achieving both aspects of the educational goal. On the one hand, for instance, personal computers* with the LOGO* language are a wonderful vehicle for developing abstract knowledge-based potency (Papert, 1980), and on the other hand, computers and video systems used by groups of people linked into networks* can be used to teach co-operation and altruism (Turoff, 1975; Stodolsky, 1981).

However, like any other pervasive technology, computers have unintended effects. The main job of society is people-making (Satir, 1972). All our artefacts, games and liturgies contribute to shaping the roles which people enact, usually in ways which are not consciously understood by very many of them (Jacoby, 1975). One of their ways of coping with life is by 'not wanting to know' about what is threatening or embarrassingly vital. Teachers concentrate on curriculum content to avoid the threatening status-game aspects of classroom life. Educational administrators and technologists often prefer not to see teachers as model human beings whom children copy. Instead, they view teaching as mainly a business of purveying information. The motor car is usually considered to be merely a means of transport, and possibly as a status symbol; but its operation as a machine to teach responsible behaviour and as a symbol of human aspirations is not widely appreciated. The telephone is seen as a communication tool (even as a democratic communication tool), but the fact that it gives a favoured status to the caller (as Intruder) was not publicly acknowledged in North America until the recent advent of the telephone non-answering machine. Television is widely regarded as simply entertainment and news, while its function as a purveyor of models (Eysenck and Nias, 1980) is ignored.

What then are the educationally important aspects of the prevalence of computers which are accidentally or deliberately ignored? How can the balance be redressed (Boyd, 1982)?

Ignored effects on competence and autonomy

As Seely Brown (1981) has pointed out, the incorporation of microcomputer chips* in our everyday machines makes our toy cars and washing machines, stoves and musical instruments incomprehensible and unrepairable. The ability to fix a toy, re-string a banjo or repair a sewing machine has given many people a sense of competence and mastery over at least part of their world. Domestic technical competency is a source of plausible hope and self-respect. People who can fix things do not feel powerless and apathetic; they feel they can do something about the problems which confront them. It is true that chip-based equipment can often be repaired by replacing a chip with its correct replacement. But there are hundreds of thousands of mostly incompatible chips. Moreover, diagnozing which component is misbehaving usually requires sophisticated and expensive tools and specialized knowledge possessed by few handymen. As knowledge of science and manual skills become less useful in daily life, their *prima facie* legitimacy in education will wane. It will probably become harder to motivate learners to attain the basic scientific competence needed as a foundation for democratic participation in this quasi-technological world.

Planning for people

Bruce Bertram (1982) has outlined some essential differences between planning for robots and planning for people:

1. planning for robots may be done by a single engineer; planning for people is planning *with* people – a social process involving negotiation of goals and procedures to accommodate conflicting desires and needs;
2. the planner of robot systems deals with facts; human planners must deal also with beliefs and often, moreover, with beliefs which influence each other recursively (eg if I believe you believe that I know you are going to trick me, then will I expect to be tricked?);
3. plans for robots are reversible; planning with people is not reversible. Past history of belief and trials influences the next step.

Unfortunately, the people introducing computers into our society are mostly used to planning for robots. Bureaucratic managers plan for robotized people, and systems engineers are usually happy only with the robot planning paradigms called the 'systems approach'. The wonderful potential of computers to enrich human learning is frequently missed because the wrong planning approach is employed.

As an example, consider the computerization of libraries. Human planning would start with conversation with scholars, researchers and students about their goals and constraints and their visions of improvement. When a scholar assembles his or her own library and makes it available to students, the methodology of co-operative scholarship is taught. The scholar selects important documents, annotates them and juxtaposes them on the shelves so as to catalyse thought. Borrowing books from such a library is like borrowing a piece of valuable tapestry. The students privileged to do so are bound to appreciate this.

It is curious that when plans are made to computerize libraries or build so-called 'information' retrieval systems, our centuries of experience with private libraries is forgotten in favour of merely automating the worst aspects of institutional libraries.

The institutional library fosters irresponsibility. It does not belong to anyone, so people steal and mutilate without a qualm. A large proportion of the documents are worthless, so losing the odd book is of no account. So much rubbish has to be waded through before anything valuable is found that most students are discouraged. These features have been carried over to most computerized information retrieval systems – which are really noise retrieval systems unless they query their users as to the value and timeliness of material in order to filter rubbish out of the data base*.

In North America, most computer searches are commercial transactions where one is charged for connect-time and data scanned, whether or not it is of any value to the user. No provision is made for the user to annotate the materials in the computer workspace. These design failures are due to planners planning for robots when they should have been planning with people. A good example of a library system (as yet unbuilt) planned with people in mind is given by Ted Nelson (1981) in his book *Literary Machines*. Each scholar builds his or her own library of documents and annotations and pointers to other documents in *one* common vast computer workspace or 'Docuverse'. Each researcher's work is directly linked to his or her sources. Any student can follow the pointers back to the original sources. Quality control in such a system is by reputation. The pointers which the student puts in for others to follow exhibit his or her judgement and either augment or weaken his or her reputation directly (Boyd, 1975).

Local effects on opportunities to perform humanly

Another area in which self-respect and competence is threatened is in the area of musical, artistic and educational performance. Using computer-based tools, it is possible for relatively few people to saturate the markets for music, art and instruction, thereby denying millions of people performance opportunities. It is interesting that the British performing musicians' union is debating a resolution to ban music synthesizers from any studio where their musicians perform. Advanced video graphics* equipment similarly enables a few people to make cheap, massively-appealing visual products for everyone and undermines the traditional role of the graphic artist.

The crux of the matter is that people's prime attention-giving time is very limited. When many people are attending to machine reproductions they have no time to attend to each other's performances. Some of the CAL* courseware* used in schools directly replaces classroom performances of *both* pupils and teachers with non-social private study (Coburn *et al*, 1982:183-5). This is very serious because, as the anthropologist Edmond Hall points out, 'man is art, and *vice versa*. There is no way that the two can be separated.' (Hall, 1976:80).

These developments are commonly regarded as merely extensions of the industrial revolution; the development that made standardized appliances, vehicles and ready-to-wear clothing cheaply available to everyone is perceived as 'good'. Unfortunately there is a profound difference between articles whose main functions are for sustenance (ie food, clothing, furniture, etc) and those whose main function is to inspire hope, such as music, art and education. Automating motor car production mainly eliminates sub-human uses of human beings, but to try to automate artistic, musical and teaching performance is to eliminate the quintessentially human uses of human beings (Parslow, 1981).

Global effects on the teaching of co-operative responsibility

It is in the area of cultivating co-operation that computers, especially in combination with the new communication technologies, offer us the greatest educational possibilities. It is in this area too, that individual and group failure to realize responsible behaviour toward this little planet's living space is most threatening.

A future *World Yearbook of Education* could be composed by educational scholars and researchers everywhere on the globe entering ideas and criticism into a common computer-communications workspace. Students anywhere could call up parts or all of the *WYBE* to read, annotate and make print-outs* as desired, at very little cost. The world's currency and commodity trade have such facilities, which they appear to be using somewhat irresponsibly at present. But education is not yet so well favoured.

Orrin Klapp has made distinctions among what he calls 'good openings' and 'good closings' and 'bad openings' and 'bad closings' being crucial to the viability of organisms, individuals and cultures (Klapp, 1978). Computers are the gate-keepers and couplers of our world telecommunications network. Most telephone exchanges are now computer-controlled; they can provide for group communications as well as person-to-person calls. In the near future both public-key-encryption for total privacy and language translation aids will be standard tariff services. When most telephones are replaced by audio/visual links based on personal computers, and when broad-band fibre-optics or direct satellite links are installed for subscriber loops, we will indeed have the basis for a 'global village' – for the rich, at least. The poor are being offered something else altogether: a limited choice of displays of a limited range of data broadcast to their television sets and radios from a centrally controlled information provider. Radios with data displays like pocket calculators as well as sound and viewdata*-type television sets can be produced in quantity for about the same price as ordinary radios and televisions. Six or seven direct broadcast satellites with large 'footprints' can cover all the populated areas of the globe. It is most likely that commercials with multi-lingual videotex* titling will soon rain down on everyone, providing a new kind of world 'educational' system.

Will these computer-communication systems teach mutual trust or co-operative responsibility (Cherry, 1971:201-5)? Whether they do or not depends on whether educators, journalists and statesmen make a public case for dedicating a large measure of our world communications capacity to truly educational purposes.

References

Boyd, G M (1982) Four ways of providing computer assisted learning and their prob-able impacts *Computers and Education* 6: 305-10

Boyd, G M (1975) The importance and feasibility of transparent universities *in* Evans, L and Leedham, J (1975)

Bertram, B (1982) *Robot Plans and Human Plans* Paper given at McGill University 17 July 1982. Bolt Beranek Newman Inc: Boston

Cherry, C (1971) *World Communication: Threat or Promise* John Wiley: London

Coburn, P, Kelman, P, Roberts, W, Snyder, T, Watt, D and Weiner, C (1982) *Practical Guide to Computers in Education* Addison Wesley: Reading, Mass

Evans, L and Leedham, J eds (1975) *Aspects of Educational Technology IX* Kogan Page: London

Eysenck, H J, and Nias, D K B (1978) *Sex, Violence and the Media* Granada Publishing Co, Paladin Books: London

Hall, E T (1976) *Beyond Culture* Doubleday: New York

Jacoby, R (1975) *Social Amnesia* Beacon Press: Boston

Klapp, O E (1978) *Opening and Closing: Strategies of Information Adaptation in Society* Cambridge University Press, ASA Rose Monograph: London

Nelson, T (1981) *Literary Machines* Ted Nelson Publishing Co: Swarthmore

Parslow, R D (1981) Computerized destruction of Western civilization *Computers and Society II* 2: 16-21 (ACM)

Satir, V (1972) *Peoplemaking* Science and Behaviour Books: Palo Alto, USA

Seely-Brown, J (1981) *Understanding Mechanistic Systems* Paper given at the AAS Annual Meeting, Toronto 6 January 1981, available from Cognitive Sciences Dept, Xerox Research Centre: Palo Alto, Calif

Stodolsky, D (1981) Automatic mediation of group communication skill training *in* Proceedings of the 25th Annual Meeting of the Society for General Systems Research: Louisville, Kentucky

Turoff, M (1975) *The Delphi Method: Technique and Applications* Addison Wesley: Reading, Mass

5. Computers and education: a solution in search of a problem?

Eric Hoyle

Summary: The fate of many educational innovations over the past 20 years does not allow one to be too sanguine about the uptake and institutionalization of computers in schools. Although many individual teachers will use a computer as a supplementary medium to their own teaching, there is little likelihood that the open, flexible resource-based school, which some protagonists believe are presaged by computers, will become a reality. Many factors will inhibit the widespread adoption of computers, such as the values and norms of teachers, their roles, professionalism and job satisfaction, and the structure, management and micropolitics of schools. Yet technical developments have reduced the size and cost of computers, have increased their flexibility and linkage with audio-visual media and have made them attractive to teachers. We are thus in a situation where computers in education have become a solution in search of a problem. Perhaps the only way forward is to adopt a school-focussed strategy of innovation whereby teachers identify the problems to which computers are solutions, and acquire the necessary skills and knowledge to utilize computers through job-embedded, in-service training.

Compared with other chapters in this book, what follows will strike a somewhat sceptical note. It is inevitable and wholly proper that other contributors, who are protagonists of the use of computers in education, should be suffused with optimism and perhaps even outright enthusiasm. I come to the issue of computers in education from an interest in the fate of educational innovations. Seen from this perspective, the potential widespread adoption of computers in schools must be treated in a most guarded manner. The recent history of education is littered with the corpses of innovations which have been abandoned and often left little trace. In the case of materials and hardware* they have often had a decent burial in the bottom cupboard of the teacher who continues to confront the perennial tasks of teaching in a highly conventional way. There have, of course, been changes in the organization and methods of teaching and learning. Classrooms *are* now different places from what they were, say, 20 or more years ago, but in truth they are not all *that* much different. Innovations have come and gone and the educational world has not been radically transformed. For a good 20 years we have been teetering on the brink of an 'educational revolution', but it has never arrived. The means to achieve this revolution have been to hand. We can all conjure up a model of a school which is truly different from that in which teaching and learning currently occurs. Such a model is usually characterized by openness and flexibility. It will include such features as interdisciplinary studies, flexible grouping, independent learning, collaborative teaching, open-plan architecture, resource centres, personalized study programmes and an Aladdin's cave of audio-visual devices and computers available both to teachers and pupils. And yet it has not happened. Disappointed protagonists of such changes have blamed costs, inflexible management, and unenlightened teachers, but the matter is much more complex than that.

Computers are now seen as the means whereby the teaching revolution might be achieved. The use of computers in education is not of course a new development. But their extensive use has been largely confined to further and higher education and to industrial and military training. Apart from one or two well-known experiments in Britain and the adoption of systems like PLATO* by a number of school districts in the United States, the use of computers in schools has been somewhat limited. Of course, factors of size, cost and complexity have had an inhibiting effect, but these are now being overcome through miniaturization, the reduction of production costs, cheaper back-up and greater flexibility. There can now be little doubt that the availability of relatively low-cost, desk-top computers coupled with advances in display technology and the availability of flexible software* and courseware* creates the potential for a transformation in teaching and learning, and a level of educational efficiency far in excess of what schools have hitherto achieved.

The uses of computers in education have been greatly extended by their increasing technical sophistication. One of the major developments has been in the varieties of computer-assisted learning* – using this term in its very broadest sense. These developments have created a potential use for computers in teaching not only in those subjects in which they have the clearest use, such as mathematics, physical sciences and some of the social sciences, but also in apparently less likely subjects such as English, history and music. The computer can thus be used in a variety of roles: drill-sergeant, game-mate, friend with the answers, and so forth. The computer assists learning but is also an object of learning in itself. If computer literacy* is a desirable aim for all pupils then practice in programming and operating will be at the centre of this. Schools are approaching the point where they can prepare their pupils for the computer-related lives which many of them will lead in the future.

Thus, the means of a revolution in teaching and learning are present, and to some degree the climate is right. Teachers and pupils almost daily encounter computers in shops, banks and offices. Friends and relatives may well have direct involvement with computers at work, and pupils may expect to have the same, or greater, involvement when (and if) they enter employment. Leisure activities are increasingly computer-controlled. If teachers and pupils do not have home computers, they will at least be familiar with the advertising that proclaims their benefits. It may therefore be thought that there would be a readiness amongst teachers to adopt computers as a means of enhancing the knowledge and skills of their pupils and as a means of encouraging the computer literacy which may come to be expected of them as adults.

Enthusiasts for the use of computers in education are using them in different ways in many areas of the curriculum. A large number have shown an interest in the adoption of computers to the extent of attending courses. However, one must be very guarded about perceiving these enthusiasts as harbingers of a massive transformation of our schools. On the diffusion curve they would fall in the categories of 'innovators' or perhaps 'early adopters'. The question, the perennial question, is not whether there will be enthusiasts who lead the way, but whether the bulk of the teaching force will ultimately be led. Time and again innovations have faltered after the initial enthusiasm wore off. In the case of computers in schools there is great potential, but their champions *must* take account of factors in the organization of schools, the professional roles of teachers, and dominant educational values if they are to succeed in their mission.

The fate of innovations

A review of the educational literature over the past 25 years would yield the impression that schooling was on the point of being transformed (or according to some accounts *had* been transformed) by innovations in curriculum, method and teaching aids. The teaching of maths was to be transformed by structural approaches, reading by the introduction of the Initial Teaching Alphabet, science by discovery learning, social studies and humanities by television and other audio-visual media and almost all subjects by programmed learning. The fate of these innovations has been variable. Some flared like nebulae never to be seen again. Others, perhaps discovery learning in science as publicized by the work of the Nuffield Foundation, gained a firmer place in the system, but even here there was frequently a disjunction between the discovery – learning assumptions underpinning the materials and the didactic use to which the materials were put. Others, such as television, are now widely used, but very much as an adjunct to the teacher's normal work, or as an interlude, rather than in any way which could be construed as constituting a radical shift in the nature of teaching and learning.

It may well be that it is too early to declare many of these innovations moribund. Studies of diffusion (eg Rogers and Shoemaker, 1971) show that when adoption is plotted against time, the result is an S-shaped wave which corresponds to the learning curve. After a brisk initial uptake many innovations reach a long plateau and will, in due course, experience another period of accelerated diffusion. We have insufficient studies monitoring the adoption process to make any generalizations – presumably because such studies would be lengthy, time-consuming, and dull. But my subjective impression is that whilst some innovations such as the use of audio-visual equipment may well be slowly creeping up the S-curve, others have ceased to spread. Case studies of schools which have attempted to transform themselves into radically different systems for educating children, incorporating many of the characteristics of the flexible school model referred to above, or which have actually been built, staffed and provisioned according to such a model, have had great problems in sustaining their charter (cf Gross, Giacquinta and Bernstein, 1971; Smith and Keith, 1971).

Schooling has changed, but it has not been transformed. Studies of innovation have time and again shown that innovations will 'take' so long as they are congruent with the values, norms, folk-ways and aspirations of the people who have to make them work. Innovation is far more rapid and, in terms of adoption, more successful in industry where market imperatives operate, where coercive means of introducing innovation are available, and where the output is products and not people. In education, normative, re-educative approaches to change are more apposite. Studies of innovation illustrate just how teacher norms operate to modify the impact of an innovation on teachers' practices. One example provides lessons for those who use computers as a means of individualizing instruction.

Carlson (1965) studied the uptake by school systems of a number of innovations which were available to American schools at the time. One of these was programmed learning which was 'adopted' by a number of schools in his sample. However, he observed the manner in which programmed learning was implemented and discovered that the teachers used a variety of techniques to ensure that the individualization of instruction did not lead to too great a disparity in achievement. One method was to teach groups rather than help individuals to solve the problems which they encountered. Another was to allow those pupils making the slowest progress to take their programs* home but to prohibit the faster pupils from doing so. A third stratagem was to slow down the faster pupils by requiring them to spend more time than the slower ones on enrichment materials. A fourth was to provide a special summer session for those who had fallen behind. The norms operating here are obviously quite complex. They could include egalitarian beliefs about the outcomes of schooling, a desire to retain control over the situation, and a continuing need to feel oneself to be the teacher of a class with whom one could identify as a group rather than with a set of individuals. The message from the research on innovation for those who wish to further the use of computers in schools is to be aware of their normative systems.

The normative context

It is beyond the scope of this chapter, and certainly beyond the competence of its author, to attempt a values analysis of the entire social and educational context in which computer-based learning* and teaching could be set. This section will not, therefore, consider the wider questions of the relationship between computers and social values: the issues of control, access, secrecy and so forth. Nor will it speculate on the relationship between computers and the contested values in education: equality, individualism, control, differentiation and the like. The section will focus on three themes, somewhat idiosyn-cratically, relating to the prevailing norms amongst teachers and will explore their relevance for the development of computer-based education.

The first theme concerns the professionality of teachers. Many innovations are introduced on the assumption that teachers are 'extended' rather than 'restricted' professionals (Hoyle, 1974). Protagonists of the innovation assume that teachers see their task in terms of a strict mean-ends rationality. The 'extended professional' is fully aware through reading, discussing with professional colleagues, attending in-service courses, etc of the latest developments in curriculum and methods in the field. He/she may, indeed, be a contributor to such developments. Having identified new developments he/she will, perhaps in professional collaboration with colleagues, carry out an initial evaluation and, on deciding that the innovation has promise, introduce it in a notional manner and subsequently evaluate its effectiveness for teaching purposes.

The 'restricted professional', on the other hand, is the good classroom practitioner who relies much more on intuition, feedback from pupils, memories of previous successes and failures and regards teaching in a much more personalized way. He/she is less aware of potential innovations than the 'extended professional' and, when aware of them, tends to be sceptical towards them. Eichholz and Rogers (1964) studied the reasons given by teachers for their non-adoption of audio-visual aids and although they were not specifically concerned with 'restricted professionals', nevertheless one may assume that the responses of their sample teachers resembled those that a 'restricted professional' might have given. They classified them as follows: Uninformed ('the information was not easily available'), Doubtful ('I want to wait and see how good it is before I try'), Comparing ('Other things are equally as good'), Defensive ('The school regulations do not permit it'), Depressed ('It costs too much to use in time and/or money'), Anxious ('I don't know if I can operate the equipment'), Guilty ('I know I should use them but I don't have the time'), Alienated ('These gadgets will never replace a teacher'), Convinced ('I tried them once and they aren't any good').

We do not know the distribution of 'restricted' and 'extended' professionals in the teaching force. 'Restricted' professionals may be found in both primary and secondary schools and might be either 'child-oriented' or 'subject-oriented' or neither. Similarly, 'extended' professionals will be found in both primary and secondary schools. The point is that if computers are to be institutionalized in schools as an integral part of the organization of teaching and learning, a substantial body of 'restricted professionals' will need to be convinced that they should acquire the knowledge and skill necessary for a successful adoption. Of course, many teachers are currently, and in considerable numbers, utilizing computers in their teaching. However, for the most part it is the secondary school teachers of maths, physical sciences and geography who most readily see the value of the computer as laboratory and the computer as tutor and calculator in their subject teaching. The problem is that the computer industry will take these swallows as a sign that summer is here (or a few Apples as signs of the harvest to come). Yet too often one has seen an innovation fail to disseminate beyond the early phase of adoption. Perhaps the great bulk of teachers are 'restricted' professionals who believe that the essence of teaching is the personal encounter with a group of pupils

where an essentially intuitive approach need only occasionally be
supplemented by more objective-orientated aids and programs which must not
in any way be allowed to disturb this traditional approach to teaching and
learning. Any attempt to institutionalize the use of computers in school must
take into account the values of the restricted professional.

A second theme concerns the values inherent in the teacher's role. By and
large teachers enter the profession because they want to work with young
people. Although a teacher may have a strong subject identity, he/she wants
to teach this subject to a group of, hopefully, eager and responsive pupils.
People do not enter teaching to achieve educational objectives in some
abstract way. They do not wish to individualize instruction as much as to
personalize instruction (Jackson, 1968a). There is ample evidence that teachers
gain their job satisfaction from the personal encounter with pupils, the here-
and-now urgency of the classroom, the autonomy which allows them to
respond to the particular nature and needs of a class, the signs of individual
progress and of the progress of a class, and the collective effort of a particular
class in achieving some goal or in producing something. On these values have
foundered so many educational innovations: programmed learning, team
teaching, resource-based learning and so forth.

In *Life in Classrooms* Jackson writes:

> Sometimes teaching is described as a highly rational affair. Such descriptions
> often emphasize the decision-making function of the teacher, or liken his task to
> that of a problem-solver or hypothesis tester. Yet the interviews with elementary
> teachers raise serious doubts about these ways of looking at the teaching process.
> The immediacy of classroom life, the fleeting and sometimes cryptic signs on
> which the teacher relies for determining his pedagogical moves and for
> evaluating the effectiveness of his actions call into question the appropriateness
> of using conventional models of rationality to depict the teacher's classroom
> behaviour. (Jackson, 1968b:151)

Insofar as the introduction of computers involves a considerable reformu-
lation of the teacher's role, strong resistance will be encountered. Much has
been written of the need for the teacher's role to become more peripheral as
independent learning becomes the norm. The teacher-as-manager, the teacher-
as-resource and similar reformulations have become popular amongst
educationists, but it may be that this is exactly what the teacher does not
want to become. It is estimated that with the PLATO system it takes the
inexperienced teacher 237 hours to produce one hour's work for a student and
the experienced teacher 26.4 hours. Many teachers may well consider that they
did not become teachers to undertake such tasks. However much it is argued
that this approach to teaching and learning is rational, economic and effective,
teachers may well wish to cling to the satisfaction of their familiar role.

The third and final theme to be considered is rationality, especially in
relation to school organization and its decision-making processes. It is
inevitable that the use of computers assumes a complex but ultimately rational
world in which, if plans are well-conceived, clearly delineated, properly
resourced, and adequately communicated, systems will be improved. But we
are all too well aware that organizations are idiosyncratic, adventitious,

unpredictable and intractable. Decision-making even at the highest levels is far less rational than we expect – or hope. With all the computer resources of the US government, decisions are more the outcome of actions taken in highly uncertain situations, bargaining within their own camps and across national boundaries as the much-cited study by Allison (1971) of the Cuban missile crisis showed. In a recent interview, Zbigniew Brzezinski, President Carter's adviser on national security, stated:

> My overwhelming observation from the experience of the last four years is that history is neither the product of design nor of conspiracy, but is rather the reflection of continuing chaos. Seen from the outside, decisions may often seem clear and consciously formulated . . . but one learns that so much of what happens . . . is the product of chaotic conditions and a great deal of struggle and ambiguity. (Urban, 1981)

What, then, are the prospects for rational decision-making in schools when at the highest political levels the process seems to be so haphazard?

The micropolitics of schools (Hoyle, 1982) have significance for the introduction of computers in two ways. One concerns the process of innovation itself. Innovation is rarely a rational matter. It is the outcome of interests, power, influence, negotiation, bargaining, career advancement and a number of other processes which subvert national plans for innovation. In any case, whilst not altogether rejecting the role of rationality as implied by scientific method, one must accept the constraints on its application to social affairs imposed by the limitations of individual and group knowledge and by the operation of conflicting interests. These constraints produce multiple and competing rationalities. Given the scarcity of resources and the competing interests of staff and conflicts in professional values, the uptake, installation and institutionalization of computers will not be the outcome of a simplistic means-ends rationality.

The second significance of micropolitics concerns the structure of a school which would be necessary should computers become the potential catalyst for their reorganization. At the present time school organization tends to be an uneasy balance between structure and autonomy (Bidwell, 1965; Lortie, 1969; Litwak and Meyer, 1974). Within a structure which has some elements of a bureaucracy coping with routine events, the teacher has a considerable degree of autonomy to teach in a creative way, which involves non-routine events. It is not easy to predict just how a computer-based approach to learning would affect this structure. It could well lead to a greater degree of bureaucratization. Organizational imperatives tend towards tight control over the use of a scarce and expensive resource; coupled with the routinization of the learning process itself, this could actually increase central control.

The obvious dangers here would be the increased control over the teacher's work and his deprofessionalization in relation to the task of teaching (although professional skills of a different kind would be required in the preparation of software, programs and materials). On the other hand it could potentially lead (at last) to the open, flexible, resource-based learning schools which have for so long been threatening to emerge, the organic-adaptive structures advocated by many management theorists. However, even this kind of system could lead to a loss of autonomy on the part of the teacher as he/she came to work increasingly in an environment which required co-ordination through collaboration, the participation in temporary teams, the making and re-making of orders and so forth. The professionality of the teacher might thereby be enhanced but perhaps at a high cost in terms of the loss of order, autonomy, and sustained relationships. Moreover, for some teachers the tasks they were required to perform could constitute deprofessionalization. Similar points were elaborated in relation to team teaching by Lortie (1964) who advocated long-term research on these issues. Significantly, team teaching did not 'take' to the degree which would have made such research crucial.

Potential strategies

The protagonist of the use of computers in education may by now feel that I have made no differentiation at all between the many different varieties of computer-assisted learning, nor even between the very different educational functions of teaching through the use of computers and teaching computer literacy. This would be a very fair and valid criticism. I have been making broad generalizations about the adoption of computers in education without dealing specifically with the variety of different uses of computers in schools for which different strategies of innovation might be appropriate. However, in partial defence, one can say that whereas individuals and even research and development units have their own views about the use of computers in assisting all forms of learning, or assisting the learning of certain sets of skills or bodies of knowledge, or enhancing the learning of certain groups – university students, military personnel, the handicapped, etc – there would seem to be very little in the way of a co-ordinated policy at national level even amongst those agencies charged with developing such a policy. Add the fact that *educationists* (researchers, developers, lecturers, inspectors, administrators, etc) are wanting to bring about changes in practitioners (teachers), and further add the compulsion on hardware and software manufacturers to create markets, then we have a situation of confusion and uncertainty.

In a perceptive book on the process of decision-making, March and Olsen (1976) argued that a decision model which depicts the sequence as one of generating alternatives, weighing the consequences of these in terms of certain objectives and then arriving at a decision, bears only a limited relationship to what actually happens. They propose instead a 'garbage can' model whereby events which can be termed 'decisions' are the outcome of the confluence of four streams: problems (eg pay, status, promotion), choice opportunities (eg staff replacements, additional resources), participants (ie the changing personnel of an organization whose different attitudes and attributes will influence specific decisions), and solutions (ie the means of solving problems in advance of the problems being identified). According to this model an organization can 'run backwards' and rewrite its own history to suggest that a decision was arrived at by rational procedures when, in fact, it was an event which emerged from the 'garbage can'. Of particular relevance here is the notion of 'solutions seeking problems'. This would appear to apply to the role of computers at all levels in the educational system. Computers can potentially provide solutions to a variety of educational problems still unformulated. The formulation of these curricular and pedagogical problems will be shaped by the availability of computer resources, but it is likely that the process will be subsequently presented as conforming to the 'rational' problem-deliberation-decision model.

Some groups have clear and limited objectives. An example would be a group of geography teachers with computer facilities in their schools working collectively under the guidance of a geographer in the department of education in the local university preparing programs for use as part of the normal curriculum of their pupils. But it is clear that in many instances schools do not know how to utilize their computing facilities and although they may have a novelty value for some teachers, this quickly wears off and the majority of teachers will remain untouched. Many local authorities are making microcomputers* available to junior schools with little expectation of how they will be used. It may be that teachers will experiment, become familiar with their operation and develop profitable uses for them. But in the light of our previous experience of innovations, this policy looks remarkably like the economics of Paschendaele. The local authorities, polytechnics, and universities will run in-service programs on computers ranging from the general to the specific and particular. Such sources will be helpful to those teachers who have some clear objective, but otherwise their impact is likely to be limited.

The strategy for the encouragement of computer-assisted learning in schools in Britain has elements of both the diffusion model – the relatively unplanned spread of new ideas through the system via a variety of media, messengers and settings – and the research, development and dissemination model through NDPCAL and other schemes. These strategies will certainly enable the teacher who is strongly motivated to adopt a computer-based approach to teaching and learning to do so readily and easily. They may eventually lead to almost total acceptance of computer-assisted learning by the great majority of teachers as part of their repertoire. But on the evidence of the past this is unlikely. This may not be important if one's aspiration is limited to the computer taking its place amongst the many other innovations of the past 20 years as an adjunct to the teaching of a limited number of enthusiasts. If, however, one's view is that computers could improve pupil learning massively, and that computers are going to become so central to the lives of future generations that computer literacy is essential, then a different strategy is needed. Richard Fothergill (in Chapter 13) describes in broad terms the strategy of innovation adopted by the Microelectronics Education Programme (MEP). The notion of recursive training is an important advance on many earlier modes of dissemination. The first stage will be to provide facilities through the regional centres for the further professional development of those teachers who already have a commitment and some expertise: the early adopters. But whereas earlier strategies have not moved beyond this stage, the MEP approach envisages that these early adopters will help to train other teachers. This is an important advance, but experience elsewhere suggests that the effectiveness of this second wave of training may be greater to the degree that it is school-focussed.

The institutionalization of computer-assisted learning will involve quite fundamental changes in the social system of the school. Some of the barriers to such an innovation – values, norms, roles, structures, etc – are quite formidable, and change could only be achieved if the school, rather than the individual teacher, became the target. Only the briefest account of this approach to innovation can be given here (*see* Hoyle, 1976). The essence of the process is school-focussed, in-service training. The school as a whole would consider the potentialities of computer-assised learning helped by an external consultant and would thus define for itself the problems to which a computer would be a solution. It would then consider the organizational consequences of such a move. If the commitment was still there, the staff would have to consider their in-service training needs. There might have to be a common element for all teachers, eg programming skills, and hence the staff as a whole would constitute the members of a 'course' to be run at the school by a consultant or by the local education authority. Staff would also have diverse needs which would need to be met through a systematic programme of in-service training. Skills would be needed, not only in the utilization of computers but also – because the school itself would probably undergo concomitant structural changes – managerial, interpersonal and planning skills.

All this is quite a tall order. However, the School-focussed In-service Training and Education (SITE) project carried out by the University of Bristol School of Education has shown both the possibilities and the problems attached to this approach (Baker, 1980). It still remains essentially a rationalistic approach to planned change and would encounter considerable resistance. It would, however, enable teachers to consider their values and commitments and to link their work in schools with the future needs of their pupils. Many teachers would respond professionally to this. They would be more likely to be motivated to acquire the necessary knowledge and skills when they saw the direct and immediate application to their own work. They would also have colleague support in their attempts to innovate. On the evidence of past efforts to introduce changes into schools, the prognosis is not good. The school-focussed approach may have little more success than previous approaches, but it is the only obvious alternative.

Conclusion

This chapter has expressed some scepticism about the institutionalization of computers in schools on any substantial scale. Many individual teachers will utilize them as an adjunct to their own teaching methods but there are strong valuational, normative, professional and micropolitical barriers. Student teachers will increasingly leave their initial training with the necessary computing knowledge and skills and this will ensure some adoption, but schools as social systems are, perhaps rightly, conservative institutions and there are limits to the degree to which individuals can change systems. One obvious way forward is for a school to make computer-assisted learning the major target for its collective in-service effort, but the catch-22 is that this in itself constitutes a major innovation.

References

Allison, G T (1971) *Essence of Decision: Explaining the Cuban Missile Crisis* Little, Brown: Boston

Baker, K (1980) Planning school policies for INSET: the SITE project *in* Hoyle, E and Megarry, J (1980)

Bidwell, C E (1965) The school as a formal organization *in* March, C G (1965)

Carlson, R O (1965) *Adoption of Educational Innovations* Centre for the Advanced Study of Educational Administration: Eugene, Oregon

Eichholz, G and Rogers, E M (1964) Resistance to the adoption of audio-visual aids by elementary school teachers pp 299-316 *in* Miles, M B (1964)

Etzioni, A (1969) *The Semi Professions and their Organization* Free Press: New York

Gross, N, Giaquinta, J and Bernstein, M (1971) *Implementing Organizational Innovations* Harper Row: New York

Hoyle, E (1974) Professionality, professionalism and control in teaching *London Educational Review* 3 2:13-19

Hoyle, E (1976) *Strategies of Curriculum Innovation* Unit 28 Open University Course Curriculum Design and Development. Open University Press: Milton Keynes

Hoyle, E (1982) The micropolitics of educational organizations *British Journal of Educational Management and Administration* 10 2:87-98

Hoyle, E and Megarry, J (1980) *World Yearbook of Education 1980: Professional Development of Teachers* Kogan Page: London

Jackson, P W (1968a) *The Teacher and the Machine* University of Pittsburgh Press: Pittsburgh

Jackson, P W (1968b) *Life in Classrooms* Holt, Rinehart and Winston: New York

Litwak, E and Meyer, H J (1974) *Family, School and Neighbourhood* Columbia University Press: New York

Lortie, D (1964) The teacher and team teaching: suggestions for long term research *in* Shaplin, J T and Olds, H eds

Lortie, D (1969) The balance between autonomy and control in elementary school teaching *in* Etzioni, A (1969)

March, C G (1965) *Handbook of Organizations* Rand Macnally: Chicago

March, J G and Olsen, J (1976) *Ambiguity and Choice in Organizations* Universitetsforlaget: Bergen

Miles, M B (1964) *Innovation in Education* Bureau of Publications, Teachers' College, Columbia University: New York

Rogers, E and Shoemaker, A (1971) *Communication of Innovations* Free Press: New York

Shaplin, J T and Olds, H eds (1964) *Team Teaching* Harper and Row: New York

Smith, L and Keith, P (1971) *Anatomy of Educational Innovation: an Organizational Analysis of an Elementary School* Wiley: New York

Urban, G (1981) The perils of foreign policy: a conversation with Dr Zbigniew Brzezinski *Encounter* May 1981:13-30

Part 2:
Computers in action

6. Towards a pupil-centred classroom

Jim Howe

Summary: Microelectronic technology has the power to amplify and emancipate the human mind. Technological aids have, in the past, failed to make much impact on classroom practice; a major reason is that they do not easily fit into the way most teachers like or expect to organize their classrooms and their teaching. Most classrooms today work on a 'bottom up' model of building up sub-skills and sub-goals to the detriment of many pupils who never achieve the skills and goals which make the effort worthwhile.

An alternative methodology is proposed of working from the top downward, decomposing a problem into more tractable parts. The computer is a powerful aide in this approach, especially when put under learner control using an accessible author language like LOGO. Examples of the success of this approach are given in the learning of reading, writing and drawing by young and handicapped children. The implications of such a methodological revolution are recognized for the syllabus, for teacher education and for support by employing authorities.

Introduction

That microelectronic devices and microelectronic-based techniques will affect the lives of everyone by the end of this century now seems beyond doubt. Perhaps the magnitude of the effect is less predictable: some view the changes taking place in the office, factory, shop and home as a natural extension of the process of industrialization that began over two hundred years ago, whereas others believe that the impact of microelectronics* on society will cause a revolution every bit as significant as the industrial revolution in which this country featured so prominently. Only history can decide which view is the right one. In the meantime, we should note that whereas the industrial revolution amplified and emancipated the power of human muscle, the new microelectronic technology is primarily concerned with amplifying and emancipating the power of the human mind. Up until now this has largely been the concern of our educational system, formally and informally: now, suddenly, technology is muscling in on the act. Clearly, this is a situation which our schools and colleges cannot stop, even if they might wish to do so. The essential problem, therefore, is their reaction to it: either they can view the new technology as an intrusion whose effects should be minimized, or they can view it as a rich source of new educational methodologies.

A recent report into the contribution of (pre-microelectronic) technology to learning and teaching in Scottish secondary schools between 1976 and 1979 concludes that technological aids, projectors, televisions, tape/slide systems, have not been integrated into classroom practice. If that is the case, it is difficult to imagine that microelectronic technology will be accepted and applied with enthusiasm. The consequences of not doing so are serious. First, it will widen even further the gap which the average pupil perceives as existing between the requirements of school and the real world outside it. Second, it will mean that the education system has neglected the opportunity to adopt new methodologies that have been urged upon it by report after report after report, eg McCann Report, 1975; Learning Difficulties Report, 1978; Education Technology Report, 1982; Cockcroft Report, 1982.

Technological failure

Clearly we must try to understand *why* technological aids have failed to make much impact on classroom practice. One issue is the availability of equipment, its reliability and its complexity in relation to staff competence. Frequently the fear that a piece of equipment might break overpowers the desire to enrich class activity, and is likely to be a particular problem in the primary school which cannot fall back on assistance from the science staff. In contrast to the primary school where the constraints are most likely to be technical, in the secondary school the main hurdle is prevailing classroom practice. Since secondary syllabuses are crowded and demanding, classroom practice is usually based upon teacher-talk, question-and-answer and assignment, in that order. Teachers see this as the most economic way of achieving their objectives – getting children through exams. You might wonder what is wrong with this approach. The answer is that it teaches children that *learning takes place through being told*. In other words, it encourages children to be passive recipients instead of active participants, a behaviour largely unremarked in a culture that has substituted passive entertainments for active pursuits. This has been well put by Holroyd (1982), in contrasting television with literature:

> The difference between television and literature is fundamental. When we read a book we enter into a secret intimacy with the author, an intimacy (as Henry Green called it) between strangers. We form our own images in our heads. But when we watch television we all plug ourselves into our sets and collectively receive identical images. Words, actions, images-in-colour, music and a firework display of technicalities: everything is supplied instantly and on a flat screen that does not allow us (as in the theatre) focus or perspective. There is little left for us to do: we are merely receivers of received pictures, in danger of becoming less like human beings and more like extensions of the set.

In making a distinction between active and passive learning, we appear to be straying into the area of value judgements, of choosing between competing beliefs about the way that children learn, and consequently the way they ought to be taught. In my view, this is unavoidable since it is this issue which is central to future success or failure in the application of microelectronics in our educational institutions.

Clearly, this last statement must be justified. This can only be done in the context of an explanation of how children learn. Consider a young (pre-school) child. In a relatively short period of time, he or she acquires two skills of fundamental importance for all subsequent activity, namely, the ability to recognize objects and the ability to use language to express intention. We might not think of these as learned skills, in part because we learn them so young, in part because the acquisition of these skills appears to be so effortless. Yet, if you try to explain the process of recognition, or the process of speech production, sufficiently precisely so as to be able to model the process by computer program*, you will find that you cannot do it. No one can: these processes are so complex that they are beyond our current understanding. William Hull has written: 'If we taught children to speak, they'd never learn'. Instead, children teach themselves to speak by an active process which involves mimicking patterns of sounds, observing the differences between their productions and other people's productions (noticeably the mother's), and making corrections to reduce these differences. In other words, learning is an active process involving the feedback of information about discrepancy, thus enabling the system to adjust its characteristics to minimize subsequent deviation. Fundamentally, this information-gathering system is akin to the information-gathering control processes found in all parts of the human body and in the majority of technological devices and systems in use today.

The child's implicit objective is to build up a mental representation of the world around him. The information with which he is presented only takes on meaning in the context of that representation. As Piaget has pointed out, the growing mental representation is manifested in the explanations a young child gives. How often do parents laugh at their offspring's explanation, when it is entirely consistent with the child's existing knowledge? Indeed, many of their explanations would have been entirely acceptable in pre-Copernican times.

If it is conceded that the pre-school child is acquiring language through his own activity, what happens when he goes to school? He quickly discovers that he has to learn a new set of rules. Creativity, activity, questioning and other forms of self-expression are replaced by methods which encourage passivity and teacher dependence, for example, teaching reading either by the whole word method or by a decoding method based on mimicking sounds made by the teachers, teaching arithmetic as mechanical manipulations governed by (God-given?) rules.

So, by the time they reach secondary school, many children appear to accept a régime in which they are the passive recipients of conventional wisdom, to be regurgitated on demand to pass exams. They play the rules of the game because it is to their advantage to do so. But what about the non-conformists? Fortunately, many very bright pupils refuse to be constrained and learn despite the system. But failures, not surprisingly, come to view school as a memorial to their own apparent inadequacies. Yet total failure need not happen. If a child has learned to recognize objects, and to use spoken language in even a rudimentary way, he is capable of acquiring essential communicative skills such as reading, writing and arithmetic. He ought not to leave school illiterate.

Implications for microelectronic technology

In a recent Bow paper, Virgo suggests that the rate of technical change has passed the point where individuals can be guaranteed a trade for life (Virgo, 1981). On present employment levels, this view is at least plausible. He goes on to argue that the educational system must adapt to changing circumstances: it ought to focus on teaching children to think, making them capable of adapting to change. Such a declaration would have been approved by Dewey, Pestalozzi and Montessori, all of whom believed passionately that children learn to think through guided active exploration and experimentation. But we have already rehearsed this belief above. The question now is how might this objective be achieved? The methodology proposed by Virgo is the computer-assisted learning (CAL*) package. Here again, we run into difficulties through sloppy usage. Computer-assisted learning is sometimes used as a general term to refer to the use of computers for teaching and learning; more often it refers specifically to the kind of program which asks a pupil questions and checks the *appearance* of the pupil's answers. (The word 'appearance' is italicized to emphasize the fact that the computer is not able to make sense of the pupil's answers.) As said above, words are given meaning in the context of stored knowledge about a situation. The computer does not have this knowledge. Instead, a CAL program is an *idiot savant*. All it does is to accept the pupil's answers as a list of meaningless symbols, and compare this list with another list of equally meaningless symbols (which represent the correct answer) supplied by the teacher. So instead of interpreting a pupil's answer, it is merely comparing two symbol patterns. If they correspond, the pupil's answer is correct; if they differ it is incorrect. Programs which offer elementary diagnosis of mistakes are simple extensions of this technique. In this case, the teacher enters known errors as symbol lists. When one of these matches the pupil's response, an appropriate message is retrieved from the computer's memory*. The problem is that many errors are unpredictable, while many others have multiple causes. So any (non-intelligent) diagnosis is of limited value. Yet the CAL program reflects prevailing classroom teaching methodology, except that the machine's control is even more brutal and exacting than the class teacher's control. As pointed out elsewhere (Howe and du Boulay, 1981), this is tantamount to turning the clock back to an earlier era in education when emphasis was placed on the acquisition of basic skills. It is an abuse of the machine in the eyes of all save those who favour a move 'back to basics'.

Alternative methodology

So, how can we use microelectronic technology to revolutionize education? How can we encourage active exploration and experimentation? First, we must be clear about the methodology which will provide the basis for techno-logical innovation. The methodology is a problem-solving methodology, where the key notion is problem decomposition. In other words, problem solving takes place within a familiar context, and proceeds by breaking the problem down into more tractable parts, solving the parts, and then combining the parts to solve the whole. This is a top-down, problem-solving strategy, working backwards from the goal (solving the problem) through a hierarchy of sub-goals (solving the parts of the problem). Each level in this hierarchy is characterized by active information gathering, including feedback of information in response to actions directed towards goal achievement. This top-down approach stands in stark contrast to the 'bottom-up' or skills approach to problem solving which prevails in classrooms today, and is expressed by a preoccupation with sub-goals, the top level goals being well beyond the sight of the majority of pupils.

There are many ways that microelectronic technology can be used to implement a top-down, problem-solving methodology in the classroom. What they have in common is a problem hierarchy, an active learner, guidance rather than control and timely feedback of appropriate information. Below we cite some examples, both to illustrate the approach and to provide evidence of benefit to the learner. Theorizing is all very well, but the acid test at the end of the day is its effect on the pupil. Ideally, such an effect should be directly observable: one has a great deal of sympathy with Papert's view that the need to apply statistical tests to data* to show effects is a confession of failure (Papert, 1980). For this reason, the examples chosen below deal with educational problems which in conventional school terms have been regarded as intractable problems for particular children. In other words, these projects help these children to learn skills which they were not able to learn previously, even when taught by specialists.

At the Australian National University, Macleod and Lally (1981) have been teaching basic handwriting skills to severely handicapped children (see Chapter 19). Their set-up comprises a display screen and a special electronic pen. Words are presented on the screen as a series of faintly drawn strokes. These faintly drawn strokes are guidelines, and the child's task is to move the electronic pen along the guideline, within a predetermined accuracy. Let us suppose the task is to teach a child to write a word in cursive script, say, his surname. The teacher uses the electronic pen to feed a specimen of the script into the computer. The computer decomposes the word into pen strokes, and writes the first stroke faintly on the screen. The child starts to track the faint stroke, and if successful, the stroke is made thicker by the computer. Then the next stroke is written on the screen by the computer, the child repeats the tracking process, and so on. If the child starts at the wrong end of the stroke, moves in the wrong direction, lifts the pen or deviates too far from the guideline, line thickening stops and a small blinking spot indicates where the pen ought to be.

The task satisfies the requirements set out above. Initially, writing a letter can be decomposed into a series of character-making strokes. When the pupil has mastered this, the segmentation can be changed to present a character as a single continuous pen stroke. Following this, a short sequence of characters can be represented by a continuous pen movement, and so on, until the word is written as a single, flowing pen movement. At each stage, the learner can self-correct his writing actions until success is achieved, by comparing his own productions (movement of the electronic pen) with those which he is expected to make (the guidelines). The differences between the two provide the information feedback which enables the pupil to acquire the skill.

Its effectiveness is hinted at by the results of a series of studies. Three pupils who could not sign their names satisfactorily despite extensive teaching were able to do so fluently, within one to four hours. A group of nine mildly intellectually handicapped pupils with handwriting difficulties learned to print lower case letters. When their performances were compared with those of a matched control group, more pupils in the computer group showed improvements. Finally, the method has been adapted successfully to teach blind children handwriting, using auditory feedback to signal deviations from the guidelines. An impressive illustration of the success of the method in improving the handwriting of a mentally handicapped boy will be found on page 197.

At Edinburgh University we have developed a computer-based system for teaching word attack skills to children with mild mental and physical handicaps (Howe, 1981). Our reading model develops the ideas outlined previously. We assume that each child brings to the reading situation a stored mental representation of the world as he has experienced it. This representation comprises both the non-verbal information accumulated through the child's actions, and verbal information which has been related to the non-verbal information through contact with older children and adults. The existence of this stored representation is strong evidence for the existence of powerful visual and auditory processing mechanisms that can select relevant information from the mass of visual and auditory data impinging on the senses, mechanisms that can cope with the very considerable variability in the quality of the sense data from one moment to another, from situation to situation. Indeed, in the absence of such mechanisms, no one would learn to see, or to make use of language.

Given this cognitive model, reading is a form of communication in which words in a text invoke stored knowledge in the mind of the reader, enabling him to create a new mental representation of the situation characterized by the words. (How closely this representation corresponds to the author's depends upon the latter's expressive skill *and* the listener's accumulated experience.) But the child who hears and speaks is already using words to invoke his personal knowledge of the world: other people's familiar utterances invoke this knowledge, and in turn his productions invoke theirs. So just as learning to decode speech involves mapping unknown sound patterns on to the stored mental representations of objects, situations, and so on, teaching a child to decode text involves teaching him to map initially unknown grapheme patterns (written words) on to these existing stored mental representations so that the grapheme patterns can become part of these representations. Then when these patterns are seen in the future they will immediately invoke the stored information, thus conferring meaning on the word(s).

But how can this be implemented in computer program form? What we need is a method of teaching reading that is pupil-centred, not teacher-centred, and puts to work the powerful mechanisms by means of which the pupil has already learned spoken language. The method developed combines analytic and synthetic phonic approaches; that is, words are decomposed into consonant and vowel sounds, and words are composed out of consonant and vowel sounds. The set-up comprises a computer-controlled slide projector and a pressure sensitive screen. Teaching materials in slide form are back-projected on to this screen. For example, to teach the final consonant *t* the child might be shown an *exemplar* slide containing a picture of a cat and the letter *t* in its final position in the word - -t. The child's task is to say aloud the name of the object, trace the shape of the grapheme with his finger and associate the final sound with this unfamiliar shape. This exemplar is followed by batches of slides presenting variants of this task. Some of the batches concerned with *grapheme* identification present a picture of a familiar object and a choice of final consonants, including the *t*; others present two or three objects, with the name of one ending with the final consonant *t*. Some of those concerned with *word* identification include two illustrations and a single word; others present an illustration and choice of three words and others an illustration and choice of two words to complete the sentence 'I see a - - -'. In practice, several final consonants, eg *d t n g* are taught together, so the child has to compare and contrast two or more unfamiliar shapes. His choice of picture, letter or word is registered by the computer when he presses the area of the screen containing it. This information is used by a control program which presents the teaching materials in an appropriate sequence. For example, when the correct choice is made, a confirmation slide containing the correct illustration and its grapheme/word is shown; when an incorrect choice is made, an information slide displays the choice made *and* the choice the child ought to have made to enable him to compare and contrast, ie extract differences, before proceeding. This control program also uses a tough all-or-none assessment criterion when deciding if a child knows a grapheme well enough to proceed through the vowel-consonant hierarchy.

Exploratory tests were carried out in our laboratory over an 18-month period to assess the effectiveness of this approach. Our subjects were four boys and one girl, from special schools in Edinburgh. Three were mildly mentally handicapped and two were mildly physically handicapped. In age, they ranged from six to eight at the start of the study; their IQs ranged from 60 to 82, and all were non-readers. From their teachers' assessments, the general picture which emerged was that of a child who is seen as being dull and not very curious, with a poorer than average memory, a limited speaking vocabulary and limited ability to express ideas. Their classroom behaviour was characterized by terms such as disobedient, disruptive, hyperactive, aggressive, non-participating and lacking in concentration.

Over the 18-month period, these children spent three periods of ten minutes per week during school term working with the programs. Two completed the available material (16 programs) and three completed half the material (one boy changed schools half way through and was replaced by another and one girl was absent for half the time for heart operations). The boys who completed showed gains of six to nine months in a year when tested on the Burt Word Reading Test; all showed gains in pre-post tests for each

program, and gains were also registered on relevant sections of Jackson's
Phonics Test. Perhaps most important, all were observed using phonic clues
when faced with new words in their classroom reading. Those boys who
completed the materials were making steady progress through a classroom
reading scheme, and were taking books home to read for pleasure.

Both of these systems can be thought of as reactive learning environments,
with the computer managing a child's progress through a problem hierarchy.
This management role might be externalized: it could be done by the teacher,
by worksheets, by pupils or by some blending of all three. Our final example
deals with a learning environment where the management is externalized in
this way. In this case, the methodology is model building. If we think about a
toy model first of all, the designer decomposes the toy into a set of parts: the
child composes the toy from this set of parts. What we want, therefore, is a
symbolic system where a child can combine the skills of the designer with those
of the assembler, for example a picture-drawing system, a tune-composing
system, a sentence-generating system. A child can explore drawing problems,
tune-composing tasks, and so on, through working with such a system because
it provides a special language for talking about the *process* of drawing, the
process of composing or the *process* of sentence construction, where this
process is a top-down problem-solving process.

As an example, let us consider drawing as a process. Suppose the picture-
drawing system's language* provides commands for controlling the movement
of a motorized pen around a drawing surface, for example FORWARD [a
distance], LEFT [a rotation]. Suppose too that the task is to draw an equi-
lateral triangle. This problem can be decomposed into parts, namely drawing
sides and changing pen direction. Next, a program can be assembled, using the
FORWARD command to draw the sides and the LEFT turn command to
change pen direction. The program might take the following form:

TRIANGLE
FORWARD 500
LEFT 120
FORWARD 500
LEFT 120
FORWARD 500
LEFT 120

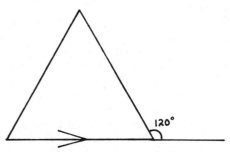

The program is given the name TRIANGLE: it can be stored in the computer's
memory and retrieved at a later time by simply typing in the word TRIANGLE.

But building a TRIANGLE requires some understanding of geometrical
concepts, such as angle and rotation. So instead of expecting a child to build
the TRIANGLE program himself, the teacher might build it and provide it as
an extension of the language. This allows the teacher to work at a higher (more
meaningful) level on the concept hierarchy. Now the task might be to draw a
HOUSE which decomposes into sub-tasks, namely draw a SQUARE then

draw a TRIANGLE on top. At this level, the child's task is to construct a program HOUSE out of the SQUARE and TRIANGLE instructions. His program might take the form:

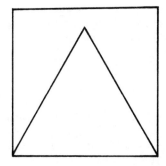

HOUSE
SQUARE
TRIANGLE

Clearly, something has gone wrong with the drawing. To find out what, he can put the computer into a state where it will step through the commands one by one. In this case, he will see that the problem arises when it has finished drawing the square. Instead of moving the pen to the top corner of the square, it starts drawing at the bottom corner. Now he can be introduced to the movement and turn commands through guided experimentation, and in due course he will produce a new HOUSE program:

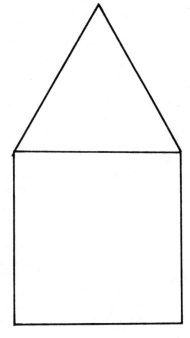

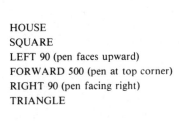

HOUSE
SQUARE
LEFT 90 (pen faces upward)
FORWARD 500 (pen at top corner)
RIGHT 90 (pen facing right)
TRIANGLE

Once introduced to the basic drawing commands, he can be encouraged to enrich his HOUSE by adding new parts, eg WINDOW, DOOR, CHIMNEY, and so on, each part being constructed out of movement and turn commands.

Of course, the problem need not be a graphical one. It might be a mathematical problem, for example finding if any of a given list of numbers are factors of a number, and finding the remainder after factorizing by that list. This problem can be decomposed into:

1. a program which tests whether a number is a factor of another one, or not;
2. a program that will find repeated factors, using program 1. as a sub-program;
3. a program that gives as the result the number left after repeated factorizing:
4. a program that solves the original problem stated above, using programs 1., 2. and 3. as sub-programs.

The final program might not be an efficient one, but it will at least be a natural one in problem-solving terms.

Several studies have supported the value of this approach, but one particular one stands out from the others. In it, two of my colleagues worked with a seven-year-old autistic boy, using a version of the drawing system described above (Emanuel and Weir, 1976). The drawing device connected to the computer was a replica of a toy robot device called a 'turtle', devised by Papert at MIT (Papert, 1980). Instead of typing in commands via an alphanumeric keyboard*, commands were entered into the computer by means of a button box, each button being labelled with a drawing to indicate its function. Pushing a button instructed the computer to move the turtle, or make it hoot, or raise or lower its drawing pen. Also when a button was pushed, it lit up and remained alight until the instruction had been carried out. To begin with some buttons were masked off to simplify the child's task.

At the start of the study, the boy was biddable and could carry out simple verbal instructions. He could utter some phrases, in parrot fashion, to express wants, eg 'more paper please'. Socially, he was quiet and gentle, avoiding eye contact. His case notes were full of the following kind of statements: 'has never made a spontaneous statement to us, except under stress', 'speech has to be prompted every time', 'no spontaneity – has to be asked again and again'. Yet, after only seven one-hour sessions working with the turtle, our autistic boy began to speak to us quite spontaneously!

From videotapes of his activities, we see him beginning to predict the turtle's actions on the basis of a growing understanding of the cause-effect relationship between his own actions, pushing the buttons on the control box, and the turtle's behaviour. Soon he begins to mimic his own button pushing actions and the turtle's responses by pressing his tummy button and moving his body, for example, pressing his tummy button and standing up, pressing it again and sitting down to act out raising and lowering the turtle's drawing pen. Clearly, these body movements are a rudimentary form of communication. Finally, and dramatically, he begins to use speech fragments spontaneously to communicate his intentions to others, for example 'Emanuel – make the turtle, goes forwards and backwards and left and right, up and down . . . . hoot'. This was no short-lived phenomenon: about a year later he was transferred out of the autistic unit because of sustained improvement in his ability to communicate with others. Since this is but a single case, carried out under laboratory conditions, we are eager to have our methodology tried out by teaching staff in institutions. With this in view, we have designed a turtle which can be driven from a range of popular microcomputers*. This is being manufactured commercially for use by both handicapped and normal pupils, in the hope that through working with it their communication skills will improve.

Transferring the methodology

Although modest in scope, the evidence is compelling. So the question is what would need to be done to transfer the alternative methodology into the classroom? As an answer, we can identify three key issues: (a) the syllabus, (b) teacher education and (c) local authority support.

Taking the syllabus first of all, not only would the content be reduced in quantity to make more time available for exploration and experimentation (a point also made in the Cockcroft report), but the ordering and grouping of topics in a subject would almost certainly change when scrutinized from a top-down viewpoint. This is a significant task, more demanding than the syllabus revisions carried out from time to time by examination authorities.

Turning now to teacher education, good in-service training would be required. This might be the Achilles heel for two reasons: lack of opportunity to attend in-service courses dealing with the approach, and lack of staff in the institutions capable of teaching the approach. In part, this is a political problem; in part, it reflects institutional inability to cope with the rate of technological change.

Finally, the attitude of employing authorities would be crucial since additional resources would be needed. No one doubts that the money is there: what one does doubt is the political will to divert it to the new educational technology from other less vital areas of local authority expenditure. Without these resources, we will not turn out more of the adaptable people that Virgo writes about. Without them, the future looks bleak for countries like Scotland which, like Korea and Malaysia, manufacture chips* but let the rest of the western world reap the profit from using these chips to build high technology devices.

Acknowledgement

My thanks are due to sponsors past and present, including the Nuffield Foundation, the Leverhulme Trust, the Social Science Research Council and the Sir Samuel Scott of Yews Fund.

This chapter first appeared as an article in *Scottish Educational Review Special Issue no 2* and is reprinted by kind permission of the editors and publishers, Scottish Academic Press.

References

Cockcroft Committee (1982) *Mathematics counts: Report of the Committee of Inquiry into the Teaching of Mathematics in Schools* Her Majesty's Stationery Office: London

Emanuel, R and Weir, S (1976) Catalysing communication in an autistic child in a LOGO-like learning environment *in Proceedings of Summer Conference on Artificial Intelligence and Simulation of Behaviour* pp 118-29 Edinburgh

Howe, J A M (1981) Teaching handicapped children to read: a computer-based approach *in Computers in Education* Lewis, R and Tagg, E D *eds* Amsterdam, North Holland

HM Inspectors of Schools (1978) *The Education of Pupils with Learning Difficulties in Primary and Secondary Schools in Scotland* Her Majesty's Stationery Office: Edinburgh

HM Inspectors of Schools (1982) *Learning and Teaching in Scottish Secondary Schools: the Contribution of Educational Technology* Her Majesty's Stationery Office: Edinburgh

Holroyd, M (1982) Seeing in the dark *Observer* 10.1.82

Howe, J A M and du Boulay, B (1981) Microprocessor-assisted learning: turning the clock back *in Selected Readings in Computer-Based Learning* Rushby, N *ed* Kogan Page: London

Macleod, I and Lally, M (1981) The effectiveness of computer controlled feedback in handwriting instruction *in Computers in Education* Lewis, R and Tagg, E D *eds* Amsterdam, North Holland

McCann Committee (1975) *The Secondary Education of Physically Handicapped Children in Scotland* Her Majesty's Stationery Office: Edinburgh

Papert, S (1980) *Mindstorms: Children, Computers and Powerful Ideas* The Harvester Press Ltd: Sussex

Virgo, P (1981) *Learning for Change* Bow Publications Ltd: London

7. The microcomputer and the teacher's needs

Bob Lewis

Summary: The stimulus to learning through activity-based problem-solving has been acknowledged for centuries and, in recent years, most curriculum development projects have promoted this methodology. The additional learning opportunities becoming available to some students through the use of micro-electronic devices provide a further dimension to the stimulus. However, whilst technology may be changing rapidly, it would be unrealistic to expect educational practice to keep pace. Whilst student pressure will speed up the process of change, major advances will not be made until the majority of teachers understand and are themselves supportive of important changes which are needed in their role. It is also unrealistic to expect the technology to solve many of the organizational and practical problems which accompany the changes believed to be desirable.

Factors which influence these changes are considered in this chapter: materials design, curriculum and syllabus change, teacher training and support.

Introduction

The thesis that understanding is best achieved by doing far pre-dates the microelectronics* revolution. Support for the thesis contained in the well-known Chinese proverb is found in the origins of school science education (Ingle and Jennings, 1981) as well as in the recent curriculum innovation in most disciplines. As has been said many times before, the problems of using computers in education are problems of education, not of computers.

The literature related to educational computing abounds with 'powerful ideas' (Papert (1980), Howe (1982), Bork (1975), Hebenstreit (1977) and McKenzie *et al* (1978)). Few acknowledge the problem of bringing such ideas to fruition in children's minds. It may be that in the present educational system, the achievement of true heuristic learning opportunities is not possible. The mere fact that 'learning' is an organized activity which goes on in a 'special place' may be a fundamental barrier. However, it is important to be positive and, accepting that schools and teachers exist, search for ways which benefit the pupils. It is almost certain that in this non-ideal world, compromises will have to be made. It seems likely that the most imaginative of the 'powerful ideas' will be the hardest, in a practical sense, to achieve; if a major objective is to make a positive impact on a very large proportion of pupils, rather modest innovations may be the only ones possible. All teachers have to make the often uncomfortable decision of where on an egalitarian-élitist continuum they are to devote most of their energies and resources. So it is, with curriculum and material developers. The philosophy of Illich (1979) and others who have attempted to define appropriate technologies will hopefully find most favour. Hebenstreit (1982) sees exciting technological mechanisms for education in his crystal ball. But, one may ask, for what proportion of children in developing countries will these be available?

It seems important to be aware of concerns such as these but no benefits will accrue to anyone unless thoughtful progress is made. Hebenstreit (op cit), supports the principle of 'CAL* software* for the teacher', emphasizing the importance of the teacher as mentor in the computer-resourced classroom, and identifies two major, manpower intensive and hence expensive problems – courseware* development and teacher training. Howe (Chapter 6), also in the context of the pupil-centred classroom, identifies the syllabus, teacher education and local authority support as key issues in the dissemination of the methodology. Some of these, and other issues will now be considered with the innovative teacher in mind.

Courseware and software acceptability

Using computers involves teachers in selecting software and ensuring that it works satisfactorily on their equipment. This section outlines the main features and suggests one 'ideal' style for designing programs*. The problems of software transferability*, so critical a decade ago, are now soluble, given a willingness to take the need seriously (Smith, 1981 and Lewis, 1981). However, the problem of acceptability is a much more difficult task. The artefacts of 'not invented here' educational material gather dust in institutes of learning and will provide exciting discoveries for a 'not invented yet' breed of educational archaeologists. There are perhaps two main reasons for the existence of such treasure troves: one is that some teachers are extremely conservative and reject materials developed by others out-of-hand. This attitude may well have become established after a number of bad experiences with poor, unrealistic material earlier in their careers. The second reason is that despite an eager willingness to experiment with new material, teachers find that much that is available is inappropriate and/or too inflexible to be adapted to their own teaching needs. One must sympathize with developers of educational technology materials which are not linked with computers, but there is no excuse for microcomputer*-based materials being inflexible. After all, the single most important feature of microelectronic devices is that they can be software controlled.

There need to be at least three elements in a CAL package of material: pupil/student notes, a teacher's guide and a computer program. The provision of a teacher's guide is of paramount importance. So often CAL material is misunderstood, and considered valueless, simply because the author(s) fail to communicate their ideas and rationale to potential users. It is essential that every opportunity is taken to maximize the chance that other teachers are able to associate themselves and their students with the environment of developers and their students. This implies a realization on the part of the developer of the learning or technical difficulties students will encounter, the various classroom/laboratory methods of organization appropriate to the package, and so on. The guide has to show that the developers have experienced the ways in which learners react to the material at a heuristic and practical level. The immediate implication of these requirements is that experienced teachers must be the prime members of the CAL development group and that trials of materials in a variety of types of school are essential.

The following check-list of questions was prepared for authors and trials teachers working with the Computers in the Curriculum Project.

Teacher's material – does this adequately provide:
a statement of objectives?
a statement of the level and prerequisite knowledge?
a statement of the rationale for the unit, its scope and limitations?
useful suggestions regarding the use of material in class, classroom organization etc?
warnings of places likely to give a student difficulty?
warnings about program limitations?
a statement of the computer model and assumptions made?
references to other sources, etc?
hints or comments on questions in the student material?
suggestions for extensions or increased flexibility?

Further consideration of the elements important in a CAL package, including reference to the needs of teachers, is contained in Peters and Johnson (1978) and Lewis and Murphy (1978).

As made clear earlier, the type of material being considered aims to improve understanding through learner activity. The way this is to be achieved will depend a great deal on how this activity is organized and will vary from teacher to teacher and from classroom to classroom. The criteria for acceptability of the learning material include flexibility in use but what is also important is some structure to the learning process. One way of achieving the latter is to provide students with problem-sheets or worksheets, designed to lead them through sections of the work. These may be considered as a framework for student activity and on the one hand may be rather directed or, on the other hand, quite open-ended. The key is that they provide stimulus and challenge for students leading to their desire to know. The motivational element cannot be overstressed. It may seem that this provision of structure to the learning negates the criteria of flexibility for the teacher, but if there is one thing that all teachers do habitually, it is to prepare worksheets for their classes. Hence, the worksheets prepared by CAL authors should be considered as exemplars of the kind of worksheets thought appropriate for use in a particular study. Teachers using the CAL package should have the flexibility of being easily able to prepare what are for them more appropriate materials for their students. The preparation of these, as with all worksheets, requires care. A check-list of questions related to their design was used by the

Computers in the Curriculum Project.

  Do the questions provide an adequate framework for students' activities
  not involving the program?
  Do the questions provide an adequate framework for students' use of the
  program?
  Is the prerequisite knowledge of the questions adequately covered:
    – in the printed material itself
    – deducible from the program
    – otherwise?
  Is the language used appropriate to the age/ability of the target student?
  Are the illustrations adequate?
  Could the layout be improved?
  Are there particular points of difficulty/confusion?

The design of pupil material for use in a particular CAL package is clearly
going to be dependent on the design of the program. It is here that most in-
flexibility may occur as it cannot be assumed that teachers are able to modify
software. Early attempts to provide degrees of flexibility in learner-program
interaction suffered from two defects:

1. the novice (student or teacher) user was given insufficient guidance and
   got lost in a forest of, sometimes technical, commands and parameters;
2. menu-driven programs, whilst providing varying degrees of both flexibility and structure, also provided options which were distractors for
   students and could seriously affect their line of thought.

Examples of newer forms of interaction are the system used by the ITMA
Project (Fraser *et al*, 1982) and the keyword system of the Computers in the
Curriculum Project (Want, 1982).

The former relates especially to teacher control during the use of programs
of the electronic blackboard type whilst the latter is designed for more general
modes of use including teacher design of adaptable student-program
interactions.

The following introduction to keyword-controlled software is taken from
course notes prepared at the Institute for Educational Computing, St Martin's
College, Lancaster.

  An important criterion for a program to be used by non-specialist users of
  computers is to ensure that the user is in control, knowing clearly how to
  make the program perform in the desired way. The phrase 'user friendly'*
  has been coined to describe this criterion. Few programs meet this requirement, yet it is crucial that they should do so if they are intended to be used
  by novice or timid users.

  The criterion is met by CAL programs if:
  a) the first-time user is guided and prompted by a dialogue in natural
     language*;
  b) the program allows flexibility to cater for the novice and yet provides
     the more advanced learner with the freedom to explore all features of
     the program at will.

The set of single-task keywords (primary keywords) meet the criterion of flexibility but may not provide sufficient guidance for the first-time user or control for the teacher to specify a certain path through the program. It is therefore necessary to be able to define 'secondary' keywords which automatically link a series of tasks (identified by primary keywords) together. When defining such secondary keywords, it should also be possible to skip the need for the input* of some values by the student. For example, the teacher may not wish students to be concerned with variations of, say, temperature and so it should be possible to provide a fixed value of temperature in the definition of the secondary keyword. Once a primary or secondary keyword task has been completed, the prompt should allow the student to enter the next primary or secondary task to which he/she has been assigned or chooses.

In order to define a dialogue for a particular group or class, all the teacher has to do is to add a BASIC DATA statement with a structure defined in the Teachers' Guide to the set already present in the program. This requires a very small amount of programming knowledge as shown in the following extract from ENZKIN, one of the CAL units in the Chelsea Science Simulation* series published by Edward Arnold (Publishers) Ltd:

Certain keywords can control not just one option but a sequence of options. This can provide a variety of predetermined pathways through the program and makes it unnecessary to type many individual keywords. For example in this example in this program the keyword START is defined as follows:

5862 DATA 'START'
5864 DATA '1, 14, 5,1, 6,8, 12,5,*,*, 8,*,*, 7,*, 13'

Therefore the following sequence occurs when START is used.

1 – RESET	all current values are cleared
14 – VALUES	table for values displayed
5 – ENZYME	enzyme 1 selected
6 – pH	a pH of 8 set
12 – VARY	5 (incubation time) is selected to vary and the user is prompted to enter minimum and maximum values
8 – VOLUME	the user is prompted to enter substrate volume and enzyme volume
7 – TEMP	the user is prompted to enter the temperature
13 – GO	the calculation and results sequence begins

Another keyword DEMO produces a sequence where no user input is required because supplied values have been entered as shown below.

5866 DATA 'DEMO'
5868 DATA '1, 14, 5,1, 6,8, 12,5,0,60, 8,2,3, 7,33, 13'

You may wish to introduce a new sequence appropriate to a particular teaching scheme. For example a lesson may be designed to investigate the optimum pH for each enzyme using supplied values for all the other conditions. A keyword such as EXPT1 may be defined in the following way to allow this investigation to be performed easily.

5875 DATA 'EXPT1'

5876 DATA '1, 7,35, 9,6, 10,1, 11,60, 14, 5,*, 12,1,*,*, 13'

When constructing these sequences it is important to consider the order carefully and to test the effect. For permanent alterations the program must be resaved. (Heydeman and McCormick, 1982)

An additional criterion for CAL programs concerns the teacher. It is desirable for the teacher to be able to make simple changes to the program in order that certain aspects be emphasized and that specific groups of students are provided with the most appropriate level of guidance or freedom. This facility gives the teacher the opportunity of tailoring worksheets or other tasks to specific learners in the teacher's own style.

One way of achieving these criteria structures the interaction around 'keyword' control of the program as it runs. Each sub-task which a student may wish to initiate, eg input the value of temperature, display a table, is identified by a specific keyword. After each task is completed, the program returns to request the next keyword. To meet the stated criteria, each keyword must be meaningful to the student and alternative keywords may be defined for the same task. Where appropriate, natural language dialogue should be used after the keyword has been chosen. For example, using the word OPTION to prompt the input of a keyword, the following dialogue may take place. The input from the student is italicized.

OPTION? *Temperature*

What is the temperature of the mixture (10-70 deg C)? *5*

+ + The temperature must be in the range 10-70 deg C Choose another value? *25*

OPTION? . . . . and so on.

Whilst some originators of materials are taking this 'open-access' view of software, a contrary trend is beginning to appear in which software is made inaccessible to teachers, ostensibly for commercial reasons of protection from copying. This is a retrograde step and indicates a narrowness of vision and an arrogance of view which implies that the material is so good that nobody would wish to change it. The printing parallel is that only the introductory chapter of a book is in black, the remainder being printed in invisible ink! There are already acceptable copyright safeguards which cover computer software. These laws should be upheld and major investment in systems software should be protected in existing established ways.

So far the main emphasis has been on the issues related to the design of materials which are capable of being used to promote learner exploration whilst at the same time carefully nurturing the essential role of the teacher. It is now appropriate to consider curriculum innovation and the syllabus changes which may be desirable.

Curriculum innovation and syllabus change

A particular feature of all activity learning is that it is seen as taking 'longer'.

A well-respected professor from a medical school once stated quite openly that his problem was getting students to remember 4000 new words; what time did he have for CAL?!

'Longer' is a relative word; longer than what? What is taking longer? Understanding something takes longer than learning, learning takes longer than remembering (which may be a transient state only suitable for the purposes of passing examinations).

Any syllabus has implicit assumptions about the methodology required to cover its aims. When it comes to the breadth of cover as compared to a depth of understanding and ability to apply knowledge, a syllabus is defined which tests somewhere on the continuum between extremes. Examinations, seen as tests of those aims, equally reflect the assumed methodology.

Many recent syllabuses assume an activity or discovery-based approach and will be found to cover rather less ground than more traditional syllabuses. Howe's 'alternative methodology' (Chapter 6), which makes imaginative use of microelectronic technology, may go too far if applied to conventional schools though it may well be an attractive solution to special problems. It may seem trite to say that a 'happy medium' is required, but that may well be the case. What is fairly certain, however, is that the experience of the use of such a methodology will assist in making the teaching in conventional areas more imaginative. In practice, it is likely that a compromise approach which tackles a series of sub-goals and views each as a starting-point either for top-down or for bottom-up progress, will be most acceptable to teachers.

In the late 1960s, it was clear that the introduction of CAL stood most chance of being a success if modest goals were set. Having just emerged from a decade of major curriculum revision, teachers would almost certainly have resisted a further revolution. The methodology had also to be established and this was attempted through the existing curriculum. The groundwork of introducing discovery-learning methods had already been done, for example, by the Nuffield Science Teaching Projects (Ingle and Jennings, 1981 which contains copious further references). Now that the use of the computer as a resource for learning is becoming acceptable to teachers, a more positive approach can be taken to the curriculum. As new waves of curriculum change occur, so the content and methodology which is considered for incorporation can be broadened to include topics which can only be handled satisfactorily by CAL methods and the extensions of activity-based methodology made possible by the increasing availability of microelectronic devices. An actual mechanism whereby this integration of CAL into the new curriculum is taking place is found in the linked working groups of the Computers in the Curriculum Project with, amongst others, the Schools Council History 13-16 Project and the Schools Council 16-19 Geography Project (Watson, 1982).

Teacher training

Before microelectronic devices can make an impact on the nature of classroom activities, a considerable amount of teacher training has to be done. This is likely to reflect the 'lateral approach' as it requires certain knowledge to be acquired through basic skills whilst at the same time inculcating an overall perspective of alternative classroom practice. Leaving aside considerations of the training required for teachers of computer appreciation, computer studies, computer science or microelectronics, etc it is helpful to consider courses at a number of levels:

1. at familiarization level – for all teachers;
2. at specialist curriculum level;
3. at teacher-author level;
4. at teacher-disseminator level.

These levels are hierarchical and each will be treated as dependant upon a previous level.

1. Familiarization

The aims of such a course are to provide a basic level of skill in using one or more microcomputer hardware* systems and to introduce a range of possible uses in schools. Typically, a 30-hour course might seek to illustrate and provide first-hand experience of:

- software at different levels (operating and elementary programming);
- setting up and care of hardware;
- experience in reading programs and making minor changes;
- technical and educational aspects of the use of prepared CAL materials;
- illustrations of microprocessors* in control application;
- possible administrative applications;
- criteria for assessing the value of materials;
- information on sources of software, educational organizations, literature and periodicals;
- alternative hardware configurations, hardware expansion;
- local support, advice, etc;
- alternative strategies for classroom organization.

This content may well be covered in a local education authority course probably best run over four consecutive full days.

Alternatively, the Open University Pack, Micros in Schools provides an excellent resource for informal in-school or individual training. It is designed to be used with a specific hardware system; the aims of the version dealing with the Research Machines 380Z microcomputer are stated as follows:

You will find in this pack very detailed step-by-step instructions for all the activities. When you have completed them, you should be able to:
- connect up, switch on and run the RML 380Z microcomputer;
- use educational material on the microcomputer;
- evaluate the educational potential of the microcomputer;
- understand enough of computer jargon to be able to express your wishes to a local computer expert. (Open University, 1982)

2. Specialist curriculum

Moving on from the familiarization course, a course of similar length for teachers of a particular discipline may be an appropriate second stage. In this the emphasis switches from the technology to the curriculum. The aim is to provide teachers with sufficient background to enable them to become fully capable of using CAL in their own teaching, and of developing their own critical approach to the innovation. The outline of courses aimed to meet these objectives and being run in our region under the aegis of the Microelectronics Education Programme (see Chapter 13) is given below:

Aims:
    (a) to consider various roles for the computer in the teaching/learning process;
    (b) to consider the use of CAL materials in a discipline in the light of current curriculum and methodological trends in that discipline;
    (c) to consider school/classroom organization of microcomputer resources;
    (d) to become familiar with two or three commonly available hardware systems and their associated software;
    (e) to explore the issues of courseware and software design and evaluation;
    (f) to undertake a modest development or evaluation project.

Schedule:
    DAY 1. The role of the computer in CAL
                Assessing the value of CAL materials
                Workshop – familiarity with hardware
    DAY 2. Discipline study –
                    Current trends in the discipline
                    CAL in the discipline
                    Workshop – available materials
                          – assessing materials
    DAY 3. Courseware design
                Software design (or specifying software needs)
                Workshop on design – small development project
    DAY 4. Workshop on projects
                Presentation of projects

Of particular importance at this level is that harassed teachers are able to make an accurate assessment of the value of new material which they discover or is brought to their attention. Related to this is peer-review of material, perhaps the most valuable form of 'evaluation' for the practising teacher. After discussion of the issues on a recent course in Cumbria, teachers decided upon a simple set of ten points which would provide the framework for a valuable, though brief, single page review:

    0. Title, target pupil, intention
    1. Initial information
    2. Teacher support material

3. Pupil material
4. How the material was used
5. Was the intention achieved?
6. Pupil motivation
7. Problems in use – actual and foreseen
8. Would you use it again? Why?
9. General comments.

The first two points (0 and 1) concern the information immediately available on reading publicity or an entry in a software directory. Points 2 and 3 aim at the existence and value of any printed materials. The following points 4 to 7 cover classroom experiences in using the material with pupils and the final points from the personal views of the material's value.

3. Teacher-author

The most common question raised when discussing the value of teachers developing materials for their own use is – how skilled do teachers have to be in programming? At the present time there is no software equivalent to the author languages* (developed for the production of drills and other didactic uses of mainframe* computers) for use in the development of simulation or modelling CAL programs. The languages which do exist in these fields are too complex for most teacher-authors to use, they are mostly mainframe-based and are not designed to produce usable products for students. One language system which may be a partial help to teachers in their development of CAL simulations (though that was not one of its design goals) is that created by R J Hartley (Hartley and Lewis, 1982).

So, if teachers are to produce their own software of a discovery-learning nature, they are left at the mercy of their microcomputer language(s), BASIC*, PASCAL or whatever, possibly helped by utilities and other structures as mentioned earlier (Smith (op cit) and Want (op cit)). Much is going to depend upon the inclination of the individual teacher concerned and upon his/her relationship with other agencies. For teachers who have no inclination to write substantial programs, it may be possible for them to contribute software specifications to a national or local project or LEA centre. It may be that colleagues or pupils can assist, but it is important to stress that the development of satisfactory programs is a time-consuming task even for an experienced programmer. Even given great enthusiasm for program writing, a practising teacher will rarely find sufficient time to create much worthwhile material especially if he/she has a family and/or a garden!

However, the other aspect of CAL development is that of specifying programs and producing the teacher and pupil material to accompany them. A team effort in both software and courseware production is likely to be essential and is educationally beneficial as experience and skills are shared.

Any course aimed at assisting teachers towards the author role should contain elements of both software and courseware design. Even though an individual teacher may concentrate on only one of these, it is essential that he/she has experienced the whole development task as the two aspects are closely interrelated. Hence, the course must have a substantial project element and be well provided with hardware. An important preliminary element to the course should be an extensive review of existing material in order that decisions may be intelligently made on graphical screen layout and courseware alternatives. It will certainly be beneficial if course members work on a project in pairs, and it may be helpful if a start is made with the same well-structured development task (SDT) for all members. In plenary session each pair should then learn from the others. Such a course requires a concentrated period to be allocated to it and a minimum of three weeks will be needed. To sustain momentum on the SDT will be difficult and elements of the project – either courseware or software development – could be held over to a further one-week course. Given a good earlier grounding in programming, teachers may find that a shorter time is adequate. There is little doubt that teachers (or anyone else for that matter) will progress much more rapidly if they use a top-down approach to their development tasks. In the context of software development, this means that whatever programming language* is used, it should be handled in a structured way and rely heavily on procedures or subroutines. In this way inexperienced programmers will find that they can extend their familiarity with the language as the need arises, rather than having to spend time on details in the traditional manner. Courseware development is best approached in a similar way with overall aims being dissected into sub-aims and ultimately into the problems to be set for students.

4. Teacher-disseminator

It may be the policy in a school or in an LEA, to identify teachers to lead the dissemination of the educational uses of computers. Such teachers are unlikely to be prime movers in the development of courses about computers if only because they will already be heavily committed and in any event are likely to view priorities differently.

To be successful in the role of disseminator, teachers need to have the experience of developing material for themselves as well as of being practitioners in the use of CAL in their own classrooms. In addition, they need to be aware, not only of CAL materials in other disciplines, but of curriculum trends in other disciplines. The elements of a course for such teachers is likely to be more a course on curriculum innovation than on educational computing. It is also essential that they are familiar with local and national sources of information and materials, have not only the support of their head teacher but also of the LEA advisers and be understanding of their policies. However, their most valuable asset would appear to be that of public relations spokesman; stories of 'sales resistance' abound.

The present wave of training courses in applications of microelectronics in schools is bound to be short-lived. A continuing need will exist for bringing teachers up-to-date with new materials and facilities. Whilst some of this may be carried out at a formal 'course' level, the most likely way of continuing to provide for this widespread need will be through less formal in-school activities. The teacher-disseminator has a crucial long-term role to play in this. Already the huge problem of primary school teacher training is on a rather close horizon in Britain. Support for those primary schools can only realistically come from their secondary neighbours.

Courses run for Cumbria and Lancashire teachers by the Institute for Educational Computing at St Martin's College take place part-time over one year. They start with a four-week, full-time block and now assume familiarity with computing, including a reasonable grasp of BASIC. In previous years it was not possible to make such assumptions and in the future the courses will evolve as the basic appreciation of teachers moves ahead. A further full-time block of two weeks follows after six months, and during this period a number of tutorial/workshop sessions are held. The content of the two-week element is designed to meet the needs course members found whilst back in school. Sessions included last year were on classroom organization, school resource priorities, computer literacy* in schools, new CAL materials, dissemination case studies, advances in hardware and recent publications in the field. Next year's course is bound to include the developments in primary schools. Course members are chosen from different schools to represent a range of disciplines from craft, through history, to mathematics and in this way are exposed to the perspectives of their peers in a way which rarely happens elsewhere.

Local support for teachers

If teachers are to engage upon what is a major innovation – for all technically, for many educationally – local support of various kinds is essential. The responsibility for technical and educational information must be vested in some institution, with people specifically designated to carry out that task for local schools. This usually implies financial provision by the local education authority.

Going a stage beyond information, a local 'software library' is needed where teachers can go to browse and borrow materials whilst assessing their value prior to purchase. Although microcomputers appear to be robust and reliable, local hardware maintenance arrangements are needed and/or for hardware loan in emergencies. For specialist 'class sets' of hardware, joint purchase by a small group of schools is beneficial, not only in making the equipment available for a term or semester, but in bringing teachers together naturally to share educational experiences and materials.

The formation of teacher-author groups with some technical and secretarial backing is an effective way for innovative ideas to be nurtured. The support for such groups may come from national projects, such as Computers in the Curriculum, or, if outward looking, even more effectively from local sources. There is a tremendous enthusiasm amongst a modest proportion of secondary teachers at the moment. The feeling that their efforts are appreciated is very stimulating, and quite small investments in LEA resources will be rewarded many times over.

However, it must be stressed that if teachers in the development or disseminator role are to make a real impact, there is no way that this can be achieved without giving them time. This is certainly costly, but secondment on a scale of one full day per week is necessary. Care is also needed to ensure that this really is time free from the perpetual day-to-day pressures, such as marking, cover for absent colleagues and other chores notorious for eating into 'free' time.

Conclusion

There is a temptation to bemoan the slow pace at which educational practice is making use of the enormous potential of the technologies. Steady progress is being made, however, despite the fundamental problems referred to in the following extract from a paper delivered by the writer in the University of Belgrade.

> Successive generations of human beings across the world are being, and it seems will continue to be, faced with a problem for which no solution is apparent. Over the last one hundred years, and perhaps throughout mankind's evolution, the rate at which tools have been developed outstrips the rate at which the subsequent human adaptation to use such tools can take place. Perhaps it is only in the last ten years that this problem has become manifest. The reason is clear; major technological change, affecting an increasing proportion of the population, is taking place within a single generation. Now for the first time, the situation has to be faced in which change has to be accepted within the working life of individual people. Adaptation to change can no longer take place from generation to generation but must be accommodated within a lifetime. There is every indication that the rate of technological development will continue to rise and hence the pressures on human beings to accept change in an 'unnaturally' short time will grow.
>
> Amongst those in society who are closest to change are teachers. They see the development day-by-day, year-by-year of their pupils and students. In many ways they are themselves agents of change as they catalyse the acquisition of knowledge and influence the attitudes of young people. Can we therefore expect teachers to be able to adapt easily to changes in educational technology or are those responsible for the change most likely to resist its effect on themselves?

The evidence of the last two years indicates a positive answer to this question. Teachers from all disciplines are involved in courses and in curriculum development. Despite current economic problems throughout the world, the next five years with yet another generation of less expensive and more powerful hardware will surely see what in educational timescales may be termed a revolution.

Acknowledgements

To my colleagues at Chelsea College and in the curriculum development projects over many years, and to Cumbria teachers who attended my recent courses and brought me closer to reality.

References

Bork, A M (1975) Effective computer use in physics education *American Journal of Physics* **43** 81

Fraser, R, Wells, C and Burkill, S (1982) Eureka, Jane-plus and Transpots: designing material for the microcomputer and teacher partnership in the classroom *in* Lewis, R and Tagg, E D (1982)

Hartley, R J and Lewis, R (1982) A computer language system for model building and experimentation *International Journal of Mathematical Education in Science and Technology* in press

Hebenstreit, J (1977) Basic concepts in information processing *in* Johnson, D C and Tinsley, J D *eds* (1977)

Hebenstreit, J (1982) Opening address *in* Lewis, R and Tagg, E D (1982)

Heydeman, M T and McCormick, S (1982) Enzyme kinetic *Chelsea Science Simulations* Edward Arnold: London

Howe, J A M and Ross, P (1981) Moving LOGO into the mathematics classroom *in* Howe and Ross

Howe, J A M and Ross, P (1981) *Microcomputers in Secondary Education* Kogan Page: London

Illich, I (1979) *Deschooling Society* Calder and Boyers: London

Ingle, R and Jennings, A (1981) *Science in Schools: Which Way Now? Studies in Education 8* Institute of Education, University of London

Johnson, D C and Tinsley, J D *eds* (1977) *Information and Mathematics in Secondary Schools* Amsterdam, North Holland

Lewis, R (1981) Mechanism for CAL origination *in* Smith, C H *ed* (1981)

Lewis, R and Murphy, P J (1978) Product design and development *in* McKenzie *et al* (1978)

Lewis, R and Tagg, E D *eds* (1982) *Proceedings of the IFIP Working Conference Involving Micros in Education* Amsterdam, North Holland

McKenzie, J, Elton, L, and Lewis, R (1978) *Interactive Computer Graphics in Science Teaching* Ellis Horwood: Chichester

Open University (1982) *Micros in Schools – an Awareness Pack for Teachers (P540)* Centre for Continuing Education: Open University

Papert, S (1980) *Mindstorms: Children, Computers and Powerful Ideas* Harvester Press: Brighton

Peters, H J and Johnson, J W (1978) *Authors Guide, CONDUIT* University of Iowa

Smith, C H *ed* (1981) *Microcomputers in Education* Ellis Horwood: Chichester

Smith, P W *et al* (1981) *A CAL Software Library Manual* Schools Council/Chelsea College: London

Want, D L (1982) Keyword driven interaction in computer assisted learning *in* Lewis and Tagg (1982)

Watson, D (1982) Some implications of micros on curriculum developments *in* Lewis and Tagg (1982)

8. Computer roles in the management of learning

Harry McMahon

Summary: Underpinning all applications of computer-managed learning (CML) is the concept of the learning cycle. The cycle begins when the student is asked to study a unit or module of the curriculum. It ends when that student successfully completes the required learning and is directed to commence study of the next logical element in the curriculum. The role of the computer in CML is to manage this learning cycle, or more precisely to enhance each individual student's learning by providing automated management of elements of the learning environment.

The computer performs a series of management functions on behalf of the teacher and the student. First, it builds a profile of the student. It acts as a testing device, generating, presenting and marking objective tests or attitude surveys which act as diagnostic or assessment tools to be used in establishing the character and quality of students' learning. It is able to record the results of judgements about students' learning made subjectively by teachers and it can store general demographic information about the students.

Second, the computer is able to make use of these measures and data to diagnose learning on an individual basis, provide feedback to students as individuals, and to route or steer them onward to the next appropriate learning experience.

Third, the computer reports to the teacher, the course designer and the administrator on the performance of students as they advance through successive learning cycles. It also provides information in summary form to support decision-making in course management, administration and curriculum development.

This chapter considers each of these management functions in turn, analyses the variety of ways in which they have been implemented in CML systems, identifies unresolved questions related to their use and looks forward to the next generation of CML systems, identifying possible trends in their future development.

Building the student profile

To support the process of managing learning, a wealth of data* about students and their learning environment must be collected by the computer-managed learning (CML)* system. The most frequently-tapped source for this information is unquestionably the objective test of cognitive understanding. As the student passes through successive learning cycles*, so-called performance data are collected. These may be the results of informal pre-tests and post-tests designed to act as diagnostic devices, or more formal assessment or achievement tests designed to provide objective measures of students' competence after an extended period of study.

The development and validation of a series of such tests and their distribution throughout a modular curriculum is a task demanding very considerable technical skill, whether or not a computer is to be used in administering or marking the tests. The perennial problems associated with writing high-quality test items have to be faced alongside the additional tasks of defining the marking and test interpretation procedures to be used by the computer. In the more sophisticated CML systems these procedures include:

○ option weighting*, where the options within a multiple-choice test item can be allocated scores other than a simple 'one for right, zero for wrong';
○ item weighting, where the score for the single test item can be weighted against a sub-total or total score by some multiplication factor;
○ group membership, where the item can be allocated to one or more groups of items possessing common characteristics, so that group scores can be calculated for sub-sections of the test;
○ two-dimensional scoring, to allow the answer to each item to be accompanied by some additional judgment, such as how confident the students are in giving their answers, or how much they would prefer to see a chosen option implemented in real life.

Such facilities for automatic test marking allow the CML designer to develop very powerful data-collection instruments, capable of establishing the students' learning status on any number of dimensions, on a regular basis over extended periods of time. For example, a course would be structured around a set of tests which measure the students' developing performance on three levels of cognitive functioning: recall, application and analysis/synthesis, four areas of content, and two levels of confidence – low and high. If large numbers of students are involved, manual collection and processing of such data would be virtually impossible. However, with careful faculty pre-planning and the help of a CML system this information can be made available and used to advantage by both students and staff as a matter of routine.

Many CML systems are restricted to the management of data which is produced by objective testing; some are inherently so restricted by design, others by their practical use. Often, the smaller systems will process data only about the current test and will not even allow for the storage of these records in a student file for later reference. However, the more sophisticated systems allow for the collection and storage of other types of information, for example, the teacher's marks on sub-sections of a student's essay, or a check-list of behaviours observed in the laboratory, or the entries in an appointments timetable, or the learning resources chosen by the student in a learning centre. These types of data, along with the results of conventional objective testing, combine to form a student profile* which is accessible at any time. The student profile may also contain demographic data about the student. Indeed it can contain any coded* information deemed by the teacher, and presumably the student also, to be of value when it comes to providing feedback on an individual basis.

Thus automated objective testing is, in these more far-reaching applications of CML, only one part of the information-gathering process. It is, or should be, but one route into a data base management system* which can readily be tailored to request, to accept and to store the gradually growing bank of data about individual students, their background characteristics, their attitudes and their understanding. However, to be of real value, both students and teachers must recognize these data as helpful when decisions are being made on diagnosing problems of learning, identifying appropriate remedial action and advising or prescribing new learning tasks.

Many problems underlie these aspects of CML. Some of them are operational, like providing sufficient disc* space for back-up storage, or simply finding the time to develop all the data-gathering instruments. But others are of fundamental educational significance: for example, before designing tests, the CML developer should address the problem of how the structure of knowledge for this particular area of knowing is to be represented to the student. Is the knowledge precise, hard-edged, tightly organized in lists, networks or hierarchies, static in time, always right and never wrong? Or is it represented as being loosely structured, problematical, forever changing and subject to the fuzzy logic of ordinary human judgment?

Most CML developers seem to prefer the first option. They are prepared to use CML systems which force this concept of knowledge upon the designer, or, given a content-free* system which would allow the alternative, they nevertheless through their testing system represent knowledge as heavily structured, tightly controlled and clearly specified. The courses which result tend to be linear in organization, with students being given freedom to pace their own learning, but not to determine the range of content or the depth and character of its analysis.

An associated issue underlying design of the data-gathering techniques to be used in CML is the designer's presumption of the nature of student learning and how it can best be advanced. At the moment, the world of CML systems is dominated by a goal-oriented management philosophy which incorporates behaviourist models of learning. Some systems designers have been so firmly committed to this view of learning that their systems will not operate in any meaningful way unless goals are expressed in the form of lists of behavioural objectives, unless progress is defined as the mastery of successive criterion-referenced tests, and unless feedback is in the form of prescriptive directions to proceed linearly or to recycle until mastery is established. Many potential users of CML systems are – with considerable justification – resentful of this notion of how student learning can be enhanced. Those who would base their learning systems design on cognitive (rather than behavioural) models of student learning need to seek out so-called context-free* CML systems. These give the designer the freedom to treat the student as an active processor of information and constructor of knowledge, as someone who has both the potential, and also ultimately the responsibility, to take over control of his or her own learning and to construct knowledge in his or her own way.

Whether the fundamental issues are faced up to or brushed aside, the CML designer faces many operational problems associated with the data collection phase of the learning cycle. The data must be defined, the structure of the information files must be decided and many technical details about the information handling resolved. All these can be rather difficult steps to understand and implement for anyone without both a computing background and considerable training on the system in use.

Faced with these difficulties, CML users have in the past tended to regress towards using only the simplest of any standard routines provided by the systems developers; hence the propensity to use objective tests with traditional multiple-choice questions and nothing else. However, the newer systems are beginning to tackle the problem; the general trend towards user-friendly* systems has not gone unnoticed in the CML field, and gradually the technical problems are fading into the background. In turn, the educational problems which have always been present are moving into sharper focus.

Feedback and routing

At some early stage in the development of a CML application, the designer must decide who is to be the prime target for the information which can be generated by the system. Is it to be the teacher acting as manager, or the individual student acting as self-manager of learning, or both in some kind of combination? If the student is seen as deserving an equal or more central position in the information system then it is critical to examine closely the feedback mechanisms provided by the CML system contemplated for use.

Several levels of feedback are possible. At the simplest level, the computer will automatically produce student reports which give the results of the test just completed, identifying right answers and explaining wrong ones. If option weighting, item weighting and group allocation of items are available, then the feedback can be more complex. It can refer, for example, to the individual student's performance on sub-sections of the test covering different content areas, different cognitive skills or different types of attitude. If the CML system allows the storage of the results of previous tests, then comparisons between current and past performance can be made and reported to the student. This allows the student to place his or her current learning status in context, over a period of time. Some systems allow the course designer access to performance statistics for the student body as a whole so that an individual student could, for example, be informed that his or her answer to such-and-such a question has also been selected by a certain percentage of the other students on the course.

All this information is retrospective. It looks back to past performance and seeks to remedy deficiencies. Unfortunately, most CML systems handle this task by confining the course designer to a very limited set of feedback options consisting of standard, automatically printed lists or tables. However, a totally different degree of freedom is reached if the designer is able to specify decision rules*, so that feedback is generated in the form of individualized letters. This facility, if it is combined with the capacity to handle the analysis of calendar dates, can be a very powerful tool in the hands of the CML course designer, especially when it is used to route* or steer the student through the individualized curriculum, to look forward as well as backward in time.

The decision rules which govern the production of individualized feedback of this type are relatively straightforward if they are related to course structures which are themselves clearly defined. In a course based on the notion that the student has to display mastery of a list of performance objectives, a decision rule might read:

IF   (a) the student has failed to demonstrate mastery of the objectives associated with this test, and
        (b) this is the first attempt on this test
THEN write in the student's letter − 'You have failed to reach a criterion score of 80 per cent on this test. Please refer to the comments on the questions you got wrong, and retake the test when you feel you have sorted out your mistakes.'

In another situation the number and range of criteria used in the decision rule could be larger, and the student record could be referenced several times before the feedback is selected for printing. For example, a decision rule for routing in a distance education course could read:

IF   (a) Today's date minus date for submission of the assignment on X is greater than 14 days, and
        (b) the student's cumulated average score in assignments to date is between 50 per cent and 60 per cent and
        (c) no explanation of late submission has been logged, and
        (d) the student has a home phone
THEN write in the student's letter − 'It is now more than two weeks past the date for submission of your assignment on X. Are you having difficulties of any sort? Please call (tutor's phone number is inserted) and let me know if things are OK with you.'

It is the content, character and style of feedback which most clearly reveals the CML designer's and users' intentions not only about how students' learning should be encouraged, but also their intentions about the location of responsibility for the control of learning. At one not uncommon extreme, control will reside in the hands of the original designer of a purpose-built system which has built-in routing rules inaccessible both to teacher and student. At face value, the modularized courseware* accompanying such a system can be very attractive in its apparent flexibility and sensitivity to individual differences. On closer examination of the feedback, however, it may well emerge that the underlying models of the knowledge domain and of the student's methods of learning are rigid, unchangeable and directed towards prescriptive and external control of student behaviour. For some educators, if CML is to be acceptable at all, its feedback-generating mechanisms will have to be readily accessible so that teachers can more readily use the system to represent themselves as they really are − to 'clone' themselves in print.

Reporting

If teachers, administrators and curriculum developers are to gain from the use of CML, then the system must provide a comprehensive range of regular reports. The more complex the learning environment, and the greater the number of students cycling through it at individual rates, the more demanding is the specification of the reporting procedures, but also the more rewarding is the implementation of a successful system. From the time when the first student enrols to the time that the last student's grades are processed, regular, reliable and up-to-date reports are required on enrolment, on individual students' performance profiles, on class lists, on attendance and on the allocation of resources. Often, one of the central reasons for using CML is to identify students who are in special need of tutorial support. In large enrolment courses the teacher cannot reasonably be expected to spend a large amount of time working in a tutorial setting with each and every student. The task of identifying the students who need this special help is made so much easier for the teacher/manager if reports are produced regularly which identify students who might fall into this category – for example, those who have suffered from procrastination in previous courses and are showing signs of dropping behind their peers. The managerial report can call the teacher's attention to the need to act as a teacher, rather than as a manager. As such, it is likely to prove popular amongst those who suspect that CML systems can come between good teachers and the students who need their skilled attention.

Teachers' knowledge of students can be greatly enriched by good reporting, but so also can the knowledge of administrators and curriculum developers about the flow of students through the course structure, about the resources deployed and how they are meeting the task, and about the performance on criterion- and norm-referenced tests.

Trends

Over the next several years anyone seeking to implement CML will have a gradually widening choice of systems. At the moment the best systems are mainframe* systems, designed to operate on large computers. However, these systems are also expensive and difficult to transfer from one machine to another. Meanwhile, a new breed of CML systems is appearing for use on microcomputers*. To date, these systems have been disappointing in that they have provided very limited sets of facilities and thus force the user into one particular form of learning management. This is not surprising since CML systems have typically made heavy demands on memory* space. Squeezing all that has to be stored into the small memories and disc space of first-generation personal computers* can only be accomplished by vigorous pruning of the range of facilities offered.

This phase of restriction on development will not last very long. Personal computers with internal memories of 256K* and disc storage of ten or more megabytes* will soon be available at prices within the reach of individual schools or college departments, and designers of CML systems will be able to take advantage of this low-cost, high-capacity hardware*.

These new systems are likely to incorporate a number of features which have not been widely available in the past. For example, students and teachers will spend more time at the keyboard* interacting directly with the machine. Students will take tailored tests at the keyboard, and receive optional individualized feedback through the screen display rather than in print. Teachers will intervene in the automatic management process more readily than was possible in the past, intercepting and adjusting communications to students in cases where the routine procedures, pre-ordained during course planning, have proved inadequate to meet unanticipated circumstances.

While CML systems will continue to support conventional learning in classrooms, libraries, laboratories and the home, there will be a trend towards increased use of interactive* computer-assisted learning* (CAL) as one of the modules for learning to which students may be assigned. When this happens, the performance data accumulated during the use of the CAL package will be transferred automatically to the student's record in the CML system. In this way CAL and CML will tend to merge.

Another likely trend will be for CML systems to separate into two very distinct types: general-purpose and special-purpose. General-purpose systems will attempt to be content-free and context-free. In theory, the systems will be adaptable for use with any subject matter and amenable to use in any learning context. However, since the concepts of scientific management underpin most CML systems designs, and since teachers who are not philosophically in tune with this approach have to date found it difficult to make extended or intensive use of CML, it may be that no system will ever be universally recognized as context-free. Some people will always presume that mechanistic use of technology is implicit, however sensitive and humane the potential uses which might be devised.

Special-purpose CML systems might not even be recognizable as CML. They will be single-application systems, pre-packaged complete with specific content, tests, feedback comments and routing decision rules. Their focus will be problem areas of the curriculum, where experience has shown that teaching in the mass, without individualization, is failing to reach institutional and national goals for education and training.

Lastly, a trend which may see the end of traditional CML as a distinct management device is the gradually rising sophistication of the information and communication systems which are being developed for use in commercial settings. These systems will spill over into education and training and could overtake and incorporate conventional CML in the process.

CML systems can bring major benefits to those involved in their use. Provided that they are user-friendly, easy to understand and easily used by the educator with relatively little experience of computer-based education, they will increasingly be used in support of learning and training in settings which involve heterogeneous student populations, large student numbers, students learning at a distance, low staff-student ratios – indeed in any settings where opportunities for regular face-to-face review of the learning status of each and every individual student are limited or non-existent. Computer-managed learning relieves the teacher of the boredom and burden of low level management tasks. But it has far more potential than that; it can allow the highest level management skills of experienced teachers to be deployed in support of all students, so that students can more readily assess themselves as learners and become active managers of their own learning.

9. The computer as a medium for distance education

Richard Hooper

Summary: Communications technology can be applied to distance education in two ways. In *live/transmitted* mode, the student learns 'on-line' from material transmitted over a distance in real-time (as with a television broadcast or remote computer linked by telephone). In *recorded/local* mode, on the other hand, the learner receives material (eg cassettes containing recorded sound or computer programs) for use 'off-line' whenever convenient. Three types of *live/transmitted* computer-assisted distance learning are described: two-way CAL (eg Prestel), one-way information retrieval (eg teletext) and computer-assisted live teaching (eg CYCLOPS). *Recorded/local* modes of learning have been advanced by the rise of the portable learning device and the personal computer. Telesoftware is put forward as a response to the problem of software distribution. It combines the advantages of both modes of distance learning by computer.

Introduction

Communications technology used in the cause of distance education can be usefully analysed and categorized in two ways.

First, communications technology can be used to transmit teaching to learners at a distance, 'live' and 'in real-time'. For example, educational radio and television could be seen as the classic examples of what I would like to call *live/transmitted* media. Here the term 'live' is being used in a particular way. It means that the student is receiving the teaching which is sent to him over a distance at a specific point in time. The maths lesson is transmitted from 9.00 am to 9.30 am. The student who switches on at 9.31 am misses it. The term 'live' is not being used here in the traditional broadcasting sense of a programme being transmitted as it is being made, ie live from a studio or outside broadcast.

The second type of communications technology for distance education can be labelled *recorded/local*. An example of this would be the same half-hour maths programme being stored on cassette or disc (audio or video) and then sent to the distant student. The manner of sending could be the postal service, a retail distribution network involving high street shops, or broadcast transmitters, for example in off-peak hours. The student could then play the recorded cassette on a local piece of hardware* with no communications/

transmission links being necessary; the student can play the maths lesson at 9.00 am or at 9.31 am. Unlike the live/transmitted technology, the student can stop and start at will.

It should be noted that this is only one way of categorizing communications technology for distance learning. Another well-known classification is one-way transmission versus two-way interaction. Broadcasting, either live/transmitted or recorded/local, is essentially a one-way technology. Computing, like the live teacher, tends to be two-way. As a rule of thumb, two-way technology is more expensive than one-way. Such a classification cuts right across the one I have adopted in this chapter, since both one-way and two-way processes can take place in either the live/transmitted or the recorded/local mode.

This chapter, then, concentrates on the computer as a medium for distance education, and reviews the role of the computer first of all in live/transmitted mode, and then in recorded/local mode.

Live/transmitted computing for distance learners

There are three types of computing for distance learners in live/transmitted mode:

1. two-way computer-assisted learning* in tutorial and/or simulation* style;
2. one-way information retrieval;
3. computer-assisted live teaching.

Two-way CAL

Two-way CAL*, in live/transmitted mode, involves the student at some kind of display device carrying out a dialogue with a computer situated at a distance from the display. The student and computer are linked together using some form of telecommunications, eg the public switched telephone network, packet switching, data* links or leased circuits. The computer works in time-sharing* mode, serving a number of simultaneous users. If the system is well designed, each user gets the feeling that the computer is personally available and adaptable to his/her requirements on that particular day.

Two-way CAL can carry out a range of teaching jobs, including transmission of facts or skills, testing, re-transmission in the light of diagnostics held in the software*, simulation of experiences for the student to manipulate, and problem-solving. In the last application, the emphasis tends to be on the student writing a computer program* to solve a problem.

This type of CAL got under way in the USA in the 1960s. Early examples tended to focus on drill and practice applications in maths and literacy. This developed into more sophisticated tutorial applications, and the computer software now tries to imitate more closely the human tutor. The most well-known example of two-way CAL is the PLATO* system; this product has been developed at the University of Illinois since 1961 under Don Bitzer and marketed by Control Data Corporation. PLATO has elegant graphics* and an author language* to help teachers construct good quality teaching materials for the system. PLATO is an intelligent computer system that can store information on the individual student's performance and route* him/her according to the achieved level of work.

At the other extreme of sophistication and cost (PLATO is a high-cost CAL system) would be Prestel, British Telecom's world viewdata* service. Prestel allows simple-minded computer-assisted learning which is reminiscent of programmed learning. Any Prestel page (24 rows of 40 characters, about 75 to 100 English words) can be simply programmed by the information provider to route to a wide range of other Prestel pages according to which keys on the keypad* the student presses. The Prestel computer is unintelligent and retains no memory* of the path of the student other than via creative use of the pre-determined routing/tree structure. The Prestel system uses the ordinary telephone lines and a suitably modified television set or viewdata terminal*. A number of organizations have experimented with CAL on Prestel: Teleview, a small information provider based in north east England; Hertfordshire's Advisory Centre for Computer-Based Education; and the Print Industry Research Association whose training materials resemble programmed learning.

For live/transmitted CAL to distance learners, both PLATO and Prestel have a disadvantage – they require the use of the telephone which increases costs. Because of telecommunications costs, allied to advances in miniaturization and semiconductors, the trend towards moving away from live/transmitted towards recorded/local has been visible for many years. Because of this trend, a new role is emerging for systems like PLATO and Prestel – the distribution of computer-assisted learning programs to remote terminals, called telesoftware*. Telesoftware will be described later under 'recorded/local'.

One-way information retrieval

The leading example of one-way information retrieval computing for education is teletext*. Teletext, like viewdata, is a British invention, whereby pages of text are sent to suitably modified television receivers using spare lines in the gaps between pictures. There are currently some 200,000 teletext receivers in the UK, the largest service of its kind anywhere in the world. Both the BBC and the commercial television companies provide teletext services. Teletext can be used not for direct teaching in CAL mode, but for transmitting key pieces of information, course or television programme notes, corrections and assignments to distant students. Teletext, like viewdata, can be updated almost instantaneously, in a way that print cannot be. Teletext is also significantly involved in telesoftware projects for educational use.

Computer-assisted live teaching

Finally, the computer has a role to play in assisting live distance teaching. The most notable example of this is the development of CYCLOPS at the Open University, which is marketed by Aregon, a leading London-based software/systems company.

CYCLOPS is an audio-visual system based on the conventional television set, standard audio cassettes and microcomputers*. It exploits the fact that microcomputers can process pictorial information into digital* form. This information can be stored on an audio cassette or transmitted along an ordinary telephone line, for playback on a television set.

CYCLOPS is both a live/transmitted and a recorded/local medium. In live/transmitted mode, it supports and extends telephone tutorial conferencing. Using a light pen* the teacher draws on the television screen, and the pictures are transmitted live down the telephone to students at other locations. In 1981-2 the Open University conducted a trial of the CYCLOPS 'remote blackboard' facility in the Nottingham area in collaboration with British Telecom. The CYCLOPS terminal, it is worth noting, is fully compatible with Prestel, ie it can access Prestel viewdata pages.

Recorded/local computing for distance learners

As already noted, the trend is well-established towards recorded/local mode. 'Speak & Spell', and the 'Little Professor', which are mass consumer products from Texas Instruments, are classic examples of recorded/local computing. In the 1960s, the Little Professor type of drill-and-practice mathematics was being done in school classrooms by large and expensive computers with many terminals linked in time-sharing mode. Nowadays such a device fits in the palm of the hand, can be purchased for a few pounds, and is available in the home.

Recorded/local mode has been given particular stimulus by the explosive growth in personal computers*: the Apple, Pet, Sinclair and Acorn/BBC variety. In the low-cost educational environment time-sharing computers plus telecommunications links cannot compete with small personal computers using discs or cassettes for storage. Personal computers can now carry out the full range of two-way CAL described above. It is significant that PLATO, in response to this changing environment, is to be implemented in a micro-computer version.

CYCLOPS also operates in recorded/local mode. In 'tape replay' mode, the pictures are recorded on one channel of a stereo cassette and the sound on the other channel. When replayed, the student sees a kind of television programme made up of animated diagrams and synchronized sound. The tape itself can be sent through the post.

There is one major problem with recorded/local computer-assisted learning. How do you distribute cost-effectively large numbers of programs to large numbers of people who are geographically dispersed? The problem is exacerbated by the fact that computer programs always have errors in them and therefore need to be maintained and updated regularly. Software maintenance at a distance and at low cost is not easy.

This problem has led to the invention of 'telesoftware'. Telesoftware is a technique whereby a computer downloads* computer programs over telephone lines to local terminals. The local terminal, which is in fact a microcomputer, then switches off the telecommunications links, and runs the program locally as and when desired. Various security devices can be used to stop pirating, and to stop usage after a certain time.

In the UK, the Council for Educational Technology is doing a lot of work with telesoftware using Prestel to download to personal computers in schools and colleges. There is also much activity with teletext services in conjunction with the BBC Computer Literacy Project (see Chapter 22). Viewers who buy the BBC Microcomputer can also purchase decoders* which allow the computer to receive telesoftware from both BBC's Ceefax teletext service and from British Telecom's Prestel.

Telesoftware has created a great deal of interest on both sides of the Atlantic. It is an elegant marriage between live/transmitted and recorded/local computing modes.

Conclusion

Education began historically as a live/local medium with no distance communication (except the length of lecture hall or church). Students went to the teacher in the monastery or the school, and sat at his feet. With the invention of moveable type in the fifteenth century, education could be recorded in book form and distributed to students at a distance. With the development of postal services in Britain from the sixteenth century onwards, the distribution of education through books became more practical, culminating in the birth of correspondence education in the nineteenth century.

In the twentieth century the technologies available to extend distance education have developed rapidly, building on the foundations of broadcasting, a mass telephone network, and computing. It is therefore not surprising that the late twentieth century has seen the growth of distance teaching systems such as the Open University and its counterparts around the world. The teacher – in recorded or live mode – can now be transported to the students. The computer is used to assist or replace the live teacher, and – more mundanely – to carry out the huge tasks of administering a distance teaching system with many thousands of students.

Since the arrival of communications satellites in the late 1950s, distance has become a much less significant factor. Given that a computer or telephone message has to travel some 40,000 miles to and from the satellite, it is of small consequence how far away the source is from the receiver, or the teacher from the student. Distance-independent tariffs are becoming a reality in telecommunications systems that rely heavily on satellites, computers and digital technology.

The modern designer of educational systems is no longer constrained by technology. The technology is there to deliver teaching quickly and accurately over vast distances. The costs are coming down in real terms since such technology is a low user of energy resources. Semiconductor advances mean that the student can afford to have a lot of storage and processing power cheaply at hand, in his own home, factory or office. The obstacles to rapid growth of distance education in the twenty-first century are social, attitudinal and political – they are no longer technological.

10. An example of a software library and its dissemination

Bill Tagg

Summary: One local education authority's approach to software distribution is presented as a case study in the problems and rewards of establishing, maintaining and disseminating a library of educational software. In the early days of mainframe computing, the standardization of terminals and display formats was achieved relatively easily by evolution. The advent of rapidly-changing microcomputer technology has demanded more positive intervention because of the greater problems of transferability. Hertfordshire has succeeded in developing software which allows users to link their microcomputers to a mainframe computer and to exchange software between the two, easily and reliably, while making it easy for a non-specialist to understand which machine is doing what. Throughout, the needs of teachers are emphasized – for training courses, user-friendly systems, good documentation and software browsing facilities, and for easy access to software produced by teachers elsewhere and from commercial sources. Programs have been distributed by telesoftware, with built-in invoicing through Prestel, and the British Telecom 'Gateway' service offers the prospect of national availability of Hertfordshire's software library at local call rates.

Introduction

This chapter is about the real world of software* distribution in Hertfordshire and further afield. It is about what is happening now in 100 establishments within the local education authority and 50 centres acting on behalf of other authorities. It is about how Hertfordshire came to its present position, about its policy of standardization, its hopes for the future and about its successes and failures. But most of all it is about what is being achieved in ordinary schools by teachers who, in most cases, accepted as an extra duty computing responsibilities within their own school or college and who, as a consequence of that acceptance, found themselves part of an interdisciplinary network* with many problems still ahead of them, but with some achievements behind them.

History

On-line* computing in Hertfordshire goes back to 1967 when, with limited experience, a mainframe* (an Elliott 803) was used to provide a time-sharing* system (three users at a time). This was followed in 1970 by a major computing installation (a DEC System 10) to serve the needs of the Hatfield Polytechnic and surrounding schools and colleges. The schools and colleges had a third of its resources and, with the establishment of the Advisory Unit for Computer-Based Education in 1973, the opportunity to collaborate and share software arose and was grasped. The coming of the microcomputer* in the late 1970s was viewed with some misgivings for, although it provided cheap computer power for the first time, it looked for a while as if the spirit of collaboration would not continue.

By this time the schools and colleges had their own machine (a PDP 11/70) and the informal 'borrowing' of software which is so easy on a time-sharing system was being threatened. A good deal of effort was required if each establishment was not to become isolated by stand-alone equipment.

Standardization

Standards started automatically – when everyone shares the same hardware* and software there are no problems in this respect. The first time any decision was needed it was to do with terminals*. Some schools and colleges had bought themselves visual display units* (VDUs) and, without any conscious effort to standardize, many had chosen the same model – the Digilog. This display allowed text 40 columns wide by 16 lines deep and was preferred because the large letters meant that it could be used to demonstrate to classes of students. Software came to be written which exploited its facilities, so what had started as a series of random decisions turned into a recommendation. Subsequently all county standards have remained at a recommendation level with the only 'carrot' being a better level of service and (usually) free maintenance.

The first microcomputers

Trying to standardize in a rapidly changing technology has its pitfalls since hardware dates quickly; today's best buy may be obsolete tomorrow. It was because the Digilog became prohibitively expensive that the first Research Machines Limited 380Z microcomputer was installed in Cavendish school, Hemel Hempstead. We had discovered that with the right bit of software, a 380Z with an acoustic coupler* could behave like a Digilog and could be bought for two-thirds of the price. Right from the start, therefore, micro-computers in Hertfordshire were linked to the mainframe and even today any school buying a 380Z is given an acoustic coupler to go with it so as to provide the link and to encourage schools to use it.

Computer-assisted learning

Many computing resources are still used to support the teaching of computer studies and the county has its own CSE/O level syllabus (see also Chapter 18). In addition, high priority has always been given to computer-assisted learning (CAL)*. Even computer studies needs a rich selection of software if children are to appreciate that computers that pay for their keep spend much more time running programs* than helping programmers to develop them. In CAL, subject specialists only find it worthwhile bothering to learn how to use the technology if the library of software available is comprehensive enough. Keeping a hundred or so programs, maintaining them, making spare copies, cataloguing them, and answering queries about them is a big enough problem on a mainframe. To look after a hundred copies of such a library is clearly much more difficult, yet this is precisely what needs to be done.

Micro to mainframe links

Linking micros to mainframes is technically easy (each is 'persuaded' that it is communicating with a terminal), but to design the software interface* so that it can be used simply by all users of computers – not just by computer scientists – is much more difficult. The third version of the software is currently operating in the schools and colleges, and the fourth edition is being tested. The software is designed to the following criteria:

1. it must be capable of allowing the micro to operate as a terminal and must allow software to be moved from mainframe to micro and *vice versa*;
2. since users are essentially communicating with two machines, it must always be clear to them which machine is receiving their input* and where messages are coming from;
3. software must not be corrupted during transmission.

Meeting objectives

Most of the Hertfordshire-produced software conforms to a set of standards designed to help the user (Tagg, 1981). This makes the programs easy to use, and also provides the user with a familiar environment – he/she feels at home because other pieces of software have communicated with him/her in a similar way and use the same conventions. The micro/mainframe interface software conforms to this standard; the distinction between the micro and the mainframe is kept clear by arranging for the cursor* to flash when the mainframe is being used and to remain stationary otherwise. As a terminal, the micro still behaves like a Digilog at present, but in the most recent version this will be an option with the micro normally behaving like a Prestel display. Error detection and correction has been implemented when software is transferred between the two machines; a sum check* is transmitted with each line and if the check fails, the line is simply transmitted again.

Teacher training

The teacher training undertaken by the Hertfordshire Local Education Authority consists of teaching some (but by no means all) teachers to write good programs in BASIC* both for the 380Z micro and for the PDP 11/70 mainframe. The dialect* available means that good structure is possible and the dreaded GOTO* statement does not have to be used in every other line. In addition, of course, all teachers need the opportunity to reflect on the place of computing within their own discipline and this means in turn that they need to use the machine, come to terms with its operating system*, and get the feel of how data processing* relates to learning and teaching within their discipline. As part of this activity, a course in the use of the micro/mainframe software is always included.

Successes and failures

During the first four years of micro/mainframe communication many lessons have been learnt in Hertfordshire. In the initial version of the interface software, the microcomputer user loaded BASIC and then requested the program from the mainframe instead of typing it in line by line. The program could then be run immediately, or could be saved as a normal BASIC program. To the user, this software looked like an extension of the cassette operating system so that he/she only needed to interact with three pieces of software: the extended operating system, micro BASIC, and the mainframe operating system. Nevertheless, it proved too difficult to be worthwhile for some of the Hertfordshire users, many of whom had come to computing as a minority activity within their other teaching and curriculum commitments. By contrast, the present software is much easier to use. This is partly because of lessons learnt about user-friendliness*; its chief advantage is that for most of the time, it communicates with the mainframe automatically, so that the user does not have to keep track of which machine is being used.

The micro software library

Standardizing on the 380Z microcomputer – not because it is necessarily the best but so that software can be exchanged – has been central to the Authority's policy. Even with only one make of micro the problems of software compatibility are quite significant. Seventeen different versions of BASIC have been used at one time or another and even now seven versions are currently being used in Hertfordshire. Different memory* sizes are one aspect of incompatibility, since users of machines with large memories often like to develop large or sophisticated programs whose coding* and data* use up most of the available space. These just will not fit a smaller machine. There is now a policy of upgrading all micros to at least 32K* bytes* of memory. Even so there are many other obstacles to compatibility. The programs can be stored on floppy discs* which may be 8 inch or 5¼ inch, single sided or double sided, or on audio cassettes, which are then played by machines which may or may not have a motor control. Since micros can come with or without high resolution graphics*, programs must either eschew this luxury or else they limit their transferability*. There are seven different printers* to support, each requiring different interfaces and special cables. Soon there will be more alternatives from microcomputer and printer manufacturers, who seem to produce new options faster than educational users can absorb the possibilities of the old. At present, software is grouped into different libraries but an attempt to qualify it further is having to be modified. In practice, for example, there is often no clear-cut distinction between software which needs discs* and that which does not. Classifying by subject, required configuration, level, style and origin is now the responsibility of a full-time librarian (sponsored for the first year by Research Machines Limited) to sort out all these problems and to co-ordinate the work of cataloguing and publicizing what is available.

Browsing

Any library of resources requires a browsing facility. For a book library this is easily achieved by arranging for the books to be displayed so that the user can take any one he/she wishes, open it in the middle, read three or four sentences and then turn over a hundred or so pages and read two or three more. Since it is not possible to do this with computer programs, some alternative facility must be provided. In Hertfordshire three parallel services are being developed to help the user to find the bit of software he/she needs.

First, every program accepted into the library is catalogued. Each entry is two pages long and, amongst the more usual information, includes a sample run of the program. Second, a file of information about all the programs is maintained on the mainframe computer as part of a generalized information retrieval system available to users. Finally, a mainframe HELP system based on the Prestel user interface is being developed (Figure 1).

HERTS PDP11/70 HELP SYSTEM   0A

HELP is available on the
following topics:

1. How to use the HELP system
2. CAL
3. System information
4. News of meetings, workshops and
   conferences
5. Micro matters

Key the number of the information you
require

Key: ⌗ to continue, 9 to exit from HELP

Figure 1 *The HELP options offered by the Hertfordshire mainframe system*

Distributing software to other LEAs

Although this 'free' system of software distribution was devised and implemented for Hertfordshire, over half the other local education authorities (LEAs) in the British Isles are using the system as well. The micro/mainframe interface software, supporting documentation* and an account number into the mainframe are provided for a joining fee of £10, which allows any one LEA centre to use the service; local software distribution becomes the responsibility of the LEA. This free service deals with all good quality software which originators are prepared to make available. Software in the public domain comprises the greater part of small scale applications software suitable for the educational market.

Going commercial

The maintenance of free software cannot continue indefinitely. As the total quantity of software and potential customers grows, so does the commitment to maintain it. Publishers are conscious of a software market particularly where there is a substantial associated printed element and they are encouraging teachers to write software for them in much the same way that in the past they have commissioned textbooks.

*Telesoftware**

Another way of disseminating software is through a viewdata* system. British Telecom's Prestel service provides access to data stored on the Prestel computers at local telephone call rates. This generalized information retrieval system provides access to different sections of the community – business, education, the general public. Through the work of the Council for Educational Technology, Hertfordshire has made some of its software available via Prestel. Because it is possible to make the microcomputer emulate a Prestel terminal, this software is theoretically available to all users. Furthermore, invoicing the user can be handled by the Prestel system itself as it has its own built-in accounting.

   One interesting development is an extension to Prestel planned by British Telecom called 'Gateway'. Through Gateway, information-providers will be able to connect their own computer to the Prestel service so that users can have access to dynamically generated pages of data from an information-providers' computer. In this way it is planned to make the Hertfordshire microcomputer library available nationally at local call rates, without having to maintain a separate copy on Prestel.

The future

Other methods of software distribution are being investigated in Hertfordshire, including broadcasting by teletext* (two Hertfordshire schools are helping to pilot a scheme being co-ordinated from Brighton Polytechnic), using bar coding* techniques and simply putting floppy discs in the post. It is too early to predict which methods will stand the test of time. What is certain is that software dissemination is essential and that it will not happen without the expenditure of resources and careful planning.

Reference

Tagg, W (1981) *A Standard for CAL Dialogue* Advisory Unit for Computer-Based Education (AUCBE): Hertfordshire County Council

11. Computers and the handling of information

Don Ely

Summary: Computers as information storage and retrieval systems are just beginning to be used in educational settings. Special systems, called data bases, acquire information, process and store it, and make it available to users. The information may be complete as it comes from the computer storage or it may be a digest of the original information which is available elsewhere.

Information systems for education may be large or small and serve students at all levels. One of the first data bases in education was ERIC, which is now operating on a world-wide basis with access in at least 20 locations outside North America and 438 in North America. Smaller data bases use microcomputers and are generally developed by local schools and school systems. Students from elementary and secondary schools as well as tertiary education are using computers to store and retrieve information from data bases. Teachers, librarians, and guidance counsellors help to create data bases and advise others about their use. Schools are beginning to use data bases with increasing frequency.

In educational settings, the computer serves as a management tool, as a medium for instruction and learning, and as an information storage and retrieval device. This chapter considers the computer as an instrument which stores and retrieves information.

Purpose of data bases

In a generic sense, all computers store and retrieve information for specific purposes (eg instructional drill and practice or mathematical calculation) but when the purpose is to obtain answers to questions which are contained in a large amount of information, a computer-based system can be used. Such systems are often called data bases*. They usually contain large amounts of information which can be instantly accessed and retrieved. The purpose of a data base is to acquire, process, and make available subject matter in an accurate and efficient manner. The computer helps to avoid the tedious and time-consuming information access problems faced by educators who have had to use various catalogues, indexes, bibliographies, and record-keeping files, often scattered across several locations.

Functions of a data base

In its simplest form, a data base is a collection of entries.

Each entry is about an entity, be it a book or person, commodity or statistic, and about its essential characteristics. At the very least, it must contain for each entity: a means of identifying it uniquely (and) an organized description of it which may be used for searching. (Townley, 1978)

It may also contain an 'address' in the system and other descriptive details such as an abstract.

There are three major functions of an information system:

1. *the production of an index* which can be used to sort, reformat, cumulate, and print information;
2. *retrospective searching* which is used to assist a user in finding specific information; and
3. *selective dissemination of information* (SDI) which locates information based on a profile generated by the user. (Tedd, 1979)

A data base can be as small as a floppy disc* used with a microcomputer*, or as large as a mainframe* computer with dozens of magnetic tapes containing information. In either case, the purpose is the same: to help a user locate information which will help solve a problem or answer a question.

Elements of a data base

Data bases are built to provide *linkages* between *users* and *producers* of information. In education, the *users* are teachers, administrators, students, librarians, and other specialists. *Producers* of information are authors of written materials such as books, research reports, journal articles and instructional materials. The *linkage* is the computer with its associated procedures (or software*) which enable users to find relevant knowledge. The critical element of the system is the way in which a user obtains information.

There are basically two types of information which can be obtained from a data base:

1. the full text or raw data; or
2. a surrogate of the text or data. When information is relatively brief, the entire item can be placed in computer storage; for example, statistical data or demographic information. However, when the amount of information is extensive, as in a monograph or report, surrogate information is necessary. In this case, there is an annotation or abstract which provides the essence of the original with some indication as to the source of the entire document or item.

A data base is a means for *users* to obtain information produced by *authors* or other originators of information. Figure 1 shows the relationship from the user's point of view. A user can have access to *full text* (solid box) if it is relatively brief and can be stored in the computer which is being used. If the content of single items is too long, access is usually by an *abstract* or annotation (broken box) which serves as a surrogate for the actual, full text item. In cases where surrogate information is given, reference to location of the full text is usually given. For example, such reference might be to a publication on a library shelf, to a microfiche in a cabinet, or to a specific person such as the teacher or librarian.

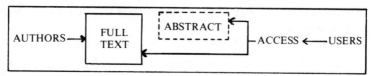

Figure 1 *Basic elements of a bibliographic data base (source: Clark, 1981)*

Additional functions of 'proactive' *acquisition*, *user services*, and *information analysis* enhances the utility of the same data base (see Figure 2).

Proactive acquisition implies that special predetermined criteria are applied to the selection of items to be placed into the system. Such criteria usually evolve from a knowledge of the user population. User services provide instruction and/or assistance to those who use the system. Information analysis grows out of the review of information going into the system for the purpose of identifying trends, describing state-of-the-art, and providing guidance for the user.

ERIC – an established data base

One of the most widely searched and heavily used bibliographic data bases in the world today is the Educational Resources Information Center (ERIC) system. Since 1966 it has systematically acquired educational documents and has annotated the periodical literature in education. Its functions are high-lighted in Figure 2.

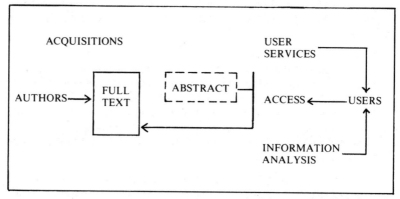

Figure 2 *Elements of ERIC: an enhanced data base with optimum features*

Access to more than 432,000 citations (as of July 1981) is available through print (*Resources in Education* (RIE), and *Current Index to Journals in Education* (CIJE)) and computer-based information systems. There are over 50 world-wide organizations that purchase ERIC tapes and provide computer access to them. From these sources more than 500 service centres provide computer searches of the ERIC data base. Individuals who want access to the ERIC data base via computer-searching can contact one of the service centres or, with a computer terminal* that can link by telephone with one of the data base vendors (eg Lockheed Information Systems-DIALOG, or System Development Corporation-ORBIT), arrangements can be made to search the data base for a fee.

A search of the ERIC data base will yield surrogate information, ie descriptive facts such as title, author, date published, publisher or journal, and an annotation or abstract of the content. Reference is made to the source which may be in the ERIC microfiche* collection (approximately 85 per cent of the documents in the data base are available this way) or the publisher source if it is not available in microfiche. Items which are journal articles give the necessary information for locating the article. In many cases, copies of journal articles can be ordered from University Microfilms International. ERIC is the best example of a large, systematic, and continuous data base for the field of education.

A counselling and guidance application

In the United States, several computer-based career planning and occupational information systems have been developed. Other systems help individuals to explore post-secondary educational options and sources of financial assistance. One such resource is the Guidance Information System (GIS) which provides access to information about occupations, colleges and universities, technical schools, and financial aid opportunities. The GIS is available to students, teachers, guidance counsellors and parents through a mainframe computer such as the one used by the Minnesota Educational Computing Consortium.

> The computerized information system aids the overburdened counsellor by encouraging students engaged in career exploration and decision-making to seek vocational information on their own. Such a system not only stores and retrieves vast quantities of data, but sorts quickly through it to find those parts which have certain characteristics prescribed by the student; and it brings together, compares and relates various bits of information, all during an interactive* dialogue with the student. (Edwards *et al*, 1978:65)

Microcomputer data bases: case studies

On a smaller scale, microcomputers are beginning to be used in education for information storage and retrieval. One obvious problem is the limited capacity of the small discs* which are the most common means for storing information. However, several projects are exploring the feasibility of using microcomputers for the purpose of building data bases. Examples from elementary and secondary schools provide case studies of microcomputer applications.

Elementary schools

In the Adams County School District of Denver, Colorado, USA, an elementary school library media specialist observed the frustration of students, teachers, and library assistants in using the card catalogue. A three-phase program* was developed using an Apple II microcomputer and a Corvus ten-megabyte* hard disc drive* (Winchester* type). The *first phase* allows students to access information by subject, author, or title as in a standard card catalogue. The *second phase* allows data entry via direct input*. The *third phase* is for general information retrieval purposes such as inventory, ordering and bibliography creation. 'The system is proving itself to be cost-effective and well worth the initial investment of time, money, and effort' (Costa, 1981).

Secondary schools

The British Library-sponsored project on 'Computerized Information Retrieval in Secondary Schools' is located in four schools in Isleworth (Middlesex), Nottingham, Leicester, and Stantonbury (near Milton Keynes). Its purpose is to develop a viable on-line* system for secondary level students (ages 14 to 18) and to introduce teachers and students to the practice of on-line searching. The equipment is a Research Machines Limited 380Z and plans for using the Commodore Pet are under way. The basic configuration contains 32K* of RAM* using double-density, two-sided floppy discs. The capacity of a small floppy disc is approximately 300 entries and about 1000 for a standard floppy disc. Each entry contains a number, a title, author(s), a bibliographic description, and keywords. Free text searches are conducted using a simple command language*. Users are drawn primarily from the fields of biology and geography since the content focusses on contemporary world problems and solutions. Information is geared specifically to topics in conservation, energy, pollution, population and raw materials (Payne, 1981).

Trends

Each of the systems described, regardless of size, attempts to put information directly at the disposal of the user. Each system has begun with the assumption that the user was having difficulty in locating needed information. Each system has developed a relatively simple direct access for which the user requires little or no assistance. The use of free text-searching techniques permits the user to query the data base using ordinary language. No special vocabulary is required to get directly to information in the data base. Most systems appear to be sensitive to the skills and needs of the user.

For many years data bases which required large capacity computers overshadowed the possibilities of the microcomputer as an information storage and retrieval device. There appear to be many programs which now use the microcomputer to store original data bases and partial files from larger data bases.

There seems to be no single educational level where the use of data bases dominate. They are being used by elementary students as well as by university students. Teachers at all levels are participating in data base development as well as learning how to use the computer in creative and time-saving ways.

Early information storage and retrieval systems used some of the basic premises and procedures of library science and, in many cases, flourished within libraries. Currently, libraries are centres of activity and, in some locations, offer access to many data bases. However, the storage and retrieval of information has gone beyond the library to the classroom, the guidance office, and even to the home.

Information storage and retrieval was one of the first uses of computers but, for schools, it has come later following the rapid development of the computer for school management and instruction. The development and use of data bases is just beginning to make headway in the world of education.

References

Clark, W Bruce (1981) Personal communication

Costa, B (1981) Microcomputers in Colorado – It's elementary! *Wilson Library Bulletin* May 1981:676-8, 717

Edwards, J, Ellis, A, Richardson, D E, Holtznagel, D and Klassen, D (1978) *Computer Applications in Instruction* Houghton Mifflin: Hanover, North Holland

Payne, A (1981) On-line information retrieval in schools *CAL News* **16** March 1981:11

Tedd, L A (1979) *Case Studies in Computer-Based Bibliographic Information Services* British Library Research and Development Reports, The British Library: London

Townley, H M (1978) *Systems Analysis for Information Retrieval* Andre Deutsch: London

Note: *The Directory of ERIC Search Services*, published biannually, is available free from the ERIC Processing and Reference Facility, 4833 Rugby Ave, Suite 303, Bethesda, Maryland 20014, USA.

Part 3:
National case studies

12. The '10,000 microcomputers plan' in France

Jacques Hebenstreit

Summary: As a result of a number of pilot schemes launched by the French Ministry of Education and the appearance of the first microcomputers on the market, secondary schools in France are currently involved in the large-scale introduction of computer technology into the educational system. This project, known as the '10,000 microcomputers plan', entails the equipping of all lycées with microcomputers and the training of volunteer teachers in their use. It aims to develop the use of computers as teaching tools in all subject areas and to familiarize students in the use of computer technology. Comparisons are drawn with a similar project in the UK and an outline is given of the training methods and the courseware and 'author language' developed. The computer's role as the tool of a new method of education, rather than as a specific training in computer science, is discussed. An assessment is made of the computer's potential in improving the teaching/learning process in tandem with current teaching aids, whilst stressing the role of the individual teacher in the successful implementation and development of the project.

The French system of education

Before examining the large-scale introduction of computer-based education in France it is worth outlining the basic characteristics of the French educational system to understand how its very structure is facilitating the introduction of computer technology.

The main characteristic of the French educational system is its high degree of centralization. All teachers from infant school to university are civil servants and, as such, are employed by the Ministère de l'Education Nationale. The content of all curricula for elementary and secondary schools (up to the age of 18) is defined explicitly, as are the number of teaching hours per week and per discipline. No change whatsoever can be made without an official decision by the Minister of Education.

For educational purposes the country is divided into 25 'Académies', each one headed by a 'Recteur d'Académie', nominated by the Minister. Although such a centralized structure has a number of drawbacks, it has definite advantages when it comes to making decisions and implementing changes, as has become apparent during the introduction of computers into the French educational system.

The period 1970-8

The first experimental introduction of computers in education began in 1970 and was limited to students between the ages of 15 and 18. From the very beginning the emphasis was on the use of the computer as a teaching tool in all subject areas. There were two major aims:

1. to investigate the use of computers as educational tools with the potential of introducing new methodological approaches to the teaching of various disciplines;
2. to encourage a type of implementation whereby interaction with the computer allows and encourages the student to take the initiative, to correct his own errors and to become more independent in his work (as in modelling and simulation*). This is in contrast to the programmed-learning type of interaction where the student is required only to respond to questions and instructions.

Implementation

To achieve these aims a number of decisions were made:

○ to train each year, on a volunteer basis, 100 secondary teachers (in all disciplines) during a full academic year in universities;
○ to rely on these trained teachers to achieve the above-mentioned aims. For that purpose, during the last three months of training, each group of three to five teachers has to design and implement a project involving an educational use of computers in a given discipline;
○ to establish a correspondence course oriented towards the application of computers in secondary education, including 'homework' to be returned for correction and a three-day seminar in a computing centre at the end of the course;
○ to define a standard hardware* configuration (16 terminals* on a time-shared* minicomputer*) to be installed in those lycées having at least two full-time trained teachers;
○ to define a standard programming language* for achieving transfer-ability* of the courseware* after it was written. The language LSE* (Langage Symbolique d'Enseignement—a symbolic teaching language) was defined at my laboratory in 1971 and implemented on the MITRA 15 and T1600, both French-made systems;
○ to arrange that after their one-year training, teachers would resume their teaching activities but with teaching loads reduced by three to six hours per week during which time they would join groups set up to write courseware packages (teaching programs* with documentation*);
○ to establish a branch of the Institut National de la Recherche Pédagogique, an existing institution of the Ministère de l'Education, with the task of centralizing, evaluating, documenting and disseminating the packages to ensure proper evaluation of and research into the results of the experiment.

What has been achieved

Between 1971 and 1976, 58 lycées received a time-shared minicomputer. Six hundred teachers were trained for a full year and 5000 followed the course by correspondence. More than 500 courseware packages were developed in LSE in all disciplines and 7000 copies were circulated on floppy discs*. In 1976, over 700 terminals were active and used for about 20 hours per week. The total cost over six years was about £10 million with half of it spent on teacher training and the other half split almost equally between hardware and the development of courseware packages.

Evaluation of the 1970-6 experiment

The full-time trained teachers were carefully selected; only about 40 per cent of them were chosen from the areas of mathematics and physics, the majority coming from a wide range of other disciplines. As it turned out, while teachers from disciplines other than maths and science experienced greater difficulties with the one-year curriculum, they produced some of the most original packages.

Most of the difficulties encountered by teachers when they began to develop courseware were caused by the official directive which stressed the importance of general educational aims rather than the specific teaching of computer science and programmed learning, and emphasized the need to develop modules based on modelling and simulation, either in closed form (guided discovery) or in open form (investigation). As a result, almost two years elapsed before the first packages appeared. However, courseware production increased steadily and about 70 per cent of the work produced was considered 'fair' to 'very good' when used by other teachers.

From the students' point of view the experiment was found to have a number of specific educational benefits. The use of computers allows the student a more active and individual role in the learning process and in certain disciplines provides an expanded field of knowledge through simulated experiments that cannot be carried out in the classroom.

Comparison with Britain's National Development Programme in Computer-Assisted Learning*, which lasted from 1973 to 1979 is instructive:

○ about 60 per cent of NDPCAL's budget was spent on staffing whereas in France the corresponding figure is around 70 per cent;
○ the evaluation of terminal use during NDPCAL showed an average of 500 hours per year; in France the terminals were used around 20 hours per week, which for an academic year of 25 weeks works out at 500 hours per year;
○ in both cases, the amount of time needed to develop a one-hour interactive* package was somewhere between 100 and 300 hours;
○ in both cases, the best packages came from teachers working in teams;
○ in both projects strong emphasis was placed on modelling and simulation in order to allow the student more opportunity to explore and develop the capabilities of the computer;

○ the experience of both projects is that the computer will not replace present methods wholesale but will complement and enhance existing practice.

An evaluation group was set up in 1976 to assess the results of the experiment and the first draft of its report presents a number of interesting conclusions:

○ about 45,000 students used CAL* in one way or another between 1978 and 1979;

○ during the 1978-9 academic year there were 6650 sessions in 48 lycées (between 27 and 501 sessions per lycée with an average number of 138);

○ during the same year CAL was used in at least five different disciplines in 75 per cent of lycées with the necessary equipment;

○ different subjects showed different levels of take-up as follows: maths: 1915 sessions; grammar and literature: 1204; foreign languages: 1387; physics: 876; economics: 599; natural sciences: 599; history and geography: 279, etc;

○ the attitude of the students was positive but almost all of them restricted computer use to between 10 and 20 per cent of their time. They all stressed the importance of human contact between students, and between teachers and students during normal classroom lessons.

The 10,000 microcomputers plan

In 1976 the first microcomputers* appeared on the market in France. With the advent of this technological advance and the accompanying decline in the cost of hardware and its increased availability, it became evident that it would not make much sense to invest in the existing time-shared minicomputers. The training of teachers was suspended but the existing groups continued to work on producing packages. Subsequently, in 1979, the French Ministry of Education and the Ministry of Industry jointly launched a five-year plan to install 10,000 self-contained microcomputers in secondary schools (11 to 18-year olds). The two major aims of this plan were the development of the use of computers as teaching tools throughout the school curriculum, not as replacements for teachers but as additional educational aids for improving and updating teaching methods, and also to accustom students to the idea that computer technology could become a normal part of their studies.

In 1978-80, 400 microcomputers were given to 159 schools, and in 1980-1, 768 microcomputers were given to 96 schools. (This worked out at eight for each school, which was considered a reasonable number because by pairing the students, half a normal-sized class could work together at the keyboards*.) Between 1981 and 1982, 2000 microcomputers will be distributed in groups of eight to 200 new schools and microcomputers will be bought by the Ministry only if they have the necessary hard- and software* to interconnect each school into a local network*. From 1979 to 1981, teachers were trained through a series of 12-day seminars in those schools receiving the new equipment. In 1982, the full-year training will start again in ten universities for a total of 200 teachers. In addition, an optional course in informatics* (three hours per week) will be started on an experimental basis in ten lycées for students over the age of 16.

In order to overcome the delays in the production of the appropriate courseware, the Agence de l'Informatique (a branch of the Ministry of Industry) has signed contracts with a number of school-book publishers to help them produce courseware packages. The Agence de l'Informatique will pay the publishers about £1000 for each one-hour package produced; the total value of these contracts is around £500,000. These packages should become available later in 1982.

Finally the Agence de l'Informatique is also funding a research and development project to develop an author language*. This is a master program that will allow the teacher greater freedom to amend and develop his/her material to fit the individual needs of students. It is hoped that the availability of such a language for CAL will reduce the cost of producing courseware by avoiding the need for lengthy training of teachers in one of the usual programming languages. It should also encourage more teachers to produce courseware by reducing the time-lag between the birth of a good educational idea and its final implementation on the computer. The estimated cost of this project is around £600,000.

Conclusion

Even though 10,000 microcomputers will be in French secondary schools by 1985, CAL will still not be fully available to every student. In France there are about two million students between the ages of 15 and 18. By 1985 there will be one microcomputer to every 200 students. This gives a theoretical average of only 20 minutes' use for each student per week! The situation becomes even worse if we are to include the 3.3 million students between the ages of 11 and 15, not to mention the 4.6 million students at elementary schools. Considering only students between the ages of 15 and 18, between 200,000 and 300,000 microcomputers would be needed for each student to have one hour of daily use. If we include all students in secondary education then about one million microcomputers would be necessary altogether. In fact, what is most likely to happen within the next five years is that some students will have a few hours' use during some weeks while others will have none at all. These figures are not specific to France; they are valid for any developed country with a population of around 50 million.

It follows that the use of CAL in schools will not be an overnight revolution, sweeping through the whole educational system instantly, as is sometimes imagined, but a gradual process extending over a longer period of time (probably somewhere between ten and 20 years). Under these circumstances, the existence of a national policy can greatly help in avoiding bottlenecks and blind alleys.

It is important to avoid confusion between training in computer science and the wider educational uses of CAL. The computer's role can be to offer a new method of education, integrated into the school's functioning, rather than merely to facilitate specific training in computer programming. It has been said that CAL has the potential for inaugurating a tremendous improvement in the teacher/learning process *provided* it is used in the right place, in the right amount, at the right moment and in the right way. This implies that *all* teachers should be trained in the use of CAL and how it can be combined effectively with other teaching aids such as books, cassettes, slides and films. After all, the final decision as to whether and how to use CAL depends on the individual teacher in the classroom.

In both the NDPCAL programme and the French experiment (often called the '58 lycées experiment') half of the money available has been spent on the training of teachers. The results suggest that this was a sensible strategy, enabling teachers to make informed choices about the range of computer technology available and to apply this knowledge to their individual teaching requirements.

The falling price of hardware should not lead to the mistaken conclusion that CAL will become a low-cost option. Although it is becoming cheaper for the end-user (ie the student or the home user) the same is not true in institutionalized education because of the cost of the necessary teacher training.

It would be of no use—and perhaps potentially dangerous—simply to install hundreds of computers in schools without support. It is well-known that even the best-designed packages can be rendered almost useless, if not harmful, in the hands of inexperienced teachers. Twenty years' experience has shown that the successful introduction of computers in any environment (business, industry, offices) is primarily a human problem rather than a technical or a technological one. In all known cases, success depends largely on the training of future users in the *reasons* for using the available software in their environment, and not on their knowledge of computers or computer science. This lesson should be kept in mind when considering the role of computers in education. It is true that helping teachers to take advantage of this new educational tool is an expensive and lengthy process. But it is the price to be paid if CAL is to realize its potential radically to renew our system of education.

13. The Microelectronics Education Programme in the United Kingdom

Richard Fothergill

Summary: An outline of the background to the Microelectronics Education Programme in the UK is given, together with a summary of its strategy. The philosophy behind the Programme is explained, with particular emphasis on the regional approach. Within each of 14 regions, the Programme is meeting three clear needs of teachers: a constantly updated supply of information, appropriate in-service training and the development of materials for use in schools. A summary of the approach to special education is provided, and reference is made to the programme of equipment provision sponsored by the Department of Industry.

Introduction

While the computer has been in use in business, commerce and government for over 20 years, it was only of peripheral interest to education until the arrival of the technology of microelectronics*. Some general courses in schools referred to it and in universities and polytechnics there were diploma and degree courses to train those whose career would involve the use of these machines. Postgraduate courses and those concentrating on data processing* for business use were also provided, and universities had large mainframe* computers to support their research interests. It was the appearance of the silicon chip* that highlighted the importance of the applications of the technology to all. Because the devices could be mass produced at little cost, their potential uses could be widely exploited throughout society, and of course within schools. The effect of their applications is affecting profoundly the way in which people live.

As the computer entered the domestic environment, its significance was clear. The 1970s had seen revolutions in electronic calculators and watches burst on the scene and saturate their respective markets. Goods like washing machines and cookers developed electronic controls to replace and extend their systems, and computer controls were introduced to improve central heating systems. On the high street, the cash dispenser attached to the bank shortened the queues and at last provided an out-of-hours money supply. Examples like these were sufficient to convince the sceptics that this was a different kind of technology from that which had gone before, one which permeated all aspects of our way of life, one which was not just a nine-day wonder, one that threatened to undermine much that was accepted as normal, one which would revolutionize employment and the way we worked through its applications in organizing information and controlling production.

The question facing government was how education was to respond. In March 1980, a four-year programme for schools, costing £9 million, was announced by the Under Secretary of State at the Department of Education and Science, Mr Neil MacFarlane. Two aims emerged as the main planks for this programme: the introduction of children to the new technology, its applications and effects, and the encouragement of teachers to make use of devices based on the technology to extend the means available to them for motivating children and helping them to learn. About a year later, the director of the Microelectronics Education Programme (MEP), supported by a small team of seven people, was in post with an active plan and strategy, operating by choice from offices in Newcastle upon Tyne. The Programme is responsible to the Departments of Education of England, Northern Ireland and Wales, and its work is undertaken through contracts arranged with them and administered by the Council for Educational Technology. Copyright in all the materials developed by the activities of the Programme is vested in the Council. This Programme is aimed at primary and secondary schools in England, Northern Ireland and Wales.

The MEP strategy

The first problem facing the Programme was the vast territory of topics and subjects that had to be covered. Because the applications of the technology are so wide, the need for education to approach them on a broad front seemed inescapable. The territory was divided into two parts, described in the Programme's 'Strategy' in the following way:

> The first covers the investigation of the most appropriate ways of using the computer as an aid to teaching and learning, as a guide to the individual child, as a learning aid for small groups of children, or as a system which involves the whole class. In principle, software* can be developed for computer-based learning* across the curriculum, but the Programme will give priority to applications in mathematics, the sciences, craft/design technology, geography and courses related to business or clerical occupations. Some attention will also be given to careers education, languages and the humanities. In addition, children with learning difficulties and special education needs can benefit from materials for use with microcomputers* as a teaching and learning aid and the Programme will therefore assist appropriate developments in remedial and special education.
>
> The second part of the territory with which the Programme is concerned is the introduction of new topics in the curriculum, either as separate disciplines or as new elements of existing subjects. The new topics (which may of course be taught at varying levels of specialization) include:
>
> 1. microelectronics in control technology;
> 2. electronics and its applications in particular systems;
> 3. computer studies;
> 4. computer-linked studies, including computer-aided design, data logging and data processing;

5. word processing* and other electronic office* techniques;
6. use of the computer as a means of information retrieval from data bases*.

In order to implement the Programme, three needs of teachers were identified which had to be met if its aims were to succeed. First, it was essential that they had information about activities and developments in the field which was constantly updated. Second, appropriate in-service training was necessary, particularly in the newer topics and in the methodology of using the computer in the classroom effectively. Third, it was clear that appropriate materials were in short supply and the whole issue of computers in the curriculum needed examination and development.

The absence of microcomputers in schools was bound to be a serious constraint on the success of the work, but there was no possibility that the small amount of money available to the Programme would be sufficient to remedy this. Indeed, it had been agreed early in its planning that MEP resources would not be used for the purchase of large quantities of equipment. A special project 'Micros in Schools', was initiated by the Department of Industry to help schools acquire computers. This gave all secondary schools the opportunity to purchase one of two microcomputers at half-price, and as a result nearly all of them now have at least one machine. A similar scheme for all primary schools was announced in July 1982. One of the microcomputers offered at this 50 per cent subsidy was developed especially for the BBC to accompany its programmes which are aimed at broadening the understanding of the general public, including teachers (see Chapter 22). The specification of the machine is an advanced one, and early indications suggest that it will become widely available in homes, so that it will be used by many children in both their domestic and school environments. One important feature of this scheme has been its insistence on at least two teachers receiving basic training on the equipment as a condition of purchase. To this end the Programme has produced and distributed an extensive packaged course, including specially commissioned computer programs*.

As a result of this initiative, the Programme could plan with some confidence that teachers could practise on and use a computer in their schools. With only a short time to make a significant impact, it was important that the initiatives started by the Programme should continue after government funding ended. Responsibility for schooling rests with local education authorities (LEAs), and it was therefore essential to involve them directly in the work of the Programme, both to attract additional resources and also to perpetuate some of the work that the Programme started. At the same time, it was hoped that such an approach would assist in disseminating the materials and ideas into schools and the minds of the teachers. In Britain, central government has little direct control over the curriculum or the level of investment in school education although signs are emerging that it wishes to increase its power; whether or not it is successful in this attempt, the role of the LEAs will remain significant.

The regional approach

The small amount of money available made it impossible to work directly with each of the 109 LEAs, and so a scheme for grouping them into regions was proposed, resulting in 14 such groups. As the requisite expertise for the whole territory of the Programme was not always available for each LEA, this regional scheme offered the additional bonus of providing groups in which better use could be made of what expertise there was. The regional approach is so crucial to the success of the Programme that two-thirds of the funding available will be in support of regional initiatives and only one-third to national ones. The three needs identified above are being met by MEP support in each region.

Information

Teachers urgently need to know what is available for them to use. Each region will therefore have an Information Centre containing a software library and other relevant teaching materials for use in the classroom, including videotapes, slides and audiocassettes, books and electronic devices. Many of these will have been specially produced by the Programme but commercially developed materials are also welcomed. Teachers calling at these Centres will have the opportunity to view and sample these, and then decide whether purchasing copies would be worthwhile. Also available is a wide range of reference information to help teachers to solve their problems, including comments from other teachers on materials and ideas from colleagues on effective ways of using them. The Centres will also help teachers locate appropriate training courses to meet their particular needs, and perhaps assist in identifying new courses that would be useful. A constant problem is the link between industry and education, and here the Centres can assist both to keep each informed of the other's activities, potential visits and demonstrations and to arrange for appropriate exchanges. By keeping in touch with curriculum development in the region and across the country, the Centres will help to maintain a close information link. This may also encourage individual teachers to bring in their own materials for sharing with others in the region and around the country. There are hidden talents that need to be stimulated.

Perhaps one of the most valuable assets of these Centres is the computer/telecommunications link between them, so that all the information available in one can be sampled and sent to another. This is based on a dedicated* word processor with its own data base that can be tapped and linked up to others for the sharing of knowledge and information. In many regions, the LEAs are establishing small centres of their own which will help the Information Centres to get closer to the teachers in their Authority, for this is the major difficulty these Centres face. With few staff and resources, and with a considerable distance between them and the edges of their region, they need to have links with people like advisers and wardens of teachers' centres who will help teachers to communicate with them.

In-service training

Each region is supporting a programme of in-service training which can be divided conveniently into four domains: the technology domain includes electronics, control technology and the practical industrial application of the devices; the computer domain covers computer studies and the study of the computer as a device, including its use as a synthesizer; the computer-based learning domain covers the use of the equipment as an aid to teaching across the whole curriculum; the communications and information studies domain includes business studies and commerce and is also concerned with the study of the changing role of information. The in-service training programme arranged within each region is a very important part of the MEP strategy and is based on the well-known principle of 'recursion'. A national co-ordinator for each of the domains has been appointed, supported by advice from a working party. It is the co-ordinators' responsibility to ensure that the MEP plans for training are carried out in each region. To help them to do this and to liaise with them, each region has appointed its own co-ordinator for each domain. These people will be doing much of the actual teaching on the courses.

The Programme has planned objectives for each domain, and two-thirds of the objectives for any course receiving financial support must be selected from them. The remaining third are decided by the region to meet the particular and specific needs of its own teachers and to respond to local conditions. Thus there is a careful balance between national requirements and the necessary support to meet local needs. To assist the regional operation, a considerable number of teaching materials have been produced and are under development; their effectiveness will be evaluated on these courses, perhaps leading to later modification. Careful monitoring will also take place to ensure that the in-service work is successful. This is the responsibility of the national co-ordinators. Based on their observations, further developments of the courses will be encouraged and more materials prepared to be used on them. Thus the monitoring can be seen as a positive means of sustaining and improving the quality of what is offered. Annual conferences for the regional co-ordinators will be used to disseminate these developments, and they will help to ensure a close liaison between them.

The target audience is that group of teachers who have a general awareness of the new technology and its effects, either from personal study or from one- or two-day awareness sessions run by the Information Centres. This is called the intermediate level. The intent of the courses is to give sufficient training for the teachers to develop some expertise in using and teaching about the technology, in other words to achieve a good understanding of it. Following the MEP courses, it is hoped that more specialized 'application-skills' courses will be established by local education authorities and institutions of further and higher education, where many teachers will take the work further. The strategy document pinpoints the importance of this:

> The reason for proposing that the bulk of MEP-stimulated training should be at
> the intermediate level is two-fold. First, there is a need to bring more teachers

who already have a commitment to new technology nearer to the point where they can make a contribution by applying innovations in day-to-day teaching in their classes and so help to build up the national pool of experience. Second, the demand to introduce a considerable majority of the nation's teachers to new technology does require a larger number of practitioners who can lend their experience to running shorter familiarization courses. This is the principle of recursive training. Teachers from all levels, primary and secondary, and from all disciplines will be encouraged to attend, as the technology affects them all.

Curriculum development

MEP takes curriculum development to refer to the preparation of materials for the enhancement of the curriculum as it is at present. However, considerable effort will also be spent on questioning current practice from the viewpoint of the effects of the technology; the Programme is keen to encourage new developments in course structure and content where applicable and to prepare new approaches for those areas not widely taught at present.

Once again the regional commitment is important, as it is necessary to capitalize on every bit of available expertise and to involve as many people as possible in helping the work of the Programme. The central team also wishes to avoid duplication and to stimulate a comprehensive spread of work in all parts of its territory. For this to occur, it is necessary to ensure good co-ordination between the regions and to monitor the work carefully. For this part of the Programme the expertise of the Schools Council and its advisers is being used. In the early stages of the work, strongest emphasis is being placed on developing a wide range of teaching materials to work right across the curriculum. Books, videotapes, tape slides, charts and overhead transparencies are being prepared to ensure that appropriate teaching for the new technologies can take place.

At the same time, the Programme is stimulating the creation of a wealth of computer programs for computer-assisted learning*. The emphasis is on modelling and simulations* rather than drill and practice or tutorial programs. The latter are more satisfactorily developed through the personal enthusiasm of an individual teacher and are more likely to be locally applicable than of interest nationally. Work on computer-managed learning* will also be encouraged in limited areas, and extensive developments in the electronic and control fields are expected. This is generally a relatively unexplored area and yet offers the potential for good returns from an industrial and commercial viewpoint. All these developments can be described as being aimed principally at curriculum enhancement.

In the area of new courses, the Programme is particularly interested in the importance of information studies. This is one part of education that will be profoundly affected by the computer, for access to information and its retrieval will be revolutionized by the technology. Up to now, education has concentrated on stimulating children to enlarge their personal stock of knowledge – their 'mental data base'; in the future this will not be so necessary. Far more important will be the abilities to use the technology to locate information and to make use of it effectively and efficiently. Thus there is a need to help all children to undertake information studies and this will be an important development for the curriculum. Attempts will also be made to analyse and amend the basic school curriculum in order to encourage a practical and useful response to the effects of the technology on society.

At national level

These then are the main elements of the regional strategy, and they are reflected in similar work undertaken on a national basis. Thus some people will be actively at work organizing the accumulation of information and its distribution through the Centres. At the same time, work on standards will be undertaken, not so much to prescribe particular styles or specifications, but to speed up the natural evolutionary processes and ensure that education is aware of and making use of the best practice. In the field of in-service training, the Programme will be supporting the development and publication of distance learning packages for primary teachers. It is also working closely with the broadcasting organizations on the development of programmes aimed both at teachers and pupils. Three organizations – Chelsea College, Five Ways School and ITMA at St Mark and St John – are also being supported from central funds as centres for curriculum development and these will be producing materials under the sponsorship of the Programme.

If there is one area where important gains are to be made from the technology it is in the field of special education, to help both those with physical and those with learning difficulties. The Programme will be supporting the same three elements, information, in-service training and curriculum development on a nationwide basis. Four information centres called SEMERCS are being set up in Bristol, Manchester, Newcastle and London to provide knowledge about devices, materials and techniques for special schools. In-service courses will be mixed between those aimed at the four general domains and ones aimed directly at teachers of special learners. From the curriculum development area, there will be a small programme arranged centrally, and all the regions will be encouraged to concentrate some part of their activities in this direction. While some work is being done on the development of devices to help children suffering from various communication handicaps, much is also directed towards computer-aided learning packages. Several of these are likely to be as useful for remedial work with children in other schools as for those in special schools.

Thus the Programme is wide-ranging and comprehensive. The resources at its disposal are limited and therefore most of its work can only be in the direction of starting projects off, encouraging other bodies like the LEAs to add their contributions to the whole activity. From a fairly strong base developed in this way, the Programme expects to provide a launching pad for further developments which will help children to understand the technology and its effects. Fundamental changes in the curriculum as a whole and even discussions on educational policy may follow, and these must form the basis for rethinking in the future. The new technology will affect society radically. How it will affect education is not yet fully understood; all that this Programme can do is to ensure that we are ready for its impact.

14. Developments in South Africa

Ivan Gregory

Summary: South Africa's economic development has led to the widespread introduction of computers in commerce and industry, and only recently to the growth of educational computing. The latter must be seen against the country's economic and social setting. The vast reservoir of undereducated and under-utilized manpower, the serious shortage of skills, the quality of life of a large proportion of the population and political discontent all combine to demand the extension and improvement of education. Asian, Black and Coloured education is characterized by high wastage rates and an inadequate teaching force. Administrative control is fragmented and most of the educands are environmentally deprived. The de Lange Committee's Report on the Republic's education (1981) suggested that the computer could materially assist educational development and recommended that it be given priority. Discussion of a number of projects reveals how computer-assisted learning (CAL) may contribute to compensatory and adult education, to upgrading qualifications, to updating knowledge and skills, and to school learning.

Some problems involved in the use of the computer are identified. Consideration of the factors influencing CAL in South Africa indicates that the main difficulties are likely to be software availability and level of hardware utilization. Any solutions will have to include making optimum use of human resources which are already scarce and positioning hardware to achieve maximum effect. Despite the computer's considerable potential, the growth of educational computing in South Africa will probably be constrained by the need to direct most of the available finance into the education of teachers and basic provision of equipment.

Like other more economically advanced developing countries, South Africa has areas which possess highly sophisticated primary, secondary and tertiary industries. In South Africa these are represented by the main urban areas and the Pretoria-Witwatersrand-Vereeniging Triangle. Such sophistication, coupled with technological advances and falling computer hardware* costs, has led to widespread and rapidly increasing use of the computer in commerce, industry, government and research. These circumstances, close educational links with western countries and South Africa's serious educational problems have led to a burgeoning interest in the computer's applications to education and training in the last four or five years.

Prior to that, most of the universities, the Council for Scientific and Industrial Research (CSIR)[1] and the Human Sciences Research Council (HSRC)[2] had been utilizing the computer for research, information storage and retrieval, and administration. However, important though these uses are for education, this chapter will concentrate on teaching and learning applications, in the fields of formal and non-formal education.

In view of the recency of computer-assisted learning (CAL)* in South Africa, it is not surprising that a national survey has yet to be undertaken. Thus, although this chapter attempts to give a balanced picture of the present situation, it cannot claim to be complete. The focus will be on the local setting, attitudes and policies, some present developments, positive and negative factors, and future prospects.

The background

To appreciate South African developments in educational computing, we need to take a look at the local educational and computer background. Interest in the computer stems from widespread acceptance of the need to improve education as rapidly as possible for social and economic reasons. With regard to the former, the Government's recognition of the social and political importance of improving Asian, Black and Coloured education is to be seen in the setting up of the de Lange Committee, appointed in 1980 to undertake 'an in-depth investigation into all facets of education in the RSA' (HSRC, 1981:1). The Committee's terms of reference included the need to 'improve the quality of life of all the inhabitants of the country' and to 'allow for the realization of the inhabitants' potential' (ibid).

The inadequacies of the work-force represent the economic reason. Statements on the labour situation by public and private sector figures are commonplace: 'South Africa is drastically short of skilled labour' (The Johannesburg Star, 12.8.82). 'The shortage of skills in the technological field is already having an adverse effect on growth and on vital research and development in the private and even more so in the public sector' (Etheridge, 1982:3). Taking the labour force as a whole, approximately two-thirds of it is Black, yet 82 per cent of Black urban male workers and 93 per cent of Black rural male workers have had either no formal education or only primary schooling (Botha, 1982). As a leading industrialist commented, their productivity must be negatively affected and the country's economic potential cannot be realized with such a work-force (Etheridge, 1982). Furthermore, de Lange states that the White contribution appears to have been largely realized, making it essential to develop the potential of the Asian, Black and Coloured[3] population (HSRC, 1981).

In its examination of the present educational situation, one of the major problems identified by the de Lange Committee is the appallingly high school wastage rate (Table 1).

White	Indian	Coloured	Black
85.40%	22.30%	4.40%	1.96%

Table 1 *Percentages of the 1963 school cohort completing 12 years of schooling (Sinclair, 1982:16)*

Teacher supply is another problem. Whilst in the White educational sector there is a serious shortage of secondary school teachers, particularly in mathematics and the sciences, the teacher shortfall in Black, Asian and Coloured education is far worse, resulting in large classes and subject shortages. The quality of Asian, Black and Coloured education also suffers from having a teaching force which is generally underqualified (Table 2).

White	Asian	Coloured	Black
3.36%	19.70%	66.14%	85.00%

Table 2 *Percentages of teachers lacking either a minimum of 12 years'
schooling or a teacher's certificate or both (HSRC, 1982:24)*

Innovation in education is never easily implemented. Its problems are accentuated in South Africa by the country's administrative structure. The fragmented control of formal education renders policy agreement and implementation highly problematic. White education is administered by the four provinces, namely the Cape, Natal, Orange Free State and Transvaal, whilst Asian, Black and Coloured education are controlled by the central government, but under different departments. To complicate matters further, education within Bophuthatswana, Ciskei, Gazankulu, KwaNdebele, KaNgwana, KwaZulu, Lebowa, QwaQwa, Transkei and Venda is the responsibility of the respective administrations to varying degrees. Despite the de Lange Committee's call for unified control of education, the South African government remains wedded to separate education departments for the different population groups (South Africa, 1981).

Computer-assisted learning is presented with further problems because most of the children of school-going age are environmentally deprived in relation to education for a technologically-orientated society, and they experience linguistic and other related problems (HSRC, 1981). An additional source of difficulties is the fact that primary education is provided in the mother tongue up to the end of Standard 2, after which Afrikaans or English is the medium of instruction.[4]

The existing computer setting has both positive and negative features. On the positive side the demand from commerce, industry and government for computer hardware and software* has attracted the major computer companies and has led to the development of a considerable marketing, technical and training infrastructure. There are also the beginnings of a domestic computer manufacturing industry, at present based mainly on imported components.

Although South Africa is only on the threshold of educational computing, at least one of its universities has been offering computer science for more than a decade, and 16 of the country's 19 universities teach the subject (Old Mutual, 1980). Technikons (polytechnics) also provide computer training, and private enterprise mounts courses in programming and systems analysis. However, training in the field of educational applications has lagged behind.

Indeed, as the de Lange Report remarks, the training of specialists in educational technology as a whole has been inadequate. A number of universities have begun to remedy the situation by including educational technology and, more particularly, educational computing at postgraduate level, and at least two universities are offering the latter in their course of initial training for secondary school teaching. Short courses and seminars for serving teachers and university lecturers are now being run, often with the assistance of overseas academics. Computer-assisted learning is also becoming a part of the conference scene, with two national conferences being devoted exclusively to the subject and a third containing computer inputs (Ballard *et al*, 1982), all within the last 12 months.

Advisory services are offered by the major computer companies, some universities (on an informal basis) and the CSIR, although the latter's contribution tends to be highly specialized. The CSIR's large scientific computing centre serves as a national centre, providing a consulting service on all aspects of computing and mounting user education courses (Jacobson and van Deventer, 1978).

Attitudes and policies

Because education lagged so far behind commercial and research computing, little could have been said about attitudes and policies until 1981, although, as has already been mentioned, computer science was developing fairly rapidly within the universities and technikons, and 1980 marked the beginning of a major computer-based education thrust at one of the former.

In terms of attitudes to the computer and the groundwork for future policies and action, 1981 may turn out to be the most important year in the short history of educational computing in South Africa. The appearance of the de Lange Report, the holding of a national symposium for schoolteachers in Johannesburg, the mounting of the first national conference on instructional computing at the University of the Western Cape, and considerable media coverage promoted a wider and accelerating interest.

The de Lange Report (HSRC, 1981) gives considerable attention to educational technology generally. It stresses the need for a national policy, and for a national programme which would include an advisory service and a co-ordinated approach to make the best use of available manpower and funds. More specifically, the computer is seen as contributing to the upgrading of teachers, particularly Black teachers, through continuing in-service programmes. The Report recommends 'that immediate attention be given to the introduction of the computer in education' and that to assist in this a research committee should be established to initiate action research (ibid: 172). Research on computer-assisted instruction* is awarded priority, along with the involvement of the post office and the national broadcasting service.

The Government's detailed response to the Report has yet to come, but its negative reaction to the call for a single education ministry suggests that a national approach to any educational matter is unlikely. In the computer field, however, there have been positive responses to the de Lange recommendations, and initiatives have emanated from other quarters. Thus the HSRC (1982a) has proposed and called for tenders for eight research projects, including a survey of the present educational use of the computer in the Republic, the establishment of criteria for software, the determination of strategies for computer literacy* and awareness, and the identification of applications in non-formal education.

The HSRC's working committee on the computer in education and training expects to have finalized its report on the minimum requirements for microcomputers* in South African schools by the middle of 1982, 'as various parties in education and the private sector are waiting for it' (HSRC, 1982b). The committee's draft report (HSRC, 1982c) is concerned with hardware specifications that will meet local needs and conditions. Although stressing that the local development of software falls outside its terms of reference, it nevertheless mentions the need for software for computer studies, CAL, and school administration.

The concern that hardware should meet local requirements bodes well for the future, but as yet the attitude to software seems somewhat ambiguous. Whilst there is abundant evidence of the need to take into account cultural and other factors when designing local software, and to exercise caution before transferring software from one cultural setting to another (I D Gregory, 1982), unadapted software is being marketed and used, and a proposal was made to include foreign materials in a local project for Black primary school children (Freer, 1982). On the other hand, there is evidence of awareness of the need to adapt imported software (Sinclair, 1982) and to develop appropriate local courseware* (Wolfson, 1982).

As indicated by developments mentioned in the next section, all the provincial education departments are interested in educational computing, although the strength of commitment appears to vary between them. Whilst it remains to be seen how much is implemented, a comprehensive report to the Transvaal Education Department (Craig, 1981) makes a series of recommendations, to be implemented over a five-year period. The proposals include the provision of computer awareness or literacy for all teacher trainers, all education students, all teachers and all pupils associated directly or indirectly with the Department, microcomputers and software for all schools on a matched funding, rand-for-rand basis, computer studies as a regular matriculation subject, a computer network*, and computerization of educational administration whenever appropriate.

Some present developments

Although educational computing is at an early stage in South Africa, a number of developments are taking place which are indicators of its potential. Further, if they are approached with wisdom and without the extravagant expectations so often associated with educational innovations, they could do much to promote and assist the growth of CAL. In this section, three developments will be described in detail: one at a university, one at an adult education centre, and one at provincial level. A number of others will be mentioned in brief.

The University of the Western Cape (Bellville) was established to cater for Coloured people, most of whom are socially disadvantaged. Some idea of what this can mean in educational terms is conveyed by the fact that between 1965 and 1976 only 154 science students out of a total of 914 completed bachelors degrees. Of the 17 per cent who did, 5 per cent took their degree in the normal three years, 6 per cent in four years, 3 per cent in five years, 2 per cent in six years and 1 per cent in seven years (Sinclair, 1982). The CAL development at the University is a direct response to student and community needs.

The University of the Western Cape possesses a mainframe*computer, with 64 terminals* on campus and the capacity for twice that number without observable reduction in response time. Its capacity can be increased further, and telephonic lines are planned to provide for up to 200 outreach terminals. The facilities are designed for the PLATO* system.

In 1982 the University began the implementation of its five-year CAL outreach plan, consisting of four linked projects. The first will develop, validate and disseminate computer-based curricula in mathematics and the sciences, in both Afrikaans (the home language of most of the community) and English for standards 9 and 10, the final years of secondary education. It involves the adaptation of American courseware, its translation, and the addition of new materials where the local syllabus expectations go beyond those of American secondary schools (ibid; Sinclair and Kansky, 1982b).

The first project aims to improve learning in the aforementioned subjects, and the prime targets are secondary school pupils, including prospective university students, schoolteachers (for upgrading reasons), and adults who wish to enhance their employment opportunities (Sinclair and Kansky, 1982b). For this purpose, an initial four computer-based learning*centres will be established within a 50 kilometre radius of the campus, each centre being provided with eight terminals linked to the University's mainframe computer (Sinclair, 1982).

As a by-product, the University put its 1982 intake of chemistry, physics and mathematics students through the materials in order to assess their entry knowledge, provide compensatory instruction, and familiarize them with the PLATO system. Student feedback on the experience was generally positive (Kansky, 1982).

The second project, scheduled for 1983, will increase the availability of the outreach CAL services. As a pump-priming operation, terminals will be placed in conveniently-located secondary schools, technikons, and colleges of education in the Western Cape region (Sinclair and Kansky, 1982b). Eight terminals will be allocated to each centre. No charge will be made during the first six months, and a body of consultants will be trained to control the centres (Sinclair, 1982).

The third project (1985-6) will be a research and development curriculum programme for mathematics and the sciences, involving the participation of secondary school teachers and tertiary level personnel. It is also intended to develop CAL expertise amongst teachers. The as yet unscheduled fourth project will focus on the improvement of language performance in Afrikaans, including its application to business, education, mathematics and the sciences (Sinclair and Kansky, 1982b).

Despite the outreach emphasis, the University is also promoting CAL on campus. In the two years of operation, over one-third of the staff has attended at least one eight-week seminar on the approach (Kansky, 1982b), and by mid-1981 ten departments other than those already mentioned had designed, programmed and tested materials (Sinclair and Dennis, 1981). At the same time, the Director of the University's Teaching Centre, which is responsible for academic planning, the improvement of teaching, and research, stresses that 'Computer-based education should not be singled out as the only medium, but as an important one in a multi-media approach' (ibid: 16).

Whilst the University of the Western Cape is the only university which has so far made a major commitment to CAL, individual departments in other universities are using it. Thus the University of Cape Town's graduate business school utilizes a minicomputer* (Miller, 1982) and the University of the Witwatersrand's chemistry department provides students in need of academic support with microcomputer materials (Bradley *et al*, 1982).

The second detailed study involves a CAL centre at a church-run, adult education complex on the Witwatersrand (Wolfson, 1982a). The complex caters for all races, but Black students predominate. The main focus is on evening study for those attending literacy classes and studying primary and secondary school subjects, and on Saturday morning tutorial assistance for undergraduates registered for the University of South Africa's correspondence courses.

Although the centre was only established in 1981, it has already provided interesting insights into the operation of computer-assisted and computer-managed learning* for adults under local conditions. The centre has proved extremely popular, despite the limited quantity of appropriate courseware. Its 16 terminals, linked to a mainframe computer in Sandton, near Johannesburg, are fully utilized in the evenings. Since most human tutoring is only available during the same hours, there is an element of competition for the students' time between the computer and the classes. Strenuous efforts are made to persuade students that the computer is an adjunct and not a substitute for classes. Interestingly, when using the terminals the majority of students feel the need for the presence of subject specialists. Shortage of time has interfered with the part-time tutors' efforts to become conversant with the system and the courseware. Similarly, although both hardware and software have usually been reliable, any fault that does occur causes a significant setback.

The computer company associated with the project has a courseware development team. This adapts relevant foreign-produced material and develops new courseware to meet local requirements, but inevitably progress is slow, especially in relation to the size of the need (Meyer, 1982). Another problem concerns hardware utilization. The study time available to the adult students means that the terminals are fully utilized for a relatively small part of each week. At other times and during the long Christmas vacation they are significantly under-utilized. Recently there has been some improvement in off-peak utilization as a result of use for mathematics and physical science by a new college of education and a neighbouring secondary school, and attendance by casual students, visiting the centre on a walk-in basis to study courses on such topics as supervisory management and data processing* (Wolfson, 1982b).

The third detailed study is at provincial level. The four provincial education authorities and many private schools are encouraging the introduction of the computer, principally at the secondary school level, for both classroom and administrative purposes. At present the emphasis is very largely on independent microcomputers. So far the Transvaal, economically the most significant province, has seen the greatest development of school computing (Craig, 1981). Thus, in 1981, 26 provincial and three private secondary schools were employing the computer for administration, and many were also using it for teaching and learning purposes. Over 2000 children are now taking computer studies as an extra-curricular subject in Standards 8 to 10, at any one of 30 centres, most of them secondary schools (Craig, 1982). The figure could rise to 5000 by 1986. Several primary and secondary schools are using CAI, particularly in mathematics, whilst in 1983 six provincial primary schools are to begin an experiment with computer-managed instruction (CMI)* for Standard 5 mathematics and five secondary schools an experiment with CAI in Standard 8 mathematics (Craig, 1981). Hattingh (1982) believes that CMI is more attractive than CAI for most teachers because the teacher remains the central figure. Computer-managed instruction is also less costly. Three extra-curricular centres for highly gifted children are equipped with microcomputers, which are used for a variety of purposes, including the study of informatics* (Craig, 1982).

In the field of Black schooling, the University of South Africa undertook research into the use of CAI for teaching arithmetic to Standard 5 children. The investigation provided useful insights into the problems that can be encountered when introducing CAI in a township environment. Work is about to begin on a new research project involving CAI arithmetic for both Standard 5 schoolchildren and adults outside the school system. The project will be located in Soweto, a very large Black township near Johannesburg, and will be controlled by the University of the Witwatersrand, assisted by private sector finance (Russell, 1982).

Finally, Madadeni College of Education, in KwaZulu, is the site of a pilot CAL project, using existing PLATO materials for English, mathematics and science. Feedback from the College's Black students is strongly positive, and similar facilities may be installed in KwaZulu's other colleges, and in the Department of Education and Culture's administrative centre (Lomax, 1982).

Positive and negative factors

As developing countries go, South Africa has a number of factors operating in its favour. Perhaps the most important is its vigorous and well-developed economy, which both requires and makes possible the large-scale application of the computer in commerce and industry. Thus the economy is at one and the same time both demanding and helping to finance the growth of educational computing. Commercial computer companies are assisting its development by providing expertise, training facilities, hardware and courseware. The country's educational links with countries like Britain, Israel and the United States provide both stimulation and additional expertise. Within South Africa, organizations like the HSRC have funds and manpower available to assist in research, and in the development of courseware. The private sector has also demonstrated its willingness to support CAL projects, particularly for disadvantaged communities.

Most of the negative factors are those found in other countries, like the general tendency to resist innovation and the concentration of resources in the developed, mainly metropolitan areas. To these should be added the fissiparity of educational administration, which must exacerbate other problems, such as limited resources and market size. Another major difficulty is that the condition of education calls for a tremendous range of software. This in turn is complicated by the country's cultural diversity.

Appropriate software is thus seen to be even more of a problem than in developed countries. Although some imported materials can be adapted, the generally poor quality of the world's existing commercially-produced software must minimize the quantity that can be usefully modified. Thus most of what is needed will have to be developed locally. American experience (Castle, 1982) suggests that production teams lead to good products. However, the same shortage of educational manpower that helps to make the computer so necessary in South Africa must impede software production, and even more so in the case of the more sophisticated design required by interactive* television (Ballard *et al*, 1982). A further difficulty is that the scale of the educational problems means a potentially heavy expenditure on hardware.

A partial answer is to be found in maximizing the return from available resources. For this, the identification of software priorities is essential. In addition, the yield from software production effort could be enhanced if materials were to be designed for more than one category of learner, eg primary school children and adult learners. Again, better resource utilization would be achieved if educational institutions in the formal system were also available for non-formal education.

The contribution that the computer can make to tackling the country's educational problems will also depend on factors outside the computer field. For instance, pre-school education for disadvantaged communities could do much to reduce school wastage (HSRC, 1981) and provide a stronger base for subsequent CAL experiences. Curriculum reform, particularly in areas which lend themselves to educational computing, eg artisan and management training (de Beer, 1982), would bring about a more economical impact on the manpower problem via both its school and training applications.

Conclusion

There are signs of a level-headed approach to educational computing in South Africa. Apart from the administrative potential of the innovation, it is being viewed as a useful contributor to learning, and as complementary to other means of teaching and learning rather than as a competitor to or substitute for the teacher.

The importance of developing the school-going population's computer awareness is achieving widespread recognition. Computer literacy seems likely to stem from awareness studies and hands-on* experience in one or more forms of CAL. Whether computer studies is necessary as a school subject is likely to be argued, with at least some academics already stating a preference for a broad educational base, leaving specialized computer work to the post-school stage (MEPV Gregory, 1982).

Presently, schools tend to favour microcomputers. Where CAL is being employed for compensatory and upgrading purposes, there is considerable emphasis on the mainframe PLATO system. The latter appears to have cost advantages for such applications, used on a large scale, but the extent of its spread will be determined by availability of appropriate courseware, reliable electricity supplies, and the quality of telecommunications.

Without a proper orchestration of public and private sector resources and effort, together with the implementation of other, related developments in the field of education, the time and energy expended on CAL cannot make the maximum impact. In a country with so many demands on its resources, this is beyond debate. Indeed, as the Government addresses itself with increasing vigour to making up educational leeway in Asian, Black and Coloured education, it may eventually decide – like less well-endowed Third World countries – that the overwhelming priority is the provision of teachers and basic equipment like buildings and furniture.

Notes

1. The Council for Scientific and Industrial Research (CSIR) is a statutory body concerned with the promotion of scientific research, principally through a number of national laboratories, research grants and bursaries, and a liaison and information service.
2. The Human Sciences Research Council (HSRC) is a statutory body, the principal functions of which are to determine research priorities, to undertake, promote and co-ordinate research, and to disseminate research findings.
3. According to South Africa's Population Registration Act, Coloureds are people who are neither White nor Black, and include Cape Coloureds, Griquas, Malays and Other Coloureds (Sinclair and Dennis, 1981).
4. The Whites acknowledge either Afrikaans (an off-shoot of Dutch) or English as their mother tongue. Most Coloureds belong to the Afrikaans language group. The 1980 Census names ten socio-linguistic peoples amongst the Black population (South Africa – Department of Statistics, 1980). In descending order of size (excluding Bophuthatswana, Transkei and Venda), they are the Zulu (5,420,882), the Xhosa, the Northern Sotho, the Southern Sotho, the Tswana, the Shangaan Tsonga, the Swazi, the Southern Ndebele, the Northern Ndebele, and the Venda (185,058). 'Other peoples' total some 185,000.

References

Ballard, L E, Gregory, I D, Hamilton-Attwell, V L, Pretorius, S J and Welch, R (1982) Development in the field of interactive television Paper presented at Instructa 82 Rand Afrikaans University Johannesburg 9.7.82

Botha, S P (1982) Manpower training in the future *in* Sinclair and Kansky *ed* (1982a)

Bradley, J D, Brink, B and Glasser, L (1982) Operational standards in computer-assisted instruction *in* van der Vyver *ed* (1982)

Castle, J T (1982) Instructional development: the team approach. Paper presented at Instructa 82 Rand Afrikaans University Johannesburg 8.7.82

Craig, J K (1981) *Computers in Education* 3 vols Transvaal Education Department: Pretoria pre-release copy

Craig, J K (1982) Personal communication

Coetzee, C J S and Geggus, C (1980) *University Education in the Republic of South Africa* HSRC: Pretoria

de Beer, D W (1982) Some perspectives from the private sector *in* Sinclair and Kansky *ed* (1982a)

Etheridge, D A (1982) Education in relation to the manpower needs of the private sector *in* Sinclair and Kansky *ed* (1982a)

Freer, D J (1982) (Professor of education: University of the Witwatersrand) Personal communication

Gregory, I D (1982) Appropriate educational technology *Media in Education and Development* 15 1: 25-8

Gregory, M E P V (1982) (Careers counsellor: University of the Witwatersrand) Personal communication

Hattingh, D L (1982) Computer-managed instruction in primary schools *in* van der Vyver *ed* (1982)

Human Sciences Research Council (HSRC) (1981) *Provision of Education in the RSA* (The de Lange Report) HSRC: Pretoria

Human Sciences Research Council-Institute for Educational Research (1982a) Letter C P Serfontein to the Rector University of the Witwatersrand Invitation to tender for research projects identified by the work committee: The Computer in Education and Training 5.5.82

Human Sciences Research Council-Institute for Educational Research (1982b) Letter from C P Serfontein to the Rector University of the Witwatersrand

Human Sciences Research Council-Institute for Educational Research (1982c) Minimum requirements for microcomputers in schools in the RSA Draft report of the working committee on the use of the computer in education and training HSR-IEC: Pretoria. Mimeographed

Jacobson, D H and van Deventer, E N (1978) Computers at the CSIR *Scientiae* 19 1: 12-26

Kansky, R J (1982a) A summary of student opinions of computer-assisted instruction in mathematics/sciences at the University of the Western Cape. University of the Western Cape: Bellville. Mimeographed

Kansky, R J (1982b) Computer-based instruction programme of the University of the Western Cape: interim report University of the Western Cape: Bellville. Mimeographed

Lomax, D E (1982) Plato-based teacher education in KwaZulu *in* van der Vyver *ed* (1982)

Meyer, W D (1982) South African secondary school curricula development program *in* van der Vyver *ed* (1982)

Miller, J (1982) Computer-aided instruction on an MBA programme *in* van der Vyver *ed* (1982)

Old Mutual (1980) Which university? Old Mutual: Claremont. Mimeographed

Russell, D D (1982) (Professor of adult education: University of the Witwatersrand) Personal communication

Sinclair, A J L (1982) The University of the Western Cape: new directions, in new ways . . . for new times *in* Sinclair and Kansky *ed* (1982a)

Sinclair, A J L and Dennis, J R (1981) Computer-based education in a developing university for a developing community: a cursory overview. University of the Western Cape: Bellville. Mimeographed

Sinclair, A J L and Kansky, R J *ed* (1982a) *Bridging the Adult Education Gap* Proceedings of a national conference on the use of instructional computing 4.12.81 University of the Western Cape: Bellville

Sinclair, A J L and Kansky, R J (1982b) *Instructional Computing Development Projects at the University of the Western Cape 1982-1987* University of the Western Cape: Bellville

South Africa (1981) *Interim Memorandum on the Report of the Human Sciences Research Council on the Inquiry into the Provision of Education in the RSA* Government Printer: Pretoria

South Africa: Department of Statistics (1980) Population Census 6 May 1980 Department of Statistics: Pretoria. Mimeographed

Van der Vyver, D H *ed* (1982) *Computers in Education* Proceedings of the South African Congress on Computers in Education SACCE 82 Stellenbosch

Wiechers, G (1982) Computer-assisted instruction in the South African context *in* van der Vyver *ed* (1982)

Wolfson, J G E (1982a) Computer-based education in a South African adult education centre: the first six months *in* van der Vyver *ed* (1982)

Wolfson, J G E (1982b) (Education consultant Control Data (Pty) Ltd) Personal communication

15. Educational computing in the Province of Quebec

Louise Dubuc

Summary: The Province of Quebec entered the field of educational computing some time ago with the establishment of a central computing network for administrative purposes in 1968 and the opening of a ministerial dossier on the pedagogical uses of computers in 1975. The chapter presents the historical evolution and actions of the two central bodies working in the field, as well as the numerous developments which are presently taking place in the educational system itself. Among these, the development of a computer science curriculum for secondary education stands as an early achievement. The chapter also points out the major problems that affect the development of educational uses of the computer. In a Province characterized by its francophone majority (80 per cent of the population), the software gap is especially great. Given that the local production of courseware is only a partial remedy, Quebec has worked out some other ideas for the solution of that problem.

In most countries, the term 'computers in education' extends to the whole range of applications of the computer in the educational setting, be it for the management function or the teaching/learning one. It follows from this global understanding that planning, budgeting and policy-making are usually co-ordinated centrally by a single body. The situation is different in Quebec, where, over the years, the concerns for management and pedagogy have been separated and have become the responsibility of two different organizations.

Educational management

The Service Informatique du Ministère de l'Education du Québec (SIMEQ) was created in 1968. Its mandate was to install and maintain a centralized computer network* linking the Ministry's mainframe* computers – which in 1980 were an IBM 370/168 and an IBM 3033 – to the terminals* located in the school boards and cegeps (1) across the province, and to provide the users with software* for the different tasks of educational management. From 1968 to 1980 numerous management packages were written. They cover payroll, scheduling, school transportation, supplies, Ministry exams and student files.

In 1980, in line with a general policy aimed at decentralization, this scene changed drastically. On the one hand, the association of school boards and the federation of cegeps individually signed with the Ministry of Education and Burroughs a contract for the purchase of minicomputers*. Under these contracts, any individual institution (school board or cegep) can acquire a Burroughs machine along with a maintenance contract at a preferential rate. The contract with the school boards amounted to $2,000,000 (Canadian) (over five years) and with the cegeps to $1,000,000 (Canadian). To win the bid against stiff competition, Burroughs promised to install a branch in Quebec.

In April 1981, SIMEQ was split up into two separate organizations. The Direction de l'Informatique du Ministère (DIM) now has the responsibility for all the computer processing for the Ministry as well as for the implementation of a plan for the computerization of its whole administrative system. The Direction des Services Informatiques aux Réseaux (DSIR) will, for its part, assist the institutions that want to use the management packages. One of its tasks will be to transfer all the management software on to the Burroughs system.

The advent of the minicomputers significantly changed the structure of the original network. First, whereas some wealthy school boards had been able to buy Hewlett-Packard HP2000 or HP3000 minicomputers on their own, all school boards now have the opportunity to purchase a Burroughs machine at a reasonable price. Second, Quebec is evolving from a highly centralized processing network to new and alternative patterns. The minicomputer can either be used as an intermediate level in a hierarchical network for the transfer of data*, ranging from MEQ's mainframe computers at one end to individual school terminals or microcomputers* at the other end. Alternatively, they can be detached from this hierarchy and stand alone at the head of a descending processing network to the schools.

The second significant feature of the changes that have taken place has to do with the financing procedures. Up until 1981, the Ministry of Education used to finance hardware* and software for its network. But in 1981 the financial responsibility (and the money) was transferred to the institutions themselves. The hardware is now purchased by the individual school board or cegep, which can adhere to the contract with Burroughs or choose any other machine. The management software is still offered by the DSIR, but the services now have to be paid for.

Pedagogical uses of the computer

Whereas SIMEQ has mostly been involved in educational management (2), since 1975, the Service Général des Moyens d'Enseignement (SGME) has concerned itself more with pedagogical aspects.

A research group investigating pedagogical uses of the computer was set up in order to gather information for policy-making in this field. Up until 1978, this group produced inventories of the experiments conducted at all levels of education (secondary, cegep, university) in Quebec. They also supported two main projects funded by the SGME, one for a computer-managed instruction* system at primary level (SAGE system) and the other for research on the use of

LOGO*. Parallel to these activities they also edited a liaison bulletin on the use of the computer in the classroom, entitled *BIP-BIP*.

A summary of the situation at that time shows that there were already many applications of the computer in the classroom. At university level most of these were oriented towards research and information retrieval from data banks*. At cegep level most applications were centred on courses in computer science, although a few experiments were using the computer as a process controller in the laboratories or as an administrative aid for the teacher (classification of the students for different instructional streams, objective test construction).

At secondary level the computer was used mostly within the teaching of computer science and mathematics. These applications were, however, quite unlike those of the cegeps. Given that the main objective of the secondary courses was to foster intellectual development rather than to educate for a trade or profession, the pedagogy was oriented much more towards problem-solving than towards the mastery of facts or specific concepts. At primary level, the main experiment was SAGE. This project involved two school boards and a team of researchers from SGME and from the Institut National pour la Recherche Scientifique (INRS). Over the years they have produced modules in mathematics, French and English and a computer-managed instruction system for individualized learning in those disciplines. The inventories have been published by the SGME and the individual experiments have been described in *BIP-BIP*.

In 1978 SGME published a position paper resulting from all the preliminary information-gathering. It contains both the general principles that should regulate the development of the educational use of computers, and also a model capable of embodying these principles. They are that pedagogical objectives take precedence over equipment and that computers should be introduced into the classroom only if their use will lead to greater efficiency in the teacher/learning process.

These principles might appear simple to an external reader, but they make sense in our provincial context where, a few years before, huge amounts of money had been invested in audio-visual equipment without bringing about any significant educational change. The authors wanted to emphasize the idea of the computer as a means rather than an end. Also, the trend towards the reduction of educational budgets was clearly visible at the beginning of 1978 at a time when the microcomputer revolution had scarcely begun. It was then important to insist on the cost-effectiveness of the investment.

The model proposed in the paper – 'Initiative locale: Développement; Essaimage; en Education' (IDEE) – adopts a rather 'informal' approach and contrasts with conventional research and development models. It suggests that any local initiative be supported by the Ministry in such a way as to foster a thorough development of local expertise. After a period of development, the experiment will become better organized and be more trustworthy; it should then become better-known and in turn will inspire new projects.

The strength of the model lies in its realism. Many experiments are led by a single enthusiastic teacher who is often inexperienced. It is important to sustain this enthusiasm and to provide the necessary guidance, in case it peters out and the potential expertise is lost. The SGME has relied on this model since 1975 and it turned out to be very effective.

The Ministry considered these proposals with a certain degree of interest but it was then mainly concerned with the huge decrease in enrolment in secondary schools (resulting from a drop in the birth rate) and with an action plan to reform primary and secondary education. Consequently, the ground was not yet prepared for any policy-making on the pedagogical uses of the computer.

In the interval, however, technology had moved into the era of cheap microelectronics* and the industry was getting ready to invade every sector of the market, including education. In Quebec the pressure of the American salesman became ever stronger, on individuals as well as on institutions, and microcomputers started to appear more frequently in classrooms, either brought in by teachers or bought by a school board or cegep (3).

The computer revolution has affected other countries as well, and many of them have reacted by launching government plans and investing a lot of money in microelectronics, so as not to be overwhelmed by a technological tidal wave coming from outside. These developments were closely followed in Quebec, and some level of awareness has been reached in educational institutions as well as among the general public. The necessity for decisions is now strongly felt in the educational world and many task groups have come together to express their opinions, needs and wishes about any future development.

Within the Ministry of Education three committees are working on development plans for the use of computers in the classroom. The 'Groupe de Travail du DICOS sur la Pédagogie' (GTDP), composed of representatives of the school boards, teachers and civil servants, has been asked to prepare a plan for primary and secondary education. Their approach is divided into three main steps: analysis of the present situation and trends, definition of orientation, and identification of strategies. During their first year they consulted all school boards and most of the teachers already involved in the use of computers at secondary level. The results were available in 1981. The Sous-Comité pour l'Utilisation de l'Ordinateur en Pédagogie' (SCUOP) performed a similar job for the collegial network of education, and their position paper was issued about the same time.

The third committee is a little different in that it is composed of decision-makers representing every sector of the educational system (primary, secondary, college, university, adult education) and that their mandate is ultimately to formulate a ministerial action plan. That committee was expected to report during 1982.

Present developments

Although Quebec has not yet voiced any official policy for the use of computers in pedagogy, many effective developments are taking place.

The first one concerns the design of an official curriculum in computer science at secondary level. For almost ten years a course called 'Initiation à un Langage de Programmation' (ILP) has been given in some schools on an experimental basis (4). Some 3000 students register for the course every year. Many of the teachers of ILP are mathematics teachers and, through their association, they have asked the Ministry to make it part of the official curriculum. Because the course differed from one school board to the next (4), a working group of three teachers and one officer from the Ministry has been set up to rewrite it according to the Ministry's standards.

The characteristics of the course are that it can be offered in the fourth or fifth grades at secondary level or in both (age 15 to 16), depending on the depth of study desired. Also, the course is machine-independent as well as language-independent, so that a teacher is not tied to specific equipment. The teaching method underlying the course is unique; called 'Pédagogie par projets' it is based on problem-solving activity applied to a project to be computerized.

Although basically inspired by the ILP course, the name of the new curriculum has been changed to 'Initiation à la science informatique'. It has been submitted to the Ministry for approval and was to be implemented in September 1982. By way of support for teachers, a methodological guide will be produced and the SGME is now making a list of student projects for the guidance of newcomers to the field.

There has been debate in some countries as to whether the use of computers should be developed in secondary education through the teaching of computer science as a separate discipline or through the use of computers in existing disciplines. The best answer would probably be 'both'. In Quebec, however, there are two reasons why the teaching of computer science as a new discipline in secondary education would seem to be a good strategy. First, whenever the Ministry officially approves a new curriculum, it is obliged to supply the necessary equipment. To teach computer science, one needs computers. Second, the use of computers in the classroom cannot develop without teachers. In Quebec, teachers have for a long time associated the use of computers in various disciplines with conventional programmed learning, and many of them react negatively to a behaviouristic approach which is more teacher-centred than student-centred.

Apart from computer science, the use of computers in the classroom is also developing along other lines. One of them is the spread of microcomputers. In the last few years the cegeps have bought around 400 micros for various pedagogical purposes. The school boards have gone the same way, buying about 150 machines (3). One interesting feature of those purchases is that some of them are large-scale, for example when a school board decides to equip a school fully. The net result of this trend is that some places can become real centres, capable of coping with a fair number of students simultaneously.

A significant line of development is the formation of user groups of computers in classrooms. In April 1981, an association was created to bring together teachers in secondary education who are already involved with the computer and those who plan to experiment with it in the near future. Many school administrators have subscribed to the association as well, in order to gather information and follow these movements more closely. This association acquired legal status in 1981. The cegep computer users decided to create a similar association at their symposium in May 1981. Both these associations will serve as centres for information and for the exchange of ideas and software; they also constitute significant pressure groups who can voice their opinions to the appropriate officials.

Experiments are also being undertaken to make it easier for teachers to get involved in the use of computers. For instance, a group of researchers from DSIR is now testing the most popular micros in Quebec to provide technical guidance to teachers. A study of the Apple, the TRS80 and the Pet has been made recently and its results will be useful to potential purchasers as well as helping the actual owners to get the best out of their machines. Another example is the SGME funding of an experiment to provide the most gifted students of a primary class with an enriched environment comprising electronic games, computers, etc. The main researcher is also responsible for the production of some courseware* for those pupils (5).

The educational use of computers could spread much faster in Quebec if two major problems were not holding us back. The first one is teacher training. The pre-service training of a teacher is a university responsibility, but only a few courses are offered on the use of computers in the classroom and they are optional. In-service training is mostly organized around the upgrading of teachers in their discipline, and no specific provision has yet been made for the pedagogical use of the computer. There are some partial remedies for the problem – training sessions, conferences, informal self-help, production of self-instructional material, etc – and we have tried most of them, but are still searching for an appropriate solution.

The second problem is the software gap. Quebec is 80 per cent francophone and, in comparison with anglophone material, there is very little production of French courseware. As said earlier, the teachers in Quebec have reacted unfavourably to programmed learning. But since computer-based materials are no longer just variants of programmed learning, and since the hardware is a lot cheaper, this resistance is slowly fading and some teachers have voiced the need for courseware. There is no quick or easy answer to this problem but a few steps have been taken towards a solution. First, the universities have started to produce (or supervize the production of) microcomputer-based materials. Second, the SGME is financing the co-operative production of educational software jointly with the cegeps and it plans to extend these efforts to secondary education.

These actions are not sufficient in the short term because the preparation of educational materials is time-consuming and meanwhile teachers are using anglophone courseware. Thus two projects are now being funded by the SGME to cope with that immediate problem. One concerns a bank of information about the francophone courseware available locally, whether produced by teachers or marketed commercially. This information has been collected in a catalogue, along with the names and phone numbers of the

156 LOUISE DUBUC

producers. The other project is to produce a check-list for the evaluation of courseware, according to Ministry standards concerning the approval of educational material. Using this check-list, a teacher should be able to separate the good material from the bad and build up a rough framework on which to produce his/her own courseware. Although very modest, these actions might be helpful to the person we want to reach: the teacher.

Conclusion

Although Quebec has not taken the same approach as many countries in dealing with the use of computers in education, it turns out that the problems encountered are similar. Time is pressing on us to solve them rapidly, but we have to keep in mind that we are working in a new field where many possibilities for development are still open. It is hard to predict exactly where we are going to be in the long term, but as long as we strive and keep on putting forward our best ideas and efforts, any problem has hopes of a creative solution.

Notes

(1) To meet the needs of six million inhabitants, Quebec's educational system is made up of 2714 schools at both the primary (grades 1 to 6) and secondary (grades I to V) levels of education, 46 cegeps (collèges d'enseignement général et professionnel which resemble community colleges – two years) and seven universities. The primary and secondary schools are grouped under 248 school boards, which are the main agencies responsible to the Ministry for administering the first two levels of education. In 1981, most school boards (210) and all the cegeps formed part of the centralized network.

(2) From 1968 to 1973 a small section within SIMEQ devoted some attention to pedagogy. This 'Laboratoire de Pédagogie Informatique' (LPI) hired a team of researchers who looked at the different possible uses of the computer in the classroom. Over the years, they supported many experiments and proposed some grounds for further development. However interesting their work was, the hardware required was at that time huge and expensive; the Ministry was not ready to consider their proposals as a priority and the team was disbanded, primarily as a result of it being ahead of its time. Some of the researchers of the LPI were later re-employed by the SGME.

(3) Quebec's educational system is not totally centralized and it leaves much administrative freedom to its institutions. The school boards receive a global sum based on a certain allowance *per capita*. Except for teachers' salaries – which are fixed centrally by a collective agreement – and except for some overriding rules, a school board has considerable freedom over the allocation of money. The level of administrative automony is greater at the cegep and university levels. There the Ministry supplies the money on the basis of a student/course formula and the institutions collect extra funds from the students themselves. This administrative freedom has permitted local purchase of computers for the classroom.

(4) In Quebec's educational system, a course can have one of three sorts of status: experimental, optional or compulsory. In an experimental course, the general structure has been proposed to the Ministry by the school board. The course is not an official one, but, if accepted by the MEQ, it can lead to official credits.

Such a course can be offered by any other school board as long as it gets permission from the MEQ. The general structure of the course will be the same in all school boards, but the specific content might differ. The optional and compulsory courses have both gone through a process of official approval and their content is defined by the Ministry.

(5) Many other researches are taking place in Quebec but it is impossible to present them all. These two were selected particularly because they concern two fields of development (hardware and primary education) which are relatively new in our Province.

16. Software and geography teaching in New Zealand

Pip Forer

Summary: Computer-assisted learning (CAL) has tremendous scope in geography teaching, especially since the advent of cheap powerful microcomputers with good colour graphics and disc drives. The main constraints are identified with special reference to geography. So far, they have consisted of a combination of limitations on hardware, lack of suitable software, weak dissemination strategies and lack of facilitation by central and regional government agencies.

The evolution of CAL in geography in New Zealand is chronicled from the importation of international mainframe-based packages to the evolution of locally designed microcomputer software. The scope of simulation is stressed in particular, as is the conjunction of data processing with high resolution colour graphics in the teaching of spatial topics including map work. In the longer term, it is anticipated that CAL will develop along lines which emphasize the encouragement of student exploration rather than computer-assisted instruction (CAI). The latent potential of colour graphics for data display and interactive map work is particularly important. Examples of such applications are given in anticipation of the future hardware and software progress which is already beginning to happen in the commercial field.

I. CAL in geography: potential and constraints

Recent developments in technology have extended the capacity of microcomputers* considerably. Apart from permitting easier mathematical analysis, current microcomputers offer the ability to process text in various ways and to draw increasingly accurate diagrams, often with colour. The presentation of landscapes, graphs, maps and imagery becomes more realistic almost daily.

Geography has a venerable history of imparting factual knowledge about different areas of the globe. It has a shorter, but nonetheless spectacular, history as a research discipline studying processes which can be simulated by mathematical modelling involving vast amounts of data*. Consequently the computer has much to offer geography across the range of CAL* varieties. Tutorial mode CAI* may offer means of imparting facts. Data base management systems* and mapping programs* can help to organize them for less formalized learning paths. Simulations* offer attractive teaching extensions in certain areas. In all, geography is a suitable case for CAL treatment. Apart from the great potential for traditional CAL, there is clearly further room for CAL innovation with the video-based developments in educational computing that have begun to take shape since 1981.

Geographers have been alert to these possibilities and generally keen to experiment with CAL. That this experimentation has been pragmatic cannot be denied. To date its links with theories of education or curriculum development have been tenuous. Geographers today are motivated but unclear as to the direction and legitimate extent of CAL usage.

Geography, in common with most teaching disciplines, reflects the society about it, current technology and the inputs from its own research techniques (Forer and Owens, 1980). To some degree this reflective relationship requires the adoption of the new technology. Yet this legitimate adoption is complicated by the arguments raised over the cost, effectiveness and appropriateness of certain CAL approaches (Fielden and Pearson, 1978). Furthermore, the demonstrable but as yet only partially assessed argument that CAL is more than just a passive medium for teaching our current course content raises queries. To what extent can CAL teach new things in new ways and cause us to reorder our priorities for the limited time available in teaching slots? The arguments of some prophets, such as Papert (1980), suggest that fundamental changes in curriculum and in the nature of schooling may result from a full appreciation of the computer's potential.

At the same time, the first words of caution are already beginning to appear in an era when practice rather than evaluation is the dominant activity. In language teaching, the experience of language laboratories has led to a certain wariness of any technology that tries to dictate the theory behind the teaching application (Farrington, 1980). The call for a greater assessment of particular aspects of CAL, including the benefits of graphics* in the school, is a necessary and overdue ground swell to further CAL development.

This chapter attempts to discuss the development of CAL in geography and to hazard some observations on the likely direction of developments over the next four to five years. Two paths are open in this endeavour. One would be to discuss in detail particular teaching applications divorced from their setting in a real-world education system. The alternative, adopted here, is to review progress in terms of the wider constraints and opportunities of existing educational milieux. What can be done ideally is of less interest than what is practically possible. The next few paragraphs outline four basic constraints on CAL. They are not exhaustive but form a basis for reviewing the framework for, and progress of, CAL in geography with examples drawn from the United Kingdom and the Antipodes.

The background constraints to geography CAL

The progress of CAL in the geography curriculum to date has been inhibited by a series of governing factors. Computer technology, by virtue of its social penetration and its teaching potential, generates an imperative for use, as we have witnessed in the past three years, but its implementation depends on four major constraints. These four are involved in a constant interplay; together they form a framework for CAL implementation, with specific implications for geography.

1. *Hardware availability*. CAL in geography is now becoming recognized as an important issue mainly because its widespread use is at last feasible. Any specific application of CAL is governed by the type of hardware* available, however, and this changes. By 1982 most Organization for Economic Co-operation and Development nations had moved towards providing every school with a microcomputer. Nonetheless not all school configurations had discs*, graphics or teletext* communications ability.

2. *Software availability*. The availability of software* tends to run in three distinct phases, particularly in countries not in the forefront of CAL or in subject areas that are slow in adopting its use. These phases are:

(a) the use of CAL by matching existing software to existing curriculum slots;
(b) the local production of CAL material to meet the needs of specific curriculum activities;
(c) the creation of CAL material for subject matter not in current curricula that can only be taught or is only relevant in consequence of computer availability.

3. *Arrangements for dissemination of material*. The successful production of cost-effective CAL material is difficult. On the one hand a large body of users is needed to carry the undoubted costs of producing quality CAL. On the other hand, the most effective CAL material is that tailored to local needs and aspirations and/or specific machines. In all cases, the policy for software dissemination is critical in efficient development.

4. *Educational policy on CAL development*. Many of the problems in areas 1, 2 and 3 relate to two factors: first, divisions were caused by geographers developing CAL of a form related to the capacities of the machines available – colour graphics on Apples, data base management on minicomputers*, for example. Second, the strong inertia in education systems acts against software progress into new CAL areas. The early rate of progress of CAL may rely heavily on the degree of central interest, funding and direction that is given.

1. HARDWARE AVAILABILITY. Until recently the main question with hardware was 'do we have a computer or a computer terminal?'* The emphasis was on possession of some kind of computing power with far less concern for the type of machine. In retrospect we can see that from the late 1970s onwards the question 'what *sort* of computing do we have access to?' was becoming more important. Not only were many more schools answering 'yes' to the original question but two new developments were offering fresh options. First, from 1975 onwards microcomputers began to appear which were soon able to provide acceptable and autonomous computing power that rivalled terminals linked to mainframes*. Second, and very significantly for geographers, these machines became possessed of increasingly fine graphics

capabilities. Parallel to this, the diffusion of cheaper disc drives* gave the first chances to embrace usages that were dependent on fast access to substantial quantities of data.

The nature and timing of the hardware resource has varied from country to country. In Britain, development of CAL in geography can be traced to the National Development Programme in Computer-Assisted Learning (NDPCAL). This project was based on mainframe computing and created a tradition in which both capital and, more importantly, human resources, became committed to the mores of mainframe computing. Prior to the microcomputer wave of the early 1980s a sound nucleus of CAL use existed. In America a similar pattern, more advanced, held. Even in 1981, a third of high schools possessing computer access were connected to an external multi-user system*. In Australia the situation between states has varied considerably (Wearing *et al*, 1976, Moore 1981), Tasmania's centralized network* system being the most ambitious.

The history in other countries has been different. In New Zealand, for instance, high costs of mainframe computing and telecommunications severely discouraged the early phases of CAL. Even university geography departments had problems with access to terminals. For a small and scattered national population, the microcomputer offered the first real chance to use CAL in the secondary sector. Free of the restrictive prejudices of the mainframe user, microcomputer technology dominated geography CAL from the start in such countries. This does have major, if short-term, ramifications. Geographers interested in CAL immediately put all their efforts into developing material for microcomputers and learned to exploit their potential without the handicap of having to unlearn a 'mainframe philosophy'. Microcomputer technology became available in Australasia virtually concurrently with European developments, and is less dependent on leads from outside than is mainframe use. A particular effect of this is that the more ambitious and demanding CAL uses, particularly CAI and data management, are tailored from the outset to the demands of the microcomputer.

In the UK, NDPCAL produced programs such as Hertfordshire's QUERY?* and the Scottish parishes data recall and mapping packages. These gave a mainframe teaching tool for geography that was both flexible and vocational. The response to the microcomputer has been to produce similar programs for smaller machines. In some ways, the non-existence of the earlier, mainframe-oriented structures has speeded innovative development in areas outside Europe and America.

For the geographer, two points need to be stressed. First, the overwhelming trend in all countries has been for a switch to microcomputers for CAL in secondary schools. This has happened almost explosively, with availability in schools moving from negligible to very high. From 1979 to 1981, New Zealand school computers went from 12 minicomputers concentrated in the more fortunate schools to 200 to 300 microcomputers spread across the majority of secondary schools. This is a typical example.

Second, hardware's capabilities are increasing all the time, and governments are trying to standardize purchasing policy. Domestically produced computers designed for education and research are emerging in various countries and attracting varying government support. In Britain these are Research Machines 380Z and 480Z, the BBC Microcomputer from Acorn, and in the most recent scheme, the Sinclair Spectrum. In New Zealand a multi-screen, graphic-based networkable machine, the Poly-I, fits the bill. These machines offer ever-finer graphics and ever-larger amounts of disc store. The horizon for CAL in geography thus constantly widens. For many uses the slower speeds and smaller memory of microcomputers is unimportant. In other areas, facilities such as graphics are simply not available on mainframes at a practical cost. The microcomputer leads in certain areas and where deficiencies exist the gap between microcomputers and larger machines is narrowing. The arrival of 16-bit processors* such as the IBM machine or the ACT Sirius will reduce this gap further. So too will the expanding power of peripherals* to provide cheap graphics and colour printing, and the arrival of videotape interfaces*and video digitizers*.

With increasing use of microcomputers, the hardware cost constraint is becoming less marked. It is becoming apparent that the real cost of computing lies in the production of software.

2. SOFTWARE AVAILABILITY. Most software to date has emerged from publicly funded development or the good offices of private enthusiasts. The UK experience under NDPCAL is a typical one and a coverage of development there is given by Cooper (1975), Shepherd et al (1980), and other NDPCAL reports. New Zealand developments are covered by Forer (1982) and Roper (1981). Most geography software development has been hosted by tertiary institutions.

As in other disciplines, geographers have tended first to write local software units that were to some extent experimental both in terms of computer use and their place in the curriculum. Many educators pass through the first phase of software use by latching on to one of these that fits neatly into their curriculum.

As an eclectic discipline, geography obtains software from many sources. Geographers have not yet fully formulated their ideas on where CAL fits into current curricula, however, nor on how current curricula may need to be modified in the light of available computing power. As the next section discusses in more detail, their demands on software have been pragmatic and catholic.

Software has been a problem partly through the shortage of suitable units. A second factor has been the need to modify programs written for a machine of one kind before they will run on another. The attempt to transfer text and number-based programs from mainframe to micro may encounter problems caused by the limits of memory* size and the number of characters per line. But programs which use graphics – especially important for geographers – are much more difficult to transfer from one kind of micro to another.

In the United Kingdom, New Zealand and Australia, government funding has helped to provide certain geography teaching units for microcomputers. These seem certain to be augmented by commercial offerings. The rapid growth in software is now beginning to provoke a review literature to monitor the quality of the goods, both through review sections of established journals and newer, special-purpose publications.

The range of software is expanding generally, particularly in those subject areas which provide a sufficiently large market to encourage development. To a greater degree than the hard sciences, however, geography has different manifestations in different national educational systems. Our international market is, and should be, more fragmentary. The costs of CAL development may have to be borne for smaller groups of teachers. Individual teachers may want many more custom-built programs to fit their own needs. Fortunately data handling and display applications are fairly universal even if the data banks* of relevance to us may be localized.

3. SOFTWARE DISSEMINATION. In most countries software dissemination is a key issue in promoting CAL. Two aspects of this process are the hardware background and the existence of recognized channels for the dissemination of software. *Ad hoc* responses in most countries have resulted in a proliferation of machine types, each with its own operating environment, and small, often competing, software dissemination units. This problem, the so-called Babel effect, has been important in both the United Kingdom and New Zealand although several groups are working on software procedures to ease portability*. Notable examples are the Institute of Educational Technology at the University of Surrey and Chelsea College's Computers in the Curriculum Project. Hardware solutions such as plug-in ROM* units offering alternative microprocessor* procedures on one machine are now also emerging, bridging the gap for instance between machines based on Z80 and 6502 chips*. In the United Kingdom, government incentives to promote domestic manufacturers seem likely to exacerbate this proliferation in the short term and the same pattern may result in New Zealand where currently the free market trend is strongly towards a single, dominant machine.

Routes for software dissemination have been slow to establish. Various clearing houses of interest to British geographers were established under NDPCAL (most centrally the Geographical Association Package Exchange (GAPE) but relevant units were also produced by the Schools Council Computers in the Curriculum Project). However, these were lacking in co-ordination and their impact was initially handicapped by the small number of active CAL users. In the United Kingdom, the microelectronics education programmes provided the first national initiatives aimed at co-ordinating the education system's access to CAL material (Bradbeer, 1981b). Elsewhere, *ad hoc* solutions are more common, co-ordination of dissemination being by interest groups, professional bodies or existing software exchanges. The indications are that leadership will emerge to streamline access to software, especially proven educational units. Developments like telesoftware* (downloading* programs into microcomputers through teletext or viewdata* systems) and the establishment of public data banks should speed this process. In theory, at least, the sampling, ordering and delivery of software should be far more efficient under such a system.

4. EDUCATIONAL POLICY AND CAL DEVELOPMENT. Central and local authorities are often slow to intervene in CAL due to the financial implications of embracing the new medium. The potential repercussions of central involvement vary nationally. In the United Kingdom with its many local education authorities, the exercise is one of co-ordination towards nationally proposed goals within the structure of multiple examining boards with requirements which sometimes conflict. Elsewhere the administrative structure is more direct. In New Zealand, which has an education system funded and administered nationally, 1981 saw considerable activity with the establishment of a widely-based Consultative Committee on Computers in Schools and the creation of some prototype programmes to develop software and train teachers. There were regional conferences on computer education which established general computer familiarization as the main priority. Within this aim, however, lay several applications within the geography area (Maths Newsletter, 1980).

Summary

CAL in geography, particularly secondary school geography, is a recent phenomenon. It has been passing rapidly through a period of enthusiast-based experiment towards a wider base of use and the production of more integrated software. The discussion above seeks to emphasize the constraints under which this process has operated. In particular these constraints vary nationally, each country developing its CAL uses in response not simply to the requirements of some idealized curriculum but also in the light of the practical constraints prevailing in that country.

II. The evolution of CAL in geography in New Zealand

Early CAL in geography: what have teachers done?

Introducing CAL into use every day, rather than occasionally by motivated enthusiasts, poses difficulties. The constraints already discussed, along with curriculum and psychological hurdles, slow down innovation. Looking at how teachers responded to early geography CAL provides insights into the pattern of CAL use that initially emerged.

What follows is based on New Zealand experience but a glance at the software library of GAPE or resource centres in other nations indicates that the example is not unrepresentative.

The early software was international and mainframe-based. Choice was restricted. Much of the early college-based material collected by the Association of American Geographers was produced in FORTRAN* and had large memory requirements (Fielding and Rummage, 1972), but the Huntington software, based on Dartmouth College BASIC*, offered smaller units with a far higher level of portability and so proved a bridge between computer technologies.

Simulation is one of the simplest yet most winning uses of computers and the later Huntington II programs in particular offer several attractive options from the geography/environmental science area (POLUT, MALAR, BUFLO). From the United Kingdom GAPE provided a useful source of more specialized units although their dissemination through schools in New Zealand was delayed by the need to embed their use in a clearly defined teaching slot. Often teachers felt that the time overhead required to introduce a class to the computer itself was too high in relation to the importance of the restricted area taught by the computer package. Significantly, the early GAPE packages were used more extensively once the first barrier of unfamiliarity with the machine had been overcome.

The most popular introductory programs turned out to be HAMURABI (DEC 1975), which is globally recognized as a good ice-breaker, and POLUT, the pollution simulation from Huntington II. Reports and evaluations of the early uses of POLUT can be found in Duckmanton (1979) and Chalmers *et al* (1980). The popularity of this unit stems from many causes:

1. it was initially in BASIC and could fit on a small micro;
2. it was superbly documented;
3. it was easily available at a minimal cost from a large number of sources;
4. it had both input* and output* specifications that were self-explanatory;
5. it was easily tailored to the local curriculum;
6. it could be combined with local field studies and data gathering from local rivers and lakes;
7. it lent itself well to a mode of operation with the teacher working the only available keyboard*;
8. minor cosmetic changes could easily be made to personalize the presentation, including changing the American spelling.

Of these attributes, numbers 5 to 8 were the most significant in distinguishing this unit from many others. These are attributes of particular importance in the initial adoption stage typified by low machine availability, low levels of official and peer support and negligible perception of the wider value of computer experience. To be attractive at that stage, a unit required above all else ease of use and the ability to amplify and expand the teaching of an important curriculum point.

The second stage of development of CAL use is now beginning to emerge and, through considerations of computer studies and computer awareness, so is some discussion on the longer-term impact of microelectronics on geography teaching.

Short-term development potential: 1982-6

This section tries to answer questions about what the general pattern of CAL geography usage is now and where, with the sort of technology in schools in 1982, it might go in the short term. The description of development to date stresses the control exercized by resource and manpower requirements. Equipment such as networked class sets and computer to videodisc* links is available now and will be increasingly cost-competitive. *When* it can be effectively and widely deployed is another matter. Consequently, in answering the two questions at the beginning of this paragraph, we will stick to a time horizon of the next five years with the assumption of single microcomputers with twin disc drives and medium resolution colour graphics* (to around 200 x 300 points on the screen). A simple subdivision of CAL into fields of particular interest to geographers is used.

Simulation

Of the various CAL modes available, simulation has for some time been favoured by secondary geographers, economists, life scientists and pure scientists (McCullough, 1978 and McKenzie *et al*, 1978 gives examples). Simulations are easy to present and usually fast and simple to develop. They can be used at various levels from simple demonstration to interaction, varying the structure of the underlying model as well as its parameters (eg the teaching scenarios in LIMITS from Huntington II). Philosophically, the main objections to simulation exercises centre on the reliability of the implicit model and the need to distinguish the model from reality in the student's mind. By comparison with doubts about some CAL practice, these are small reservations indeed.

In geography, simulation is most applicable to physical processes but is also useful in human geography which tends to dominate the time devoted to teaching in many secondary schools. Apart from the spatial simulations offered by GAPE and the Schools Council Project, simulations from neighbouring areas of study can be of considerable value, as in the case of the demography programs and data bases offered by the American software centre Conduit. Second-generation machines with good graphics output have offered the chance to provide summary displays of results in a more amenable form, although some caution may be needed with certain graphics applications (Preece and Lewis, 1981). The established popularity of simulations will ensure their continued development. The trend of improving graphics makes certain simulations such as spatial diffusion and competition for land more attractive. The main problem here seems to be that of computing power. For instance, a disease diffusion simulation on a 16 x 32 grid can take up to ten minutes between responses. Also processor speeds may limit the graphics capabilities, in contrast to the past when text-based output so frequently crippled the full display scope of certain simulations. Here 16-bit machines, better BASIC compilers* and other advances keep pushing the frontiers of our expectations back.

Computer-aided instruction

Tutorial-type CAL, sometimes called CAI, has as yet seen little development. In part this is due to limitations of memory and storage capabilities of the earlier microcomputers which in this case were perhaps fortunate. Certainly, as a means of imparting any but the simplest concepts, CAI is open to attack on a variety of methodological grounds. It is also the most intensive resource user of all the CAL modes, usually involving long periods in development, one-to-one computer access, high inherent program redundancy and large amounts of back-up storage.

Nonetheless, CAI in its simplest drilling forms is of great value in primary schools (Fiddy, 1981a, Jones, 1980). Furthermore, these simpler applications are likely to be those that will be, and are, emerging in the commercial informal education sector through language and maths training devices. Geographic training that embodies graphics has already emerged with the PET commercial programs that teach place location in regions of England and Wales. This plays HANGMAN with the pupil using town names whose location is specified on a screen map. The factual side of the discipline, the hang-over from 'Capes and Bays', can benefit considerably in this area.

Possibilities for this increase considerably thanks to the appearance of CAI author languages* on microcomputers. For instance, the University of California at San Diego PILOT language offers both sophisticated graphics editing*, sound creation and screen interaction as part of its wares. One of its demonstration programs tutors a pupil in understanding map locations and map keys through interaction with a screen map. This form of simple CAI offers an extremely attractive option, particularly for remedial pupils. Such drills will in any case surely emerge in the commercial sector to replace the 'swot cards' currently in use to impart facts in preparation for certificate examinations.

Data, graphics and maps

The most exciting things in CAL start to happen when data and graphics are put together to produce thematic maps in graphic mode. These combinations link most closely to computer use outside of education. The development of general-purpose software tends to bring together educators of different disciplines, a very useful result in the early days of trying to interest the majority of the teaching body in CAL. Although these developments are not excessively hard to program, this form of software has been surprisingly slow to emerge; an exception is the Computer-Assisted Cartography package produced by Carl Youngman (1980) for the Apple (illustrated in Figure 1). This is an area of considerable potential, and in many cases it can fit into existing timetables via project work. The sophistication and nature of much of this work varies considerably. Much of the benefit lies in the simplest, illustrative applications. Graphs may be more interpretable than tables of statistics, and maps are virtually essential in geography classes.

Earlier programs sought to draw maps with line-printers* on mainframes, eg SYMAP, while microcomputer emulations emerged at a later date, eg CLAMP (Forer, 1979). The Computer-Assisted Cartography mapping suite for the Apple is shortly to be supplemented by developments elsewhere (Smart and Jennings, 1982). The idiosyncratic nature of the graphics commands makes many of these programs hard to transport to other machines, but character-based mapping programs, even on an 80-column printer, can be used to produce simple area shaded maps. Perversely, the technically superior graphics of most microcomputers in education are slower, less able to show large numbers of areas in a variety of colours, and less easily able to give hard copy than the nominally cruder character-based software. However, they are far more flexible in displaying material such as flow and pie charts, and can be used to produce quite high quality area shaded maps, as Figure 1 shows. Cheap colour printers, particularly useful for geographers, are now becoming available.

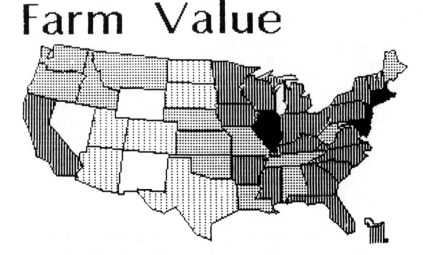

Figure 1 *Cartography on low cost microcomputers: the CAC Apple example*

Hardware and software now exist to allow the use of interactive* graphics to create maps and associated data banks for oneself, particularly maps of point patterns. These can be entered using a digitizer. A typical classroom project studying the location of urban facilities would involve field surveys to collect data which could be entered together with a map outline. It is then possible to use the computer to locate areas of the city that have differing levels of access to urban facilities such as post offices. This is illustrated on Figure 2, in which the little X's show the locations of the post offices in the Christchurch Urban Area (plotted from a data base). The large crosses and lines are the result of student interaction. The centre of each large cross is a home location and the user has specified a search range for postal facilities. The computer links the facility to the home location by a diagonal line and shows the search range by the size of the cross-hairs drawn.

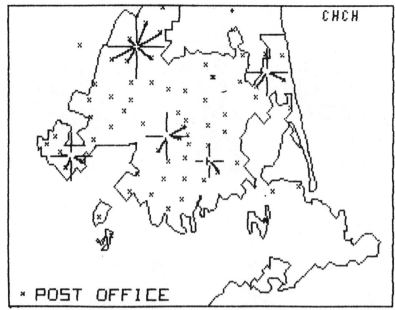

Figure 2 *Data display for exploring concepts. The map illustrates an analysis of access to postal services in the city of Christchurch*

The real hindrance to wider use of mapping and data banking software is usually the difficulty of obtaining the data in machine-usable form. The arrival of projects providing specific data on disc and the prospect of telesoftware (downloading programs through schemes such as the Council for Educational Technology's Prestel umbrella in the United Kingdom) will open up this area much wider. The geographic and mapping aspects will become a part of a larger shift in teaching options. One interesting set of possibilities is posed by programs such as the Topographic Mapping Program (Apple Special Delivery Software), which allows the user to create a spatial data base of spot heights and then display this in one of seven ways. The example here (Figure 3a) represents mesh overlays of an area of spectacular fjord country around Milford Sound in New Zealand. The user has specified different angles of view and vertical exaggeration in each case.

This sort of software raises interesting issues. It is cheap and provides a tempting way to extend and modify some of our geographic material (as does the faster but cruder 3-D representation of an area in Figure 3b). With the increasing availability of printers capable of 'dumping' the entire contents of a screen (including graphics), the data can now also be printed out. The mesh overlays each take about two minutes to draw. Faster micros will bring this down to a more acceptable time for interactive use. Such developments and their logical extension clearly will both extend and modify areas such as the teaching of map interpretation.

As geography is not a primary school subject, little has been said of pre-secondary developments. There is considerable room for the application of

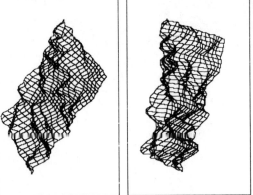

a) Three views of a fjord landscape using different viewpoints and vertical exaggeration

From ESE, skewed   From NE, downwards

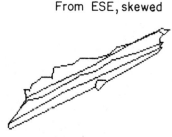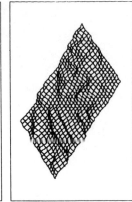

From the North at sea level   From the West at sea level

b) Viewing island landforms with the aid of a fast 3-D graphics utility

Figure 3 *Two examples of 3-dimensional data display.*

graphics in early schooling. The language LOGO* teaches certain geometric properties to young children in maths classes. Quite soon several languages or programs will be able to extend this idea to map work and the formal interpretation of this form of imagery. The maps may be crude and simple but the pupils will increasingly be able to explore aspects of map making through simple exercises in map creation and interactive interpretation.

A final aspect of data management is the bibliographic one of handling various references. Again this is an area which will involve several disciplines and where current software is far from ideal. However, projects such as the British Library's attempts to get information retrieval into schools (Payne, 1981) can in the long term only result in significant shifts in what geographers view as possible and desirable. The potential scope of the teacher and class to undertake exploratory projects is greatly enhanced by these advances in the display of information and structured access to it.

Gaming

A final area where CAL has proved useful is that of gaming, where computer management offers considerable benefits in extending the scope and accuracy of games (Forer, 1977, 1979; Walker and Graham, 1979). Game progress can be monitored and the value of debriefing after games enhanced by replay and analysis of the action. Multi-player gaming, however, is harder to fit into the curriculum than data-base projects and again its benefits are disputed. However, one- or two-player, short teaching exercises with a gaming aspect fit well into geography, particularly those areas where competition or individual decision-making is important.

III. Mid-term directions

From the comments above, certain trends are apparent, which are summarized in the table below. While the timing is specifically related to New Zealand, the progression is applicable more widely. The number of stars indicates the importance of work in the specific categories while the comments box expands a little on the focus of the trends.

Area of application	Phase I 1978-9	Phase II 1981	Phase III 1985 (est)	Comments
Simulation	*****	****	***	Physical and macroscale socio-economic models with documentation and increasing scope for local data input.
CAL ⟨ Basic drill	*	*	**	Factual base of geography plus map
Tutorial CAI			*	skills.
Data banking	**	**	***	Programs using both public data banks and locally acquired field work data in a spatial setting.
Interactive mapping	*	**	****	
Gaming		*	**	Some solo but important developments for study of interactive group processes and decision-making.

Table I *Software emphasis in geography CAL*

The table above suggests that school CAL will follow a path where the computer offers an exploratory avenue to students. The more rigid CAI uses, based on simple formal models of learning processes, will be less in evidence.

It is profitable to look outside current educational practice, however, to consider what other possibilities may emerge. These are almost certainly going to be based on two developments. The first of these is the advent of cheap multi-user microcomputer networks which will encourage interaction between students. It will also enable far greater use to be made of local data when many machines can share a large hard disc* drive (Bradbeer, 1981a). Some of the wider implications of networking have been outlined by Dwyer (1981). To social scientists interested in processes of group interaction and competition this is noteworthy.

The other breakthrough will be in the extension of graphics beyond the display of information or simulation. Graphics capture has become increasingly easy thanks to cheap digitizers and frame grabbers*. When the link into fast access, high storage videodisc technology becomes more widely available it will open tremendous vistas to a spatial and landscape discipline. Where relatively simple concepts require sophisticated presentation for their transmission this technology has immediate potential. Geomorphic process and landscape is one example, land use, transition and urban landscape a second, and assessment of the visual impact of industrial projects a third case where television imagery could be of great value when linked to a computer which can control the sequence of presentation in reaction to student response. The 1982 arrival of Apple SUPER-PILOT complete with built-in videodisc access commands surely heralds the start of the full integration of this technology.

The wider use of graphics will come more quickly through conventional computer generation and have clear relevance for a spatial discipline (through the introduction of LANDSAT* imagery in a pedagogic form, for instance). Readers who are tempted to be sceptical about likely development times for this may recall the rapidity of progress in commercial games and think again. Video and arcade games are considerably ahead of educational software in production and the lesson is clear: commercial software for microcomputers offers good graphics and animation*, and is often (eg in war games such as COMPUTER BISMARCK), set in sophisticated and valuable simulation models. Commercial software is frequently of educational value. The views of New Zealand's South Island in Figure 3b for instance were produced from an author program designed for use in writing space war games. This moderately sophisticated 3-D display package by Bill Budge is only one of several available that widen CAL horizons. There are exciting possibilities for role-playing fantasy games where a party of individuals explores a maze of unknown rooms and tunnels or a mapped landscape. The program ADVENTURE is the mainframe progenitor of all of these. In each adventure the player interacts with a fantasy environment, discovering through experiment the lessons to be learnt and dangers to be avoided. In current versions of these programs the player can see a map and/or graphics picture of each new room as he encounters it and his progress is managed by the computer. Both the individual's characteristics and the environment about him are monitored and updated as a result of interaction with the environment. The computer is deeply engaged in data management, rather than merely providing a simple simulated environment as in many computer games.

The player must learn this new world from scratch and by discovery. The games are highly motivating and can stretch both the computer's and the player's capacity to the full. They allow the player the freedom to explore. Clearly such games offer a direct opportunity to geographers to simulate the process of exploration in the age of discovery. More generally, though, these games are of interest for their inherent properties of motivation, exploration and liberation; they offer a good pointer for fruitful third-generation software development in geography CAL. Such approaches already have adherents but the impact of their adoption may not leave geography unaltered. Dwyer (1974) anticipated this almost a decade ago.

CAL in New Zealand, as exemplified by geography, has made very rapid progress. The microcomputer has allowed educational applications to by-pass the mainframe and to take advantage of the rapid pace of hardware developments which are particularly relevant in the graphics area. We are now approaching the take-off point where future progress will be based on exploiting new developments in commercial and entertainment software for CAL, rather than waiting for new hardware developments.

Acknowledgement

This paper was written while the author was Visiting Research Fellow at Bristol University on sabbatical leave from the University of Canterbury. He appreciates the assistance of both institutions.

References

Bradbeer, R (1981a) How I plan to spend the money: an interview with Richard Fothergill *Educational Computing* 2 3: 22-6

Bradbeer, R (1981b) Exciting prospects for networks *Educational Computing* 2 6: 27-31

Chalmers, A, Thompson, W and Keown, P (1980) The use of a computer based simulation model in the geography classroom *New Zealand Journal of Geography* 67: 6-9

Cooper, Z A (1975) Computers in secondary school geography *Computer Education* 19: 8-14

DEC (1975) *101 BASIC Computer Games* Digital Equipment Games, Digital Equipment Corporation: Maynard, Mass

Duckmanton, N (1979) Computers in the classroom *in* Forer, P C ed *Geography, Simulation and the Computer in Schools* 42-9

Dwyer, T (1974) The significance of solo mode computing for curriculum design *EDU* Sept 1974

Dwyer, T (1981) Multi-micro learning environments: a preliminary report on the SOLO/NET/works Project *Byte* January 1981:104-114

Farrington, B (1981) Computer based exercises for language learning at university level, *Paper to the CAL81 Symposium, Leeds, 8-9 April 1982*

Fiddy, P (1981) *The Microcomputer: An Ideal Assistant in the Infant Classroom* Unpublished paper gives to the CAL81 Symposium on Computer Assisted Learning, Leeds

Fielding, G and Rumage, K W eds (1972) *Computerised Instruction in Undergraduate Geography* Technical Paper No 6, Association of American Geographers

Fielden, J and Pearson, P K (1978) *The Cost of Learning with Computers: report of the Financial Evaluation of the National Development Programme in Computer Assisted Learning* Council for Educational Technology: London

Forer, P C (1977) Gaming the space economy: a teaching simulation and its context *in Proceedings, 9th New Zealand Geographical Society Conference* Dunedin, Christchurch, NZ

Forer, P C ed (1979) *Geography, Simulation and the Computer in Schools* Canterbury Branch, New Zealand Geographical Society: Christchurch, NZ

Forer, P C (1982) *Report on Computer Assisted Learning in the United Kingdom with Particular Reference to the CAL81 Symposium at Leeds* New Zealand Department of Education: Wellington, NZ

Forer, P and Owens, I (1979) Frontiers of geography in the 1980s *New Zealand Journal of Geography* 67: 2-5

Hooper, R and Toye, I (1975) *Computer Assisted Learning in the United Kingdom: some Case Studies* NDPCAL/Council for Educational Technology: London

Jones, R (1980) *Microcomputers: Their Uses in Primary Schools* Council for Educational Technology: London

McCullough, L (1978) *Basic Interactive Computer Models in Population Dynamics* Department of Geography, University of Queensland

McKenzie, J, Elton, L, and Lewis, R (1978) *Interactive Computer Graphics in Science Teaching* Ellis Horwood: Chichester

Maths Newsletter (1980) Proposals for computer education in New Zealand high schools *Maths Newsletter* Department of Education: Wellington

Moore, W (1981) Catching up in the computer race *Education News* 17 7: 16-19

Papert, S (1980) *Mindstorms: Children, Computers and Powerful Ideas* Harvester Press: Brighton

Payne, A (1981) On-line information retrieval in schools *CAL News* 16: 11

Preece, J and Lewis, R (1981) *Improving Students' Data Interpretation Skills via CAL graphics,* Unpublished paper given to the CAL81 Symposium on Computer Assisted Learning, Leeds 9.4.81

Roper, K (1981) The implications of new technology for secondary teachers *Paper to the Gisborne In-Service Training Seminar* Gisborne 16.10.81

Schools Council (1979) *Computers in the Curriculum: Geography* Edward Arnold: London

Shepherd, I D H, Cooper, Z A and Walker, D R F (1980) *Computer Assisted Learning in Geography* Council for Educational Technology: London

Smart, N and Jennings, R (1982) Microelectronics technology and geography in the Scottish secondary school *Scottish Educational Review* Special Issue 2: 23-33

Walker, D R F and Graham, L (1979) Simulation games and the microcomputer *Simulation/Games for Learning* 9 4: 151-8

Wearing, A J, Cass, B W and Fitzgerald, D (1976) *Computers and Teaching in Australia* Australian Advisory Committee on Research and Development in Education Report No 6, Australian Government Publishing Service: Canberra

Youngmann, C (1980) *CAC-Apple: a Mapping and Data Management Utility for the Apple II* Morgan-Fairchild Group: Seattle

Part 4:
Computers and the curriculum

17. Computers and teacher education

Benedict du Boulay

Summary: The student teacher learns her subject, learns about teaching and learns about children. The computer can play an unique role in each of these enterprises. It can simulate a piece of arithmetic, a child with a misconception or a whole class of children. In each case the student teacher can conduct experiments with the simulation to deepen her understanding of the system in question. This role of computer as simulator cannot be duplicated by any other medium; only the computer has the versatility and reactiveness to make simulations educationally feasible. There is also a more indirect use of computers in teacher education. Tutorial programs embody teaching strategies whose principles are open to inspection and discussion. So we can expect such programs, as they become more intelligent, to be increasingly used as a source of educational case studies.

Introduction

The computer can be employed in colleges and departments of education in just as many ways as in any other educational institution. For example, it can sieve access to information, conduct a tutorial dialogue, become a simulation* or provide any of the many other services described elsewhere in this book. Thus, in order to examine its impact on the education of student teachers, we need to keep in mind what distinguishes their education from that of other groups of students. Put in its baldest terms, student teachers predominantly learn about three things: the subjects they are to teach, techniques for teaching them and how children learn. This chapter describes examples of the use of computers in teacher education that illustrate these three tasks. My purpose is not to give a wide-ranging survey but to indicate some possibilities, based on the question: what unique contribution can the computer make to teacher education? My contention is that the computer offers something new and valuable to teacher education, something that cannot be imitated by other means. The computer is not just a novel presentation medium for conventional teaching material.

Programs as case studies for observation

Let me distinguish, at the outset, two ways in which the computer can be employed in teacher education. The first puts student teachers in the role of *users of programs** which attempt to teach them some skill, provide them with facilities for exploring some domain or give them a tool for undertaking some task. The second puts them into the role of *observers of programs* as material for the study of learning and teaching, in much the same way as videotapes of good and bad classroom episodes are currently used, say in microteaching.

This section concerns the second – the indirect – use of programs, which is as yet undeveloped, but will increase as the availability, quality and intelligence of teaching programs improve. Used in this indirect mode, the power of a tutorial program as a focus for the study of teaching is that the principles by which it makes decisions about teaching actions can be stated precisely. It is then possible for student teachers to observe the educational effectiveness of those principles with a view to deciding how they should be modified in order to produce better learning. A nice example of this is Burton and Brown's program WEST which coaches children in a game that requires them to practise certain arithmetic skills (Burton and Brown, 1979). The game is like snakes and ladders but the players have to do a small sum in order to determine their move.

Experience with an earlier version of the program had shown that children tended to play very conservatively, using only those few arithmetic rules with which they felt comfortable. So they tended not to practise the very rules in which practice was most needed. The problem was to develop a program which encouraged children to use a wider range of arithmetical skills while maintaining the stimulation of using a game, without making the program so didactic that it became overbearing and ungamelike. In a college or department of education, student teachers could observe children using the program in order to examine its educational effectiveness.

The program is based on a set of a dozen principles. Surprisingly, many of the principles are concerned with *preventing* the program from making too many tutorial comments. The authors' theory of coaching is based on the idea that a single, well-timed and apposite tutorial comment is more effective than lots of advice, even if that advice is in some sense good. Indeed, so unobtrusive is the advice giving that some (adult) players claimed not to have been advised at all after a session, even though they had in fact been given one or two suggestions for better play.

One of the values of such a program in teacher training is that it raises the issue of 'what to say' and 'when to say it' in a very concrete manner. The teaching principles are quite explicit and open to discussion, analysis and (in principle) to experiment. A refined version of the program could allow student teachers to change the teaching principles and observe the new behaviour of the program and its effect on children.

However, there are problems in implementing a program in which the teaching principles can be varied, even when the particular set of principles can be stated precisely in English. The main difficulty is that in most teaching programs the teaching principles are not kept in one place where they can be easily modified. At best they will be explicit but distributed through the program, and at worst they will be implicit in the way the program works and thus not open to any kind of modification at all except by rewriting.

O'Shea's (1979) quadratic tutor is one program which has a set of modifiable teaching principles. This program teaches a method for solving quadratic equations. Its teaching principles form a sufficiently self-contained component of the program to enable a supervisory part of the program to run teaching experiments automatically, with a view to improving the teaching principles as given. Clearly such a program could be adapted for use by student teachers who would run the experiments, instead of having them run automatically.

Simulation programs

This and the following sections are concerned with student teachers as users rather than as observers of programs, and describe three systems designed expressly for student teachers. In each case the computer acts as a simulation with which students can conduct various kinds of educational experiment. So the emphasis is very much on hands-on* activity by students whereby they themselves control the interaction with the computer rather than the other way round. Again, much of the work described concerns mathematics. This should not be taken to mean that it is only in the domain of mathematics that computers can help in the training of teachers. It is rather that the most accessible examples concern mathematics. I do not discuss any example of a program that teaches in the traditional computer-assisted instruction* sense, ie that presents text and then asks questions. Of course there are any number of such programs which student teachers may use to learn some topic and many other programs that students may find useful in their professional roles, such as a timetabling program. This is not to say that such programs cannot be used profitably in teacher education, only that there is little of interest to say about student teachers as users of such programs.

My three examples cover learning a subject, learning about children and learning about teaching. In dealing with learning a subject, I will concentrate on those student teachers who find mathematics difficult and unpleasant. I will describe a system which enables such students to investigate areas of mathematics which they find troublesome. Here the computer becomes a mathematical laboratory with which the student can conduct mathematical experiments.

Student teachers must also learn how children think. Partly this comes from their own experience on teaching practice, partly from discussion with their peers and with teachers, and partly from more formal work in psychology within their training programme. The computer can play a part via the powerful educational tool of simulation. The program simulates a child with a particular arithmetic misconception and it is the student teacher's task to diagnose this misconception or bug* given only the answers produced by the 'child' to a series of sums proposed by the student teacher. Some of the child's answers will be correct, some not, depending on the sums chosen and on the nature of the bug, and both types of answer act as clues to the child's underlying difficulty.

As well as learning how children think, the student teacher must also learn teaching skills. Some of these skills will be concerned with effective methods of helping an individual to learn and understand an idea and will necessarily be closely associated with the notion of diagnosis introduced above. Other skills will be concerned with the broader managerial issues of how to handle groups of children in order to maintain an educationally effective classroom. Again the computer can play a part by simulation, though this time it simulates a whole class rather than an individual child. The student can try out different teaching actions on this 'class', having established the class's current state, and see how these actions affect the state of the class. For example, the student may decide to set some written work at a particular stage in a lesson only to be told that the pupils are getting restive and that there are still 20 minutes to go before the end of the lesson. Here as in the previous example where the computer simulated a child, the advantage is that the student can try out a variety of experiments without endangering either real children's learning or her own position with a class.

Learning a subject

In some ways, a student teacher learning mathematics faces much the same task as any other student who must learn mathematics at the same level. What is different is that the student teacher learns the subject with a view to re-explaining it to others. This puts a different emphasis on how she should learn it compared with other learners. This distinction does not arise from the extra burden of learning a set of techniques for teaching the subject, but is concerned with the manner in which the student teacher must master the subject in order to be able to cope with the misunderstandings and difficulties of pupils. For example, a student teacher training for primary school may need to re-examine much of her understanding of arithmetic, not because she cannot carry out arithmetic procedures correctly but because she may not have fully articulated to herself the logic underlying those procedures. Without understanding the logic she will be in a weak position to adopt any but the teaching strategy of 'do this and this because I tell you to'. Playing with BUGGY is likely to sensitize her to the idea of bugs in children's symbol manipulation procedures, but learning how to remove those bugs or to discourage their emergence requires a different approach.

One of the classic problems of teaching arithmetic has been how to teach about the multiplication and division of fractions. There are two reasons for this. First, the procedures involved seem rather arbitrary and strange. Second, any metaphors used early to explain about addition and subtraction of fractions break down when applied to multiplication and division. For example, what does it mean to multiply 1/2 of a pie by 2/3? Various positions are held about this problem, ranging from 'avoidance' – there is no need to teach these fraction manipulations at all – through 'authoritarian' – just tell them the rule and hope for the best – and 'theoretical' – describe the rules as a kind of arbitrary symbol game that can be played – to 'explanatory' – try to find some way to justify the way the rules are. My own work with student teachers is based on the last of these positions and has used the computer to build a dynamic system which students can use to create a picture that illustrates these fraction operations (du Boulay, 1980).

The program works by first drawing a thin pencil-like shape on the computer terminal's* screen. The student is then invited to type in a fraction of her own choice. The effect of this is that a second pencil is drawn, beside the first, whose length is in proportion to the first according to the fraction that she entered. So entering 1/2 gives a pencil half as high, and entering 3/2 gives a pencil one and a half times as high. The student then types a second fraction that has the effect of producing a third pencil whose height is in proportion to the second pencil according to this second fraction. The combined effect of the two fractions, and the consequent relation between the first and third pencil, give a visual illustration of fraction multiplication. Put more formally, the fractions are considered as length transformers which can be sequentially combined. So if the two fractions entered are 2/5 and 3/4, the overall effect is that the third pencil is 6/20, ie 2/5 × 3/4 times the height of the first one. Using this as a basis, other fraction ideas can be explored visually, such as fraction equivalence (ie 2/3 has the same effect as 4/6) and the idea of a fraction inverse (ie 2/3 exactly undoes the effect of 3/2). Subsequently, the mysterious rule for dividing fractions, 'turn it upside down and multiply' can be given some sort of justification, in terms of a series of length transformations.

Now this program is very simple and only deals with a very restricted issue, but it serves as an illustration of an important point in teacher education: there are student teachers going into primary schools who really have no idea of the reasons behind some of the mathematical rules they will be expected to teach. What the computer can do in these cases is provide a mathematical 'apparatus' which embodies the rule and allows students to give some meaning to a rule which they probably already 'know' at a formal level.

The fraction program allows only a highly constrained dialogue between student and computer, in that all the student can do is choose her fractions and see what happens. She cannot alter the way that the program works. A more radical approach based on Papert's (1980) ideas has the student teacher learn a programming language* such as LOGO*, so that she then has the full power of the computer at her disposal and could, if she wished and was able, herself implement the fraction program or any other. The facility with which this could be done depends crucially on the quality of the programming language employed, and in this respect LOGO, though certainly not perfect, has many good features. My own work with student teachers explored an approach similar to that proposed by Papert, and was concerned to teach student teachers to program in LOGO and then have them explore mathematical topics that they were finding troublesome by writing programs embodying those topics. One aspect of this work which the student teachers found valuable was the chance to be honest about their mathematical difficulties. The whole emphasis of the work was on developing programs and trying to understand why they did (or more often, did not) work. It was much more acceptable to the student teacher to initiate a discussion by saying that she did not understand quite how to write a program to add fractions (say) rather than having to admit that she did not understand how to add fractions. The computer was both a catalyst to mathematical discussion and a scapegoat for difficulties.

Learning about children

One of the many problems of teaching arithmetic is diagnosing the causes of children's mistakes in their written sums. Sometimes mistakes are a result of carelessness, tiredness and a lack of concentration, but often they arise from some misconception about how to do the sums in question. A single misconception may have an effect in a variety of situations. For example, misapplying a rule about 'carrying' may produce wrong answers in both addition and multiplication sums. Likewise misapplying a 'borrowing' rule may show up in both subtraction and division sums. Conversely, a child who misunderstands these rules may still get some sums correct because those particular sums did not require him to use his faulty rule. In some situations the only evidence available to the teacher is the child's written work, eg when homework or a test is being marked. In these cases the teacher will not be able to see the child doing the sums or ask him for reasons for these answers and will have to perform the diagnosis as best as possible with the available information.

BUGGY is a program designed to give students practice in diagnosing children's arithmetic difficulties (Brown, 1978). Its educational objectives are, first, to alert student teachers to the idea that children sometimes misapply certain rules consistently (ie mistakes are not just random). Second, it trains student teachers in effective diagnostic procedures, for example, to resist the temptation to jump to conclusions too early on the basis of insufficient evidence. Notice that the program is not concerned with helping students learn about children's understanding of the logic underlying arithmetic procedures. It is concerned solely with the procedures for manipulating symbols on paper.

The program gives students practice in the diagnosis of addition and subtraction bugs in sums such as 453 + 62 or 2987 − 1403. The program embodies an analysis of how the skill of addition, for example, is broken down into a hierarchy of sub-skills, such as adding up two digits in a single column. Sub-skills may themselves be broken down into sub-sub-skills and so on. There is also a representation of the ways that these sub-skills can go wrong and the program simulates a child with a bug by arranging for one of the sub-skills to be set to one of its incorrect forms. The selected sub-skill will then work consistently but incorrectly whenever it is called on. Of course in some situations the chosen sub-skill may not be needed and the child will get the sum correct. However, if the sub-skill is used then its incorrect result will be incorporated into the child's working with the consequent possibility that the answer to the sum as a whole will be wrong.

It is the student teacher's task to diagnose which is the incorrect sub-skill by setting the simulated child a series of sums and observing its answers. The program starts by choosing a bug and displaying a sum that incorporates that bug. The student then suggests further sums to which the computer provides the simulated child's answers. When the student thinks that she knows what the bug is, she can ask to be tested on her hypothesis. The program does this by asking the student to predict how the simulated child would answer to a series of sums chosen by the program. If she fails to predict correctly, she returns to the earlier data-gathering stage where she has to suggest sums. Note that the program sometimes simulates a child and sometimes an examiner.

Burton and Brown have conducted a small informal evaluation of their program and found that students, who started out by treating the simulated child as just 'dumb' and 'stupid', changed their attitude and began to take a more professional view and became interested in developing systematic explanations for the child's behaviour. One question raised by this program is how far these techniques can be applied outside mathematics. This is, what other areas are there in which children exhibit consistent errors that can be explained in terms of underlying bugs?

Learning about teaching

The computer can as easily simulate a class of children as a single child. The program I outline next is an adaptation of a simulation program originally used to train doctors in dealing with emergency patients (Kemmis et al, no date). In its original form, the program starts by describing a patient who has just been admitted to hospital in an emergency. The patient has a set of 'vital signs', such as heart beat, breathing, etc, which give clues to his underlying condition and to the steps needed to improve it. It is the student doctor's task to decide what to do, and she must do something. There are choices about conducting tests to gather more information and about giving treatments. The difficulty is that both tests and treatments have associated 'costs'. That is, each takes a certain amount of time, and time is valuable and running out for the patient. Each may also have undesirable side-effects which may actually make the patient worse. As the student works with the program, she sees time ticking away and the changing (possibly deteriorating) state of the patient. If she is unsuccessful in her choice of tests and treatments she will kill her 'patient'.

Dunn (1980) has exploited the analogy between this situation and that of a student teacher learning to manage a class, to recast the program in a form suitable for use by student teachers. Now the 'patient' is a 'class' and the vital signs are its attentiveness, its degree of restlessness, the state of knowledge of the class members and the match between its activities and the lesson objectives. Time ticks away here, too and the student teacher has available both 'tests' and 'treatments'. Tests are concerned with establishing the state of the vital signs of the class, eg their knowledge or restlessness, and treatments are the activities that the student teacher and the class engage in. These include the children reading, writing, discussing, looking at visual aids, preparing for written work and being controlled by the teacher. Of course, when the class is in certain states, some treatments are likely to prove not only ineffective but positively detrimental. The program will terminate the lesson early if the class gets too noisy or confused.

The program provides various kinds of feedback both during the lesson and at its finish. For instance the student can obtain a print-out* showing the changing profile of the 'vital signs' and the teaching decisions she took which produced that profile. This enables her to re-run the same lesson making different decisions and observing the new outcome.

Underlying the teacher's version of the program is a model of how classroom interactions work. That is, a model which, given a state for the class, specifies how a teacher's action will affect that state. As presented, the program embodies a very simple model whose details are open to question (and to a certain amount of empirical study). But, in principle, this kind of simulation program could become a very useful way for students to try out teaching experiments. Like aircraft pilots in a flight simulator, they can practise emergency procedures until they become second nature. The difficulties are the usual ones with simulations; first, it may be hard to implement an accurate simulation because we do not know enough about detailed classroom dynamics and, second, there is still the unresolved issue about how far and in what ways practice with such a simulation would transfer to the real classroom. As far as I am aware, no evaluation of the effectiveness of this particular simulation has yet been conducted.

Conclusion

I have indicated how the computer can offer something new and valuable in teacher education, whether the student teacher is a program user or a program observer. In each case, the computer is doing a task that cannot easily be duplicated by other means. The three systems which I have described give student teachers hands-on experience of the computer's power to simulate. Such systems can help student teachers learn about their subject, learn about teaching and learn about children. In addition, as teaching programs become more versatile and intelligent, we can expect to see the programs themselves being used as the focus for discussion among student teachers about learning and teaching.

Acknowledgements

This paper was written with the support of the Sloan Foundation while the author was a visiting fellow at the Center for Human Information Processing, University of California. San Diego.

References

Brown, J S and Burton, R R (1978) Diagnostic models for procedural bugs in basic mathematical skills *Cognitive Science* 2: 155-92
Burton, R R and Brown, J S (1979) An investigation of computer coaching for informal learning activities *International Journal of Man-Machine Studies* 11 1:5-24

du Boulay, J B H (1980) Teaching teachers mathematics through programming *International Journal of Mathematical Education in Science and Technology* **11** 3: 347-60

du Boulay, J B H and Howe, J A M (1982) LOGO building blocks: student teachers using computer-based mathematics apparatus *Computers and Education* **6** 1: 93-8

Dunn, W R (1980) *The Development of a Computer Assisted Learning Program on Classroom Management in the Primary School* Department of Education: Glasgow University

Kemmis, S, Atkin, R and Wright, E (no date) *How do Students Learn? Occasional Publication 5* Centre for Applied Research in Education, University of East Anglia: Norwich

O'Shea, T (1979) A self-improving quadratic tutor *International Journal of Man-Machine Studies* **11** 1:97-124

Papert, S (1980) *Mindstorms: Children, Computers and Powerful Ideas* Harvester Press: Brighton

18. Computer studies and computer education

Derek Esterson

Summary: This chapter traces the development of computer studies as a formal examination subject in the secondary schools of England, Wales and Northern Ireland. The genesis of the subject is traced from the initial point where there was a marked mathematical bias, to the present emphasis on information processing. Problems of inadequate equipment and teacher training are identified. There is also an account of the wide variety of computing courses available below degree level in colleges of further education for those intending to pursue both industrial and commercial careers.

Computer studies, or what is in practice often synonymous, computer science, has come to be a distinct school subject in England and Wales and Northern Ireland. It is not to be confused with informatics*, which seems to have originated in the USSR, but which has been espoused most enthusiastically in France and which presupposes the existence of fundamental laws, for the communication and processing of information, which require investigation and understanding. Inevitably there will be elements of computer studies which impinge on informatics, but in the pragmatic manner of the education systems of the United Kingdom (apart from Scotland) computer studies has not necessarily sought the formal justification of being a distinct discipline, but it has been introduced into schools in one way or another because teaching children about computers is believed to be important. This teaching has developed a range of syllabuses whose general outlines will be given later and which include less detailed studies appropriate for all children, embodied in the slogan of the British Computer Society 'Computer Education For All'. In Scotland, an interim report published in 1969 was in favour of an 'Introductory Course for the great majority of pupils', but felt that computer studies should not be developed as a subject discipline in its own right.

The distinction is drawn, therefore, between formally established courses of computer studies leading to examinations and qualifications, and an ill-defined 'computer education' designed to produced an awareness of the social, industrial and commercial impact of computers without necessarily involving learning much about how they work or even of how to use them. Whether it is necessary that the great majority of children should acquire this awareness is a matter for debate. Opponents of the idea point to other technological developments, such as the motor car or atomic energy, which have had or will have a profound effect on our lives, and argue that the need for an understanding of these is no less. Proponents insist that the use of computers, particularly in the age of microcomputers*, will be so all-pervasive and significant as to constitute a special case. In any event, there have been some attempts to put across this 'awareness', sometimes as much to enable pupils to make a sensible choice of subjects for public examinations, when the time comes, as for any social purpose. Perhaps the most notable of these was 'A Course on Information' by Norman Longworth of IBM to design a study, in the secondary school classroom, of the way information is generated and processed. Although this is not overtly linked to the use of the computer, inevitably such use suggests itself. The course has not gained wide currency, perhaps because there are few teachers able to teach it. Computer studies, on the other hand, has become established as a school subject in its own right, attracting an ever-increasing number of candidates for its examinations (see Figure 1).

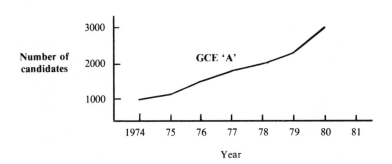

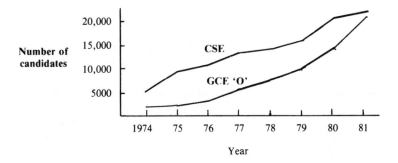

Figure 1 *Growth in presentations for computer studies examinations 1974-81*

The information presented in Figure 1 relates to the current school examination system in England, Wales and Northern Ireland where there are two kinds of public examination available to children. The General Certificate of Education (GCE) is intended for the academically most able and offers examination at Ordinary (O) level for 16-year-old pupils, who may leave school at that age, or who may proceed to Advanced (A) level, which is the common requirement for university entrance. For the less academic, but those nevertheless deemed capable of formal examination, there is the Certificate of Secondary Education (CSE). This exists in three modes: for Mode 1, the examination is set and marked by an external regional body; for Mode 2, the examination is set by the school but moderated and marked by the external regional body; for Mode 3, the examination is set and marked in school, but moderated externally.

The first computing examinations appeared in the early 1970s. Not surprisingly, the initiative was taken by teachers of mathematics and this was reflected in the early syllabuses. The Advanced level of the GCE was heavily biased towards numerical analysis and the early CSE courses (Mode 3 as specified above) contained much about circuits, logic and memory* devices and possibly gave currency to the fiction that mastery of binary* arithmetic was a necessary prerequisite to understanding computers.

An unusual feature of computer studies has been the inclusion of a significant element of practical work, attracting between 20 per cent and 50 per cent of the total marks. The practical work has to be undertaken throughout the course and generally requires the demonstration of programming skills, but students are frequently allowed to undertake more discursive projects, for example the description of an application of computers. At the Ordinary level of the GCE, computer studies arrived comparatively late on the scene in 1974 and differs from CSE courses only in its more academic approach and less marked emphasis on practical work. In any case, plans are far advanced to merge the CSE and GCE O level examinations. The intervening years have seen a gradual change to the point where there is almost an anti-mathematical slant to syllabuses and much stress is placed on the importance of data processing*. At the nub of a computer studies course is the computer as processor of information; mathematical data constitutes only one of the many sources from which information may be processed.

What, then, is expected of children who undertake computer studies? The syllabuses in the various regions have a great deal in common, reflecting the influence of the Schools Committee of the British Computer Society, which has done much of the work in defining syllabus content. The history of information processing is considered significant. Early syllabuses concerned themselves with the mechanization of arithmetic, usually starting with the abacus and making much of the difference between Chinese and Japanese variants! Napier and Babbage had their part to play, not forgetting the romantic interest of Byron's daughter, Lady Lovelace, whose true role is consistently undervalued. Oughtred and Hollerith and, of course, von Neumann, all take the place of kings and queens of traditional history. The invention of printing has latterly been given more significance, and attention is given to established methods of filing information and the operation of accounting machines and such like.

Under the general heading of computer concepts, we find consideration of the input*/processing/output* cycle, latterly in the order output/input/processing. The examinations have in the past been concerned with detailed descriptions of peripheral* devices, of the nature of main memory and external memory, including its physical construction, speed of operation and price. Students have been expected to determine the best equipment for a particular job and to assess the merits of punched cards* and paper tape*, or even to explain how a barrel printer works! Fortunately, this is now giving way to a requirement for general understanding.

Having mastered these concepts (or not as the case may be), the student is required to look at the application of computers in commerce and industry. He or she is likely to be taken to visit an installation at a bank, insurance company, warehouse or mail order company, to gain insight into the real use of computers. It is not unusual for the examination to ask for a description in some detail of an application of computers with which the student is familiar. Students may also be expected to specify equipment suitable for particular applications. Over the years, the emphasis on information processing has steadily increased. Attention is paid to the collection and validation of data*, and pupils are encouraged to design their own experiments and carry out their own surveys. For CSE and GCE O level only the rudiments of file processing are dealt with, but in GCE A level this topic is given detailed consideration. Systems analysis and design are dealt with at the appropriate level, with due attention being paid to both computerized and manual systems. Fundamental to the processing of information is an emphasis on the notion that the value of the information depends on the quality of the data.

Naturally, programming plays a central role in the courses. In theory considerable latitude is allowed in the choice of language* but in practice BASIC* is almost universally offered, although at GCE Advanced level COBOL, ALGOL and FORTRAN* are fairly common as additional languages. There is also some assembler* or pseudo-assembler language work, which is thought to reinforce comprehension of how a computer works. Every effort has been made to set high standards of documentation* which are of particular relevance to the practical work. It has been found difficult to examine programming skills in the written examination and there is a growing tendency to confine questions to the diagnosis and correction of error, or the discovery of a process carried out by a section of program*, or the dry running of a program segment with appropriate data. Students are expected to apply their knowledge to the solution of specified problems, increasingly with an algorithmic* flavour. Because of the difficulty experienced in assessing programs written during the formal examination, candidates are often asked instead to produce flow diagrams or other logical descriptions of their solutions.

A knowledge of formal logic is demanded by some syllabuses and students may be expected to deal with the input and output of simple combinations of gates* to about the complexity of a half adder at GCE O level, and rather greater at A level.

The social implications of the use of computers bring in subject matter of a different kind. Students are encouraged to consider the impact of automation on the types of job and levels of employment likely to be available in the future. The possible effects of data banks* on personal freedom and privacy are considered. Generally, questions in the examination require discursive answers and the less academic pupils find these more difficult than those in other sections dealing with factual matters.

Finally, most syllabuses are concerned with the staffing and structure of data processing departments. Various job functions are expected to be known, from the humblest punch operator to the director responsible for data processing, and questions may be asked in the examination about the relationships between different people helping to operate a computing department. There is a tradition in UK schools that courses are non-vocational and it is only in this section that overt attention is paid to possible careers in computing. Recently, the bodies responsible for administering the London Region examinations have put forward a new technique involving the distribution of case studies to pupils a short time (14 days) before the written examination. Questions are then asked in the written examination about the case studies.

The various bodies administering these examinations have attempted to define the minimum facilities and staffing required for satisfactory courses to be run. These have proved unenforceable, but, as far as computer facilities were concerned, they have suggested that batch processing* turn-round time should be no worse than three days, and that the facilities should be guaranteed for the duration of the course. In the past, schools have obtained computer facilities in a wide variety of ways. Sometimes they would be provided by the local authority, either from the town hall or through a higher education institute, and sometimes a local company would be the benefactor. More and more, schools are becoming self-reliant as a result of acquiring microcomputers. It is true that computer facilities have been inadequate and this remains a major difficulty for the satisfactory performance of the practical work.

The staffing of courses has posed particular problems. Few teachers have much experience of computing, either in commerce and industry or in their own education. The early pioneers were nearly all teachers of mathematics who were self-taught in computer studies. These pioneers now play a key role in providing in-service training for teachers of the subject with less experience. Despite strenuous efforts to involve teachers of other subjects, reinforced by the grave shortage of mathematics teachers, the great majority of those who wish to teach computer studies are mathematicians. It has to be said that because of the inadequate training and experience of the teachers involved, the standard of the courses is not entirely satisfactory, and additional training will be necessary. The in-service training of teachers is the responsibility of the local authorities. A number of polytechnics and universities have provided courses for this purpose, supplementing those of the authorities themselves.

Also of interest are the courses which have been run in conjunction with the ICL/CES series of books which support computer studies as covered by the CSE and GCE O level courses. In order to rationalize and accelerate the provision of in-service training, the British Government's Microelectronics Education Programme (see Chapter 13) has designed a 40-hour course for intending teachers of computer studies.

Turning from the secondary schools to the colleges of further education, which by and large cater for the needs of non-degree students over 16 years of age, we find a somewhat different situation. While GCE O and A level courses are offered, often to students too old for school, there is also a range of courses with direct vocational aims. Colleges of further education try to respond to the specific needs of local employers and provide, for example, programming courses in particular languages. There is in addition a wide range of courses under the aegis of the Business Education Council (BEC) and the Technician Education Council (TEC) designed to provide personnel at technician level for commerce and industry. These are modular in structure so that computer education may be incorporated into a large number of courses. Both full-time and (for those in employment) part-time courses are available. BEC courses may lead to a first certificate (one year part-time) or a first diploma (one year full-time or two years part-time) and consist of compulsory and optional modules relevant to careers in business, finance, distribution and public administration. Elements of Data Processing is an option module covering the key types of information and their sources, the principles of data handling, data processing machines and the relationships between people involved in data processing.

Having completed the first diploma or certificate or a recognized equivalent, a student may proceed to what is known as a BEC national course. Here again, a certificate or a diploma is available covering many vocations. There are two option modules relevant to our subject—Data Processing and Computer Studies. The Data Processing option aims to make the student an educated user of the computer in a business environment. Students are required to comprehend the nature of information needed to run a business, to understand the basic principles of data collection, validation and processing, and be able to identify the most appropriate equipment for carrying out the processing. It is considered important that students appreciate the nature of the discipline imposed by the use of computers and are familiar with accepted standards of operation and documentation. Attention must be paid to the work of various data processing specialists in devising cost-effective solutions to data processing problems.

The Computer Studies module is more general and superficial and is intended for those involved in accounting, sales and production planning and personnel. Students learn the principal components of a computer system and their interaction. Elementary programming is used to develop problem-solving abilities. A working knowledge of systems software* is expected. Emphasis is also placed on an appreciation of the effects of the widespread use of computers on society and the need for safeguards. Practical work is designed to relate to other modules of the course.

Assessment of the student's attainment combines (i) a formal externally set and marked examination, (ii) BEC moderated work assignments and (iii) an oral test held in conjunction with employers.

TEC courses are intended to train technicians to work in all areas involving engineering and science. There is no TEC equivalent to the first level of BEC, and the structure of courses is somewhat different, comprising what are called units and half-units. A half-unit normally involves 30 hours of normal study and the full unit 60 hours. These units are graded 1 to 3, 3 being the most difficult, and a TEC certificate must contain at least two level 3 units. Units may be externally regulated, or (very frequently) locally constructed and subject to moderation. There are five half-units involving Computer Studies in any depth.

At level 2, the Use of Computers unit gives an introduction to the uses, principles and applications of software. Students study the purpose of software and learn the simpler aspects of programming in a high-level language*. They see examples of scientific computation, real-time applications and commercial data processing.

The Computer Assignments unit, also level 2, gives practice in the use of the computer. Each student carries out three assignments, of which at least one is concerned with analysing a case study and at least one involves developing a simple high-level program to solve a specific problem.

At level 3, we find Programming in FORTRAN or some other suitable high-level language. This covers the distinction between programming in a scientific and in a commercial environment, with emphasis on the solution of scientific or engineering problems. Simple numerical analysis and elementary statistical techniques are covered. Again at level 3, the Use of Computers extends to the level 2 course of the same name by dealing with more detailed problem analysis, more complex programming and the use of programming aids. There is also a level 3 half-unit for Computer Assignments.

For courses designed to provide training for careers in computing, a somewhat different pattern has emerged. Here the courses are sponsored jointly by BEC and TEC. Once again, there is a certificate and a diploma course, and these are modular in design, following the BEC pattern. Eight modules constitute the certificate and 12 the diploma, and only one of the diploma modules offers a choice of options. Beyond this are higher certificates and diplomas. These have a common core to which are added modules of local design, but moderated by BEC/TEC.

The certificate and diploma courses aim to produce junior operators or junior programmers and the module headings give a good idea of the course content. Introduction to Computing is the foundation of the courses. This is followed by Information in Organizations and People and Communications. Quantitative Methods deals with the scientific/mathematical side. Then, for the certificate, there is a choice: either the three modules Programming Concepts, COBOL and a Programming Project; or Operation Concepts (two modules) and Operating Practice. For the diploma, all modules must be taken, together with an optional topic. Assessment is a mixture of time-constrained examinations and the evaluation of in-course work.

At the higher level, the courses are in the main offered by polytechnics and require for entry any BEC or TEC national certificate or diploma or equivalent qualification. If such a qualification does not include computer studies, a foundation course must first be taken. The core material comprises High-Level Programming Methodology, Computer Systems Architecture, Systems Methodology, Organizations – Policy, Accounts and Funding, Quantitative Methods, Communication and Project Implementation, Computing (including Elementary Programming), Organization—Structure and Practice. The separate sections make up what are known as study areas and for the higher certificate the core makes up three-quarters of the course, while for the higher diploma it is half the course. A higher certificate takes two years part-time and one year full-time and a higher diploma three years part-time and two years full-time. As elsewhere, assessment is a flexible compromise between formal examination and in-course assessment.

In the future, computers will play an increasingly important role in our everyday lives, both in the home and at work. It is therefore essential to educate both young and old in the uses of computers and the associated area of information processing, enabling them to gain an understanding of what computers are, what they can do and how they should be employed efficiently. Computer studies is now included in school syllabuses and it is essential that this process of integration be a continuous one and that schools educate their students in the practical applications of computers rather than in the more theoretical/philosophical aspects of computing and computer-based technology which were espoused in previous years.

19. The promise of micro-computers in developing basic skills

Mike Lally and Iain Macleod

Summary: This chapter describes applications of computer-based exercises in developing handwriting, reading and number skills with children who have learning difficulties. By placing emphasis on means of student/machine interaction which are appropriate to the learning tasks, new and more effective teaching strategies have been developed.

In computer-based handwriting exercises, students use a digitizer pen to track various letter shapes on a graphic display. The display can be deliberately offset from the pen and writing surface so that visual and muscular feedback are separated. The overall effect is to facilitate the transfer of control of letter formation from the visual feedback used by beginning writers to the muscular feedback which is characteristic of fluent writers.

A touch-sensitive display surface and computer synthesized speech are used to teach beginning reading skills to pre-literate children. Exercises for whole-word recognition, sentence-building and reading comprehension are discussed. A program for teaching elementary number concepts, based on Piaget's theory of cognitive development, is also described.

These exercises demonstrate that by taking account of various psychological principles of skill acquisition, computer-based instruction programs can provide highly effective learning environments. Attention is given to means whereby research advances can be made available in mainstream classrooms. In particular, the potential of computer-based networks to facilitate management and delivery of special education services to students isolated by geographical and other factors is discussed.

Introduction

It is essential for students to achieve competence in basic skills such as reading, handwriting and understanding of elementary spatial, temporal and numerical concepts. Failure to acquire these abilities can seriously impede further learning and have far-reaching effects on a student's self-image, motivation and employment prospects. While most students make satisfactory progress using traditional methods of instruction, some 10 to 15 per cent of beginning school students encounter significant difficulties. In particular, students who have specific learning disabilities or intellectual handicaps may require a great deal of specialized assistance.

Computer techniques have the potential to overcome many of the limitations of traditional media in developing basic skills. Research into computer-assisted instruction*, particularly teaching of arithmetic and reading, has been pursued for more than 20 years. Much of this work has been rooted in programmed instruction concepts, using the computer simply as a fast and flexible teaching machine to present instructional material, to control the sequence in response to answers given by students and to record results. Basic skills packages are now available on microcomputer* systems of the personal* or home computer type and via interactive* terminals* on remote time-sharing* computers (eg PLATO*).

With the proliferation of microcomputer systems and interactive terminals in schools, computer-aided development of basic skills – principally arithmetic and reading (Mason and Blanchard, 1979) – is gathering momentum. The overall extent of the practical benefits achieved with basic skills packages has not yet been established. Setting up and performing a rigorous evaluation, then analysing the results, is a process which can take many years. Given the dynamic nature of CAI*, the results will then be of only historical interest – witness the large-scale evaluations of PLATO and TICCIT which began in 1972 (Alderman et al, 1978). It is already clear, however, that CAI can lead to substantial gains with students who have learning disabilities or who are disadvantaged (Osin, 1981), or who need remedial work (Poore et al, 1979).

Some basic skills packages retain a strong programmed instruction flavour and fail to make creative use of the computer's capabilities. Together with other groups around the world, the Information Sciences Laboratory in the Australian National University's Department of Engineering Physics is investigating potential advantages of computer-aided skill development, with the aim of using the computer's unique characteristics to implement new and more effective teaching strategies. The team involved in this project, which started in late 1974, includes educators, engineers, computer specialists and psychologists. A basic principle we have followed is to emphasize educational objectives and to devise means of student/computer interaction which fit the learning tasks under study. It may well be that this priority has been maintained at the expense of complexity in the supporting software*, high computational overheads and the need to develop new interface* devices. Much of our research has been conducted in small computer-based learning* laboratories at two sites in Canberra – The Woden School (which caters for mildly intellectually handicapped school students) and the City Educational Clinic (which caters for students of average or above average intelligence with specific learning disabilities). These laboratories facilitate involvement in the project by students and educators, allow realistic evaluation of the techniques developed, and are helping to speed the process of making improved techniques available to a broad spectrum of students in need.

Computer-aided development of basic skills

This section describes several applications we have studied in examining the potential benefits of computer-based exercises, and gives examples of the results obtained with learning-disabled students.

Handwriting

Analysis in the light of established principles of skill acquisition (Welford, 1976) reveals several shortcomings of the usual methods for teaching handwriting (which are mostly variations of tracing and/or copying). It is easier to acquire motor skills if the learner makes active decisions and at the same time is helped to be accurate and consistent in producing the motor patterns. Tracing promotes accuracy in the patterns produced but requires little thought or active decision-making in shaping the letters or sequencing the strokes; the converse applies to copying. Some means of transferring control of the skill from conscious to largely unconscious processes, so that control becomes 'automatic', is also needed. Neither copying nor tracing offer much assistance to the learner in the transfer of control from conscious visual feedback to faster unconscious muscular processes, and the teacher can offer little direct guidance at this stage. Students are left to grasp relationships between these processes through repetition; many fail to make this step and never become fluent handwriters.

We have developed computer-based handwriting exercises which enable students to be both accurate and active learners: accuracy of response is maintained even though students have to predict the sequence of strokes to be followed in order to complete letter shapes. This is achieved by using exercises with varying degrees of computer guidance, and by informing students quickly of any incorrect movements, thus localizing the consequences of wrong choices and interrupting the development of erroneous patterns. A much greater degree of control over the handwriting process is possible than with conventional techniques. At the same time, students are encouraged to think about what they are doing. Thus, the procedure adopted emphasizes the *process* used in handwriting as well as the appearance of the *product*.

Equipment used for these exercises included a 25cm square display screen, on which fine detail can be drawn by the computer, and an associated digitizer* pen which is the size and shape of a thick pencil. The computer calculates the pen position from the lengths of two fine strings attached to the pen tip which pass through eyelets above the display. The pen position as calculated is indicated by a square cursor* box drawn on the display. A switch inside the pen indicates whether it is up or down and the impression of writing is given by drawing a thin (1mm wide) lighted track under the pen tip as it is pressed down and moved around the display. Handwriting exercises involve students tracking a series of line segments, which can range in complexity from individual strokes to complete words, according to their developing abilities.

To track successfully, students press the pen down at the beginning of each guideline and move along it within an accuracy defined by the size of the cursor box (which varies from 4 to 15mm square). The student aims to keep the cursor box centred on the track, although tracking continues as long as some part of the cursor box overlaps the track. As students track successfully, the thin guideline changes into a thicker path (2mm wide). If the student starts at the wrong end of a stroke, lifts the pen or moves too far off the guideline, path filling stops and a small blinking spot (4mm square) calls attention to the point where the pen should be.

Various letters of the alphabet are tracked during training sessions. Only portions of the outline of some letters are visible prior to tracking, although strokes for the complete letters are stored and the same criteria for successful tracking apply. The incomplete stimuli encourage students to think about what they are doing and to predict letter shapes from memory. The amount of support given by the computer can be reduced as the student's competence grows. For children of lower ability a larger cursor box is used. Their attempts to approximate letter shapes using gross motor movements cause the computer to draw well-formed model letter shapes on the display screen. Thus, children see the desired product rather than their own possibly ill-formed attempts, although the pen movements used in performing an exercise are stored and can be viewed on completion. As students' skill improves, the cursor box is gradually made smaller so that their movements are shaped to become more and more like those required to produce the desired model letters without computer support.

This procedure is effective in improving handwriting skills both with intellectually handicapped school children (Macleod and Procter, 1979; Lally, 1982) and with non-retarded children who have a specific learning difficulty. An example of the improvement in the handwriting of a ten-year-old intellectually handicapped and visually impaired boy called James, is shown in Figure 1. His writing before any computer-based training is shown in 1a, after two months of daily 15-minute sessions in 1b, and after further training using a magnified visual display in 1c. Note the dramatic reduction in size and improvement in control.

Figure 1 *Handwriting samples from a ten-year-old intellectually handicapped and visually impaired boy. Original records have been copied and reduced as per scale shown: a) initial samples; b) after computer-based training; c) after further training.*

Methods which make it easier for students to explore relationships between the visual feedback used by beginning writers and the muscular feedback used by fluent writers are currently being investigated (Lally, 1982). Visual feedback plays a significant role in positioning writing on the page, maintaining alignment and spacing between words, and in correcting (over a period of time) any distortions which are creeping into letter shapes. However, the importance of muscular feedback in handwriting can be demonstrated by the relative ease with which most people can write individual words legibly with their eyes closed. In general, fluent writers form strokes much faster than can be achieved with purely visual guidance.

When the cursor box and visual track are moved away from directly under the pen tip and displaced upwards by about 15cm, students see their writing separately from their hand and finger movements. In order to predict and control the cursor box movements and writing produced on the display screen, they need to attend to non-visual feedback from hand and arm movements.

Magnification can be used with the displaced pen/display configuration, such that small pen movements result in larger visual movements on the display. This feature aids the generation of muscular feedback appropriate to the final skill. While pen movements are of a size requiring finger movements rather than whole-hand and arm movements to direct and control the cursor box, the visual letters produced are large enough for the learner to see what is happening. Initial results indicate that this configuration is successful in training students to use non-visual processes to control their handwriting (Lally, 1981a). For example, Figure 1c demonstrates the further improvement in James' handwriting following two months of training with the magnified visual display.

Reading

A lot of early schooling is spent in acquiring beginning reading skills. There are several component skills which need to be learnt, such as left/right sequencing and an ability to recognize individual words, either by their overall shape or by sounding them out. A traditional method of teaching whole-word recognition is the use of 'flash-cards'. A teacher shows the class a word written on a card, says it out loud and gets the class to repeat it, with the aim of establishing visual/auditory association by repetition. This procedure does not make efficient use of highly trained teachers' time nor does it take proper account of individual differences.

Computer synthesized speech has improved in intelligibility to the point where it is now a practicable means of communicating with students, thus overcoming obvious limitations in the use of written information to convey instructions and information to pre-literate students. In order to teach students a beginner's reading vocabulary, we have developed a computer-based program* whereby students are presented with various arrays of words to be learnt. These words are displayed via a translucent plastic overlay on a matrix of buttons. (In a later version of this program, the words are drawn on a touch-sensitive display screen*.)

The computer gives instructions such as 'Press *had*'. If the student responds correctly, this word is highlighted (by backlighting on the button box or by a flashing border on the display screen) and the computer says the word three times to help promote the desired visual/auditory association. If the wrong word is pressed, eg 'has' instead of 'had', then the computer responds with 'You got *has*, try again, press *had*'. Otherwise, if no response has been made after a pre-set time interval or if more than one error has been made, the correct word is highlighted. When the correct word is pressed after prompting, the machine says 'Right, but try again, Press . . . .'. The same word is presented until the student responds correctly within the given time interval. New words are presented only after correct responses so that the learner is not confronted with too many different and unknown words, but rather deals with a subset of words until these are correctly recognized. At the end of each set of 16 trials, the computer gives verbal results to the student.

A five-hour training program, over a four-week period resulted in a group of intellectually handicapped students increasing the number of words correctly recognized from an average of 39 to an average of 69 (Lally, 1981b). This improvement was maintained six months later (71 words recognized), even though no further computer-based training took place. Grocke (1981) has shown that this same paradigm, using the touch-sensitive display screen, is effective with children of average intelligence who have a specific reading disability.

Many other aspects of reading instruction can be investigated with the added flexibility of the touch-sensitive display. For example, students enjoy building sentences using this equipment. A word type menu is displayed on the screen: 'e' signifies words beginning with the letter 'e', 'adjective' means a variety of adjectives and so on. As their sentences evolve, students specify their chosen category for successive words by pressing the appropriate section of the menu, which causes a selection of words of that category to appear. Words chosen by the students are then written in sentence form at the top of the display screen and read out via a voice synthesizer, thus giving verbal feedback and allowing self-correction if a sentence is not what was intended.

The aim in reading is to derive the meaning of whole passages of words: fluency in reading requires more than ability to recognize each word. The 'Cloze' procedure, wherein students must identify words which have been omitted from passages, has received much attention in this area (Jongsma, 1971). Students need to read the passages in order to obtain contextual cues (both semantic and syntactic) for the missing words. Although this procedure has been used for some time in assessing students' ability to comprehend reading material, its potential as a training procedure has not been fully realized (Gunn and Elkins, 1979), partly because of the difficulty of monitoring a student's progress and giving appropriate feedback.

A modified Cloze technique exploits our equipment's flexibility and presents exercises in reading comprehension. For each missing word in the displayed text, students are given a choice of words and receive feedback and assistance as they work their way through the passage. If students cannot recognize a word on the display screen, they simply press on the word and the computer speaks it out, thus allowing them to progress independently through an interesting passage which might otherwise be too difficult. This procedure has proved to be effective both in teaching children to read for meaning and in helping them to develop better overall reading strategies (Grocke, 1981).

Concept formation

Piaget (1928) argues that concepts of space, number and time develop as a child interacts with the world. The child is forced to elaborate his/her concepts when their application leads to contradictions. Enhancing the environment so that a child can recognize that these concepts are inadequate is one way of promoting cognitive development. Such a learning environment must be challenging but must also provide the child with a conceptual frame of reference.

We have investigated a computer-based learning environment for developing conservation of number in children with mild intellectual handicaps, which aims to focus attention on contradictions in their cognitive judgments. Conservation of number is exemplified in the ability to know whether two rows of counters have differing numbers of counters when placed in lines with differing spacing. Students faced a colour television monitor with a button box in front of them. Two rows of squares, each row having a different colour, orientation and spacing, were displayed on the screen. On some trials there were equal numbers of coloured squares whereas on others, one row had one extra square. The child was asked, via synthetic speech, if both colours had equal numbers of squares. The child could respond by pressing a coloured button if he/she thought that colour had more squares or alternatively a button with an ' = ' sign. The computer repeated the child's response and said 'Let us count them'. A button numbered '1' then lit up. When this button was pressed the computer said, for example, 'One blue' and moved one of the blue squares across to the bottom right hand corner of the screen, then said 'One green' and moved a green square to a position alongside the blue square in the bottom right hand corner. A button numbered '2' then lit up and after it was pressed, the computer counted and moved the second squares.

All the squares were thus paired off, so that the equality or lack of it in the numbers of squares became obvious to the child. Little introductory training was needed for students to perform the task. They saw themselves as being in control by manipulating the buttons and coloured squares and seemed to enjoy the interaction. Most children's concept of number improved, although their strategies did not generalize well to other conservation tasks, for example length, and their performance depended on the way in which questions were worded (Lally, 1980).

Potential advantages of computer-based exercises

CAI enables teachers to use media for information display and student response in ways which are more appropriate to teaching certain skills than those traditionally employed. This and other capabilities of information processing technology give computer-based exercises a number of fundamental advantages. Predominant among these is the fine moment-to-moment control which can be exercised over the learning process. Other advantages include the availability of support which allows students to work independently, individualization of curriculum material and consistency of presentation.

Certain psychological principles of skill acquisition (Welford, 1976) can profitably be employed in providing a highly structured but flexible learning environment which (a) presents routine skill development exercises in an attractive format, (b) focusses attention on currently relevant aspects of the task (and student performance), and (c) minimizes extraneous distractions.

Exercises in skilled motor performance should enable students to develop higher-order control processes which incorporate the various perceptual and motor components of the skill so that smooth co-ordinated motor patterns result. This development is facilitated by providing both spatial and temporal consistency in visual and kinaesthetic feedback. Computer techniques can provide the necessary feedback on moment-to-moment performance (Macleod and Lally, 1981).

Errors need to be minimized, to prevent students practising and hence learning incorrect material (and therefore later having to unlearn it). Learning is facilitated when students have to make active decisions even though, in a yet-to-be-mastered skill, this increases the probability of errors. The conflict between preventing errors and making active decisions can be minimized by providing students with a degree of computer support appropriate to their changing level of skill. In the handwriting exercise, for example, the changing cursor box size means that students initially receive more computer support than they do when their skill improves. Thus, there is a trade-off between errors and active decision-making. The bias can change from minimizing errors to encouraging active decision-making as skill level improves.

Students can be motivated to learn a skill through an appreciation of the value of that skill, enjoyment of the learning activity and an expectation of success. For students conditioned to failure in basic skills, the radically different appearance of computer-based exercises may allow a fresh start to be made. Student fascination with technology, together with the semi-mystical powers commonly attributed to computers, gives an enhanced expectation of success. By working through exercises in a sequence of simple steps with computer guidance and assistance, students can move on to meaningful material earlier than with traditional methods. Continuous monitoring of performance allows the presentation to be modified according to the student's changing abilities so that the task is challenging but error rates are kept low. Automatic prompting following repeated errors or slow responses avoids extended failure. The above features help to maintain self-confidence and motivation throughout a learning session.

CAI can combine movement, colour, sound, etc to help focus student attention on the exercise being performed and also on those aspects of the learning task which are relevant at each stage. By presenting a complex task as a series of steps, the information pertaining to each step can be displayed only after the preceding step is successfully completed. In handwriting, the steps can be as simple as individual strokes (which avoids distraction by succeeding strokes) or as complex as complete words.

An incidental advantage of computer-based exercises is the ability to keep records of performance throughout each learning session. These records can be very useful in determining the optimum length and frequency of exercise sessions, and in monitoring a student's overall progress towards instructional goals.

Bringing research advances into the classroom

It is now clear that CAI can complement, extend and enhance existing methods for the teaching of basic skills, and that it can be unusually effective with disadvantaged students, especially those with specific learning disabilities and intellectual handicaps. The problem is to make these research advances available to the widest population of students, particularly those who are not achieving their potential in basic skills. Dramatic improvements in computer and data* communications technology make implementation of classroom portable microcomputer skill-development systems a practical possibility. Although inexpensive systems of this type could soon become a standard teaching tool for beginning school students, the best use of computer exercises will involve participation of teachers with the specialist educational knowledge and sensitivity to relate individual student needs and learning characteristics to the strengths and limitations of this new teaching tool. Thus, these microcomputer systems will not replace teachers but will give them a sophisticated and powerful tool to exploit.

Our ultimate aim is to adapt skill development techniques to suit the wider educational community after they have demonstrated their educational validity with restricted populations. Experience with young children of normal ability, and with students referred to our project by school counsellors and health professionals, confirms that the techniques developed are appropriate (with minor modifications) to a broad range of students.

In Australia, and other countries, the provision of specialist educational support services to the wider community is made more difficult by the low population density outside the major cities. It is important to remedy latent problems in basic skills before they interfere with other aspects of a student's academic and social development. In general, such skills are best taught via brief but frequent exercise sessions. However, students tend to be most widely dispersed (and most difficult to reach) in their early years at school, when they could receive most benefit from specialist help with basic skills.

Fortunately, developments in data communications and computer technology facilitate the establishment of networks* for improved management and delivery of special education services. A network we have proposed for Australian schools takes advantage of microcomputer-based student terminals to provide skill development exercises at the point of need, and facilitates co-operation between specialist and classroom teachers in catering for individual student requirements (Lally and Macleod, 1982). A central support computer is linked via telephone lines to interactive student terminals located in mainstream classrooms, and maintains files for each student participating in the program regarding lesson plans, progress against instructional objectives, etc. Using a network of this type, specialist teachers will be able to oversee remedial instruction in basic skills for students at remote sites, with only occasional visits to participating students and their classroom teachers.

A network of the type described promises to provide better access to special education services for geographically isolated students (particularly those in rural elementary and primary schools). It also promises to improve the position of students who are isolated educationally by factors other than geography, in that they have needs and abilities which differ markedly from their peers, making it difficult to provide appropriate services in an economic and convenient manner. Examples of students who may fall into this category are those who are gifted or who speak English as a second language. Thus, the flexibility of microcomputer-based learning units and the capabilities of electronic communication promise to alleviate the barriers of isolation which disadvantage many students.

Discussion

The particular skills examined above, namely handwriting, reading and concept development, form only a part of the spectrum of skills for which microcomputer units are appropriate. Possible further applications include development of: coding strategies for sequential memory (with particular application to telephone dialling skills); improved articulation and inflection in deaf students' speech via real-time displays of articulator positions and speech characteristics (Fletcher, 1982); more fluent signatures for blind people, by transforming visual information into auditory and tactile form (Macleod, Jackson and Eulenberg, 1980); and hand-eye co-ordination via exercises akin to video games.

There are both advantages and disadvantages of computer-based exercises compared with traditional classroom activities, and the best results will usually be achieved by a combination. The interaction between student and machine is usually highly structured; the student has to respond in the manner expected by the machine. This can be a limitation in the language skills area, for example, where it is important for students to be able to express their own thoughts rather than being constrained to make selections among multiple-choice answers – which is unlikely to promote creativity. Another limitation with computer-based exercises concerns difficulties in trying to diagnose errors in the process used by a student to arrive at an incorrect answer.

Well-structured computer-based exercises are very successful at capturing student attention and obtaining concentrated effort at the given learning task.

The interaction tends to be both intensive and enjoyable, and much of the success of these techniques may derive from the higher proportion of 'on-task' time achieved compared with that in a traditional classroom. A once-daily 15- or 20-minute exercise session can lead to substantial gains. This style of usage avoids issues which might arise if students were to spend much of their school day interacting with machines rather than people, and does not compromise the very important (but usually implicit) function of early schooling of developing students' interpersonal skills.

The computer-based learning laboratories at The Woden School and the City Educational Clinic have proved to be particularly suitable environments in which to conduct research, and we have been able to elucidate some of the many components involved in basic handwriting and reading skills. While the current emphasis in this project is on bringing the benefits of our work to the wider educational community, we are continuing work on fundamental issues with learning-disabled students. Two points which have been emphasized by this work are the central role of directed attention in handwriting, reading and concept formation, and the power of computer-mediated feedback as a tool for both investigating and facilitating skill acquisition.

Computer-based exercises have the potential to effect a substantial reduction in the time required by mainstream students to achieve competence in basic skills. Initially, these exercises could help to lift overall standards through being used selectively to assist students who have fallen behind their peers and to provide challenging enrichment material for able students. Subsequently, as microcomputer skill development units become more widely available and as curriculum materials improve, these units could become a standard instructional medium for most students. The consequent effects on school curricula could well be dramatic, given the proportion of class work during early school years which is currently dedicated to basic skills.

References

Alderman, D L, Appel, L R and Murphy, R T (1978) PLATO and TICCIT: an evaluation of CAI in the community college *Educational Technology* **18** 4: 40-5

Fletcher, S G (1982) Seeing speech in real time *Institute of Electronic and Electrical Engineering Spectrum* **19** 4: 42-5

Gladstones, W H *ed* (1981) *Ergonomics and the Disabled Person* Australian Government Printer: Canberra

Grocke, M A (1981) Computer-assisted reading instruction for intellectually handicapped children *in* Gladstones, W H 47-52

Gunn, V P and Elkins, J (1979) Clozing the reading gap *Australian Journal of Reading* **2**: 144-51

Jongsma, E A (1971) *The Cloze Procedure as a Teaching Technique* International Reading Association: Newark, Delaware

Lally, M R (1980) Computer-assisted development of number conservation in mentally retarded school children *Australian Journal of Developmental Disabilities* **6**: 131-6

Lally, M R (1981a) Computer-assisted handwriting instruction for intellectually handicapped children and the role of visual and kinaesthetic feedback processes *in* Gladstones, W H 53-8

Lally, M R (1981b) Computer-assisted teaching of sight word recognition to retarded school children *American Journal of Mental Deficiency* **85**: 383-8

Lally, M R (1982) Computer-assisted handwriting instruction and visual/kinaesthetic feedback processes *Applied Research in Mental Retardation* **3** (in press)

Lally, M R and Macleod, I D G (1982) Computer-based management and delivery of special education services *in* Sale, A H and Hawthorn, G (1982) 588-97

Lavington, S H *ed* (1980) *Information Processing* **80** Amsterdam, North Holland

Lewis, R and Tagg, E D *eds* (1981) *Computers in Education* Amsterdam, North Holland

Macleod, I D G, Jackson, J J and Eulenberg, J B (1980) A multisensory electronic system for developing handwriting skills with blind trainees *in* Lavington, S H (1980) 945-50

Macleod, I D G and Lally, M R (1981) The effectiveness of computer controlled feedback in handwriting instruction *in* Lewis, R and Tagg, E D *eds* (1981) 291-6

Macleod, I D G and Procter, P S (1979) A dynamic approach to teaching handwriting skills *Visible Language* **13** 1: 29-42

Mason, G E and Blanchard, J S (1979) *Computer Applications in Reading* International Reading Association: Newark, Delaware

Osin, L (1981) Computer-assisted instruction in arithmetic in Israeli disadvantaged elementary schools *in* Lewis, R and Tagg, E D (1981) 469-75

Piaget, J (1928) *Judgment and Reasoning in the Child* Routledge and Kegan Paul: London

Poore, J H Jr, Qualls, J E and Brown, B L (1979) *FSU PLATO Project: Basic Skills in Math for Florida High Schools (final report)* Computing Center, Florida State University: Florida

Sale, A H and Hawthorn, G (1982) *Proceedings of the 9th Australian Computer Conference* Australian Computer Society: Hobart

Welford, A T (1976) *Skilled Performance: Perceptual and Motor Skills* Scott, Foresman and Co: Glenview, Illinois

20. The student experience of computer-assisted learning

Diana Laurillard

Summary: The chapter begins by considering what, in essence, CAL provides for the student. It then considers what kinds of learning activities we wish to encourage in students, and how we might exploit the medium of CAL to achieve this. The design process is discussed in relation to a particular package (on economics) in order to elucidate the issues that a designer must attend to. Finally, the discussion is concluded by developing some basic design principles for CAL packages.

Introduction

The real point of using computers in education is to help students learn more effectively. There is a widespread belief that they can do this, and indeed there is a good theoretical case for it: computer simulations* can open up new areas of the curriculum; the computer provides an active learning environment for the student; it is capable of giving instant feedback; CAL* packages can be individualized to a greater extent than many other forms of teaching, and so on. In theory, it should be an excellent learning method. However, the practice sometimes falls short of the promise, and it is the purpose of this chapter to consider how the practice might be improved to bring it more in line with the hopes and expectations.

The problem is to design CAL packages in such a way that students derive genuine educational benefit from using them. To this end it is important that teachers and designers should understand the students' experience of using such a learning aid. What types of thinking can be promoted using CAL, and what design features contribute to the kinds of cognitive activities we want to encourage in students? If we want them to understand satellite motion, what sequence of mental events should that process of understanding consist of, and how can we design the package to promote it? These are difficult questions to answer for any learning method, and the study of CAL is less advanced than most, so the answers are still incomplete. This chapter is an attempt to formulate the questions and to indicate some preliminary answers.

Characteristics of CAL

A typical CAL package consists of a computer program* that is easily operated on a remote terminal* or self-contained computer with output* (text and graphics*) on a screen, sometimes accompanied by written notes. The aim of the package is normally to enhance students' understanding of a difficult topic. The students' experience of this kind of learning task is that he or she goes to a special piece of equipment, reads some instructions and perhaps a written introduction to the content, then runs the program, sitting in front of a terminal, typing input* from a keyboard*, and looking at the output on the screen, perhaps for half an hour to an hour. There may be a teacher to supervise if the student is one of a group, but, even so, this is essentially an individual learning method. Its educational success depends very much on what the program (and perhaps the accompanying text) requires the student to do. If the input-output interaction in the program is carefully thought out, it has the power to make the student think intelligently about the subject matter, as we shall see. It also has the power to bore him to distraction so its design is all-important.

What the student learns from a CAL interaction is closely related to what he or she pays attention to, and what kinds of mental manipulation he or she performs upon it. This, in turn, is related to what a learning task requires and to what it allows. The task for the CAL designer is to create a program that both requires and allows the student to pay attention to the topic, and to think about it in a productive way.

The tools at the designer's disposal are relatively few, which simplifies the description of the task. The forms of input a student can make are:

Numbers	(eg values of parameters, numerical answers)
Letters	(eg choice of options, verbal answers)
Graphical positions	(eg points on graph, vertices of a line drawing).

The forms of output the designer can build into the program are:

Pictures	(eg diagram of electrical circuit)
Graphs	(eg population curve)
Colour	(eg chemicals, maps)
Words	(eg hints, explanations)
Numbers	(eg results of calculations)
Animation	(eg the trajectory of a projectile)
Sound	(eg reinforcement bleeps, music).

The basic elements are few, but the presentations and combinations of these are, of course, endless. As in the case of the medium of text, it is pointless to start from what the medium can offer and work backwards to what the student needs. For that reason, we start with what kinds of learning activities we want to encourage in students, and then determine how we might exploit the medium of CAL to achieve this.

A case study

In order to illustrate the design process it is essential to go through a particular case study: the more intricate points cannot be discussed fully without reference to some content. The choice of content for a general readership is always a problem, but perhaps the choice of a mathematical concept within the social sciences will be reasonably meaningful to most people.

Suppose, for example, the student has to master an understanding of the concept of 'price elasticity' in economics. It is important first of all to know what kind of difficulty students typically have with the concept (if they have very little then no CAL package is necessary, of course). The teacher may already know something about this from experience with examination answers or tutorial discussions. In the case of price elasticity for example, a common mistake is to associate the calculation with a single value of price and quantity rather than with a relative change from one value to another. This is defined in Lipsey (1975: 103)[1] as:

$$\text{Elasticity} = (-1) \frac{\%\text{ change in quantity demanded}}{\%\text{ change in price}}$$

The minus sign is only there to make elasticity of demand a positive number for convenience. This ensures that the more responsive a quantity demanded is to a change in price, the greater is its price elasticity. Without the minus, the opposite would be true, which would conflict with our everyday use of language.

The value of the concept is that it differentiates between commodities for which a small change in price has a major effect on demand (which would be true of some non-essential goods which are therefore price elastic), and those for which a large change in price has a very small effect on demand (true for some essential goods, which are therefore price inelastic). In addition to understanding how the concept is defined, students also have to become familiar with using it to describe actual economic situations.

An analysis of the learning activities we want students to undertake begins by considering (a) what they should pay attention to, and (b) what kinds of manipulations they should perform on the data they are given. We have already identified a difficulty that students have, and this suggests that we must ensure that their attention is focussed on the fact that to calculate the elasticity you need *two* values of price and demand. We have also established that one objective is to get students to apply the concept properly, so we must give them the opportunity to do this.

There are many ways in which we might attempt to focus students' attention, and practitioners of media design are well aware of techniques such as a zoom, a close-up, colour, etc depending on the medium, but we want to engage the students' interest, not simply by perceptual tricks, but through the *meaning* of the topic. We shall therefore eschew gimmicks such as flashing arrows and try to create some *intrinsic* motivation for the students.

One of the most powerful ways to do this is to create a problem, with a goal to be achieved by employing a strategy, or making some moves each of which has feedback on how successful or unsuccessful it was. Anyone who doubts the value of this only has to consider the enormous success of computer games with people of all ages. They have exactly these characteristics. The challenge for the educator is to find a way of building this format into an educational package. In the process of making decisions about the next move, based on information about the success of the previous one, the student will be attending carefully to some aspect of the content, and should be making some rational decisions about what to do next. The *kind* of decision will depend on the nature of the entries the program asks for; the *quality* of the decision will depend upon the perceived meaningfulness of the feedback the program gives.

In considering how to design the program to achieve our particular objective, we must provide a goal for the student, the means to 'make a move' (ie some form of input) and the feedback on the success of each move (ie some form of output).

Suppose we begin with the goal: for a given commodity and demand curve (Figure 1), find a position on the part of curve where it is price inelastic ($E < 1$).

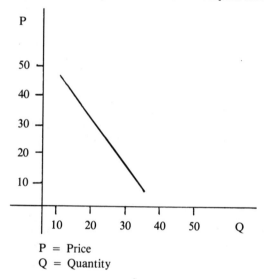

P = Price
Q = Quantity

Figure 1 *Demand curve for commodity* X

The curve is virtually a straight line, which occurs if the elasticity varies with price with high elasticity occurring when prices are high.

What choices of input should we give to the student? We could program the computer to produce a list of possible actions, eg:

P1 – enter initial value of price
P2 – enter new value of price
Q1 – enter initial value of quantity
Q2 – enter new value of quantity
E – calculate elasticity
N – analyse new demand curve.

This means that the students are left alone to work out their own strategy for answering the question. The list *suggests* that they need two values each of price and quantity, but does not explicitly draw it to their attention. They may still try to calculate elasticity with only single values, in which case this option should have a program trap* which would ask the student for both values if one is omitted. A further problem with this approach is that there is no built-in check on whether the student has reached the goal. Again, a trap could be inserted which would not allow the student to move on to a new demand curve until he or she had inserted appropriate values. The remaining problem is that some students will have very little idea of where to begin—we are assuming, after all, that they do not understand the concept, and that is why we need a program.

An alternative approach is to lead the student through the problem by requesting input as in Figure 2.

INITIAL VALUE OF P? *20*
NEW VALUE OF P? *25*

Figure 2 *Input format (student input italicized)*

It is then possible for the program to calculate corresponding values of Q (given the curve), percentage changes in both and hence the elasticity, so that the dialogue might look something like Figure 3.

ENTER VALUES OF P TO IDENTIFY A PART OF THE CURVE WHERE ELASTICITY<1

INITIAL VALUE OF P? *22*   INITIAL VALUE OF Q = 20
NEW VALUE OF P? *15*   NEW VALUE OF Q = 25

CHANGE IN P = 38 PER CENT   CHANGE IN Q = 22 PER CENT[1]
∴ E = .57

GOOD YOU FOUND A POSITION IN ONE GO.
DO YOU WANT A NEW DEMAND CURVE?

Figure 3 *Dialogue Mark I (student input italicized)*

[1]Percentage change in P is calculated in terms of change relative to the average price, ie 22.5 in this case.

There are several problems with this design. First of all, because the program calculates the values of Q, there is no check that the student understands where these come from. It would be better to ask for these to be entered, so that the student is *forced* to interpret the diagram in order to read off and enter the values. These should be checked for accuracy by the program. The same point applies to the calculations of percentages; the program should only carry them out in order to check that the student has done them correctly. Finally, the calculation of E should also be done by the student, with the program providing a hint (eg E = percentage change in Q / percentage change in P) only if they enter the wrong value.

At this point, if the student has found a value of E greater than 1, then he/she repeats the procedure. If he/she finds that further away from the centre of the curve E is even greater than 1, then he/she must go in the opposite direction to find an E that is less than 1. During this process the student will be making decisions about entries that focus attention on the way E varies along the curve, on the relation between changes in P and changes in Q, and in aspects of the calculation. This is in line with what we need, except that there is always the danger that the student guesses an appropriate value of P on the first trial, which means that there is no need for any interpretation of

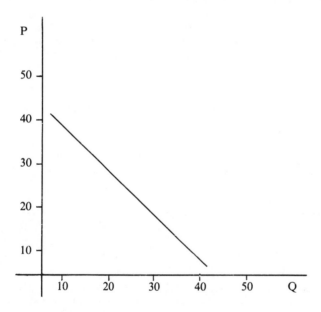

INITIAL VALUE OF P? *10*   INITIAL VALUE OF Q? *35*
NEW VALUE OF P? *12*   NEW VALUE OF Q? *32*
% CHANGE IN P? *18*   % CHANGE IN Q? *9*
E = ? *2*
NO E = (% CHANGE IN Q) / (% CHANGE IN P)
E = ? *.5*
GOOD. NOW TRY ANOTHER INITIAL VALUE OF P.

Figure 4 *Dialogue Mark II (student input italicized)*

the result in relation to the curve. One way round this is to make the goal less easily guessed, eg 'Find a point on the curve where the elasticity is equal to 1'. This would have all the virtues of the above design, but would make it very unlikely that the students would guess an appropriate value on the first trial and they would therefore be forced to make further decisions based on the feedback given. The design would now give a dialogue similar to that in Figure 4.

If it is important for students to gain an intuitive feel for the relationship between the value of E and the position on the curve, then the package will be improved by scoring the number of trials it takes for a student to find a particular value of E. In order to reduce the number of trials they require, students will have to pay attention to precisely how the value of E varies along the curve. In the present design the student will do this with a particular problem, but will not necessarily transfer this information to the next one. If the students experience a series of outcomes such as those in Figure 5 then they might be expected to use the experience of the earlier results to deduce that the position where $E = 1$ tends to be around the point where a 45° line from the origin intersects the curve. They would be motivated to look for such a relation if they want to gain a better score, and this finding would prepare them for the mathematical derivation of this characteristic later.

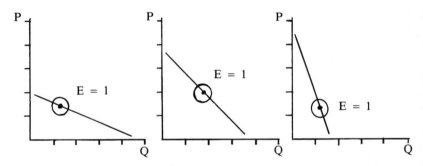

Figure 5 *Sequence of possible graphical feedback*

The design process illustrated by this example begins with some basic principles – provide a goal, give meaningful feedback, etc – but does not determine a unique design. Once an idea for a design is generated it must then be examined in terms of the interaction it provides, the experience it offers the students, and the kind of thinking it requires of them.

There is still the possibility that because the Mark II design does not *require* students to attend to the fact that two values of P are needed (it only *allows* them to) then this point will still be missed. The open-ended option list design would fare better from this point of view, and was only rejected because of its complexity for the beginner. By the time this dialogue-style interaction has been completed, the student would be in a better position to attempt the open-ended form, and this would make a good second part to the package.

Conclusion

The design procedure discussed above has grown out of experience of designing and evaluating a wide range of CAL packages. These studies show that CAL is capable of stimulating students to interpret diagrams, experiment with ideas about simulations, develop visual representations of concepts, and to reason successfully about theoretical topics.[2, 3]

The medium is certainly *capable* of all this, but it does not *guarantee* it because good package design is crucial. If the structure is too open-ended, then at the beginning students may be at a loss to know where to start or what is wanted of them; if the program does not require enough of the student – if it does too much for them, as in Mark 1 above – then the students will take a purely passive attitude.[4, 5] If there is no meaningful feedback then the student has to resort to guess work, and this has little or no educational value.[6, 7]

To summarize then, here are some basic design principles that a CAL designer might bear in mind when designing a package:

1. provide a goal for the student to aim for;
2. design input that requires attention to specific details,
   decisions about relations,
   calculation exercises;
3. provide meaningful feedback that assists decisions about entries,
   checks correctness of entries,
   provides hints,
   indicates when goal is achieved;
4. make the structure simple (while bearing in mind the possibility of future development).

Whether the teacher is thinking about the design of a new package, or evaluating an existing one, these are important issues to bear in mind. In either case, the fundamental question is: 'does this force (or at least encourage) the student to think in a productive way about the important aspects of the subject?' – and this has to be asked of each part of the interaction. It makes the design stage a difficult and complex creative process, and it always takes longer than seems reasonable (at least 100 hours for a one-hour package). Because, ultimately, it is the students' learning outcome that this technology is supposed to improve, it is important that the package design be considered always from the students' point of view.

References

1. Lipsey, R (1975) *Introduction to Positive Economics* 4th edn Weidenfeld and Nicholson: London
2. Laurillard, D M (1978) Evolution and evaluation *in* McKenzie, J *et al eds Interactive Computer Graphics in Science Teaching* Ellis Harwood: Chichester
3. Laurillard, D M (1978) Evaluation of student learning in CAL. *Computers and Education* Vol no 2 pp 259-65

4. Cox, M J (1981) Developing computer-assisted learning for a vibrations and waves course *in* Wildenberg, D *ed Computer Simulations in University Teaching* North Holland: Amsterdam
5. Marante, G M (1980) Cognitive activities related to student learning through computers *in* Winterburn, R and Evans, L *eds Aspects of Educational Technology XIV* Kogan Page: London
6. Laurillard, D M (1981) The promotion of student learning using CAL *in* Wildenberg, D *ed Computer Simulation in University Teaching* North Holland: Amsterdam
7. Marante, G M and Laurillard, D M (1981) *A View of CAL in the light of Conversation Theory* Internal Paper, IET, University of Surrey (to be published)

21. Computer-based approaches to overcoming language handicap

Leo Geoffrion

Summary: Handicaps such as cerebral palsy or deafness often result in severely deficient English language skills. Current psycholinguistic theory suggests that four key elements are essential for proper language remediation. These are the centrality of meaning for language acquisition, the importance of personal involvement in the learning process, the major role played by egocentric language in reinforcing emerging skills, and the need for fostering autonomy. The Talking Typewriter, CARIS, DAVID, and LOGO are all examples of computer-based approaches consistent with these principles. Severely handicapped children who have used these approaches often surpass initial expectations of performance substantially. Significant social growth frequently accompanies these academic gains.

Introduction

The ability to communicate is fundamental to social and educational growth. Without adequate communication skills a person cannot benefit from the wealth of information shared through speech and print. This includes information on social values and expectations as well as intellectual material.

Communication handicaps can arise from a variety of sources. Sensory deficits such as deafness block speech perception. Cognitive difficulties such as aphasia and autism disrupt the ability to understand or process language. Finally, motor handicaps such as cerebral palsy prevent accurate production. While the causes of each are very different, the results are often similar. A person unable to communicate suffers serious educational and social restrictions. Mental retardation is a common misdiagnosis for all these handicaps, despite ample research that cognitive skills can develop without speech (Furth, 1966; 1971; Vernon, 1968).

Current attempts to remediate communication handicaps have not been very successful. The typical hearing-impaired student graduates from secondary school seven years behind his or her non-handicapped classmates in reading, English, and other language skills (Kyle, Conrad, McKenzie, Morris, and Weiskrantz, 1978; Trybus and Karchmer, 1977). Likewise, these deficits continue throughout the adult years (Hammermeister, 1971). Comparable data for aphasic and expressively handicapped students are not available, but informal experiences suggest that their progress is often not much better.

Marked individual variations are also common. While the average communication-handicapped individual faces a limited vocational outlook, some become successful in careers which depend on excellent communication skills (cf Kiser, 1974, Fourcin, 1975 for some typical biographical accounts). Thus it is tempting to believe that significant educational potential exists within communication-handicapped individuals, provided their language problems can be surmounted.

This chapter describes attempts to use computer technology as a language development tool. Computer-based approaches hold great promise because of their ability to create stimulating environments which accommodate the special needs of severely handicapped people. This chapter examines some of the literature supporting this belief along with projections for future development of computer-based communication systems for handicapped individuals.

A communication rationale

Communication consists of the sharing of information among individuals through a mutually accepted code system. It can take several forms including speech, print, and signing. Communication even spans time and distance through books and telecommunication devices. Communication serves a variety of purposes including social contact, amusement, learning and need-gratification.

The approach to communication development advocated in this chapter is based on four major principles. The first principle is the belief that meaning is the central element controlling language acquisition. The child learns language in order to communicate rather than communicating in order to learn language. Infants start conversing with messages whose grammar is ambiguous although the pragmatic intent can be inferred (cf Bloom, 1970). Gradually, the child's language evolves into more mature forms approximating that of Standard English. The explicit correction of grammatical errors plays only a minor role in this evolution. Developmental research shows that most parents will correct their children when the child's message conveys incorrect meaning or contains socially unacceptable material, but are often oblivious to flagrant grammatical error. Slobin (1979) proposes a different mechanism for grammatical development. He finds that parent-child conversation is often marked by interchanges whereby the parent paraphrases, repeatedly varying the syntax while keeping the meaning unchanged. He speculates that this phenomenon may facilitate the child's awareness of words as language units.

A second key element is that language is learned when it serves a valid personal function for the child. Simple exposure is inadequate. Todd (1972) demonstrated that hearing speech on television or radio is insufficient for speech development if speech serves no communicative value within the child's environment. Similarly, the children of immigrant families do not learn their parent's native language unless it is used in parent-child interactions (Ervin-Tripp, 1971).

A third element is that language play, the use of language for egocentric purposes, facilitates communicative and cognitive growth. Young children often produce a regular stream of chatter while playing. This language production is egocentric in character because it is not intended as communication with others. Vygotsky (1962) has argued that this language play forms the basis for cognitive development in children by guiding attention to characteristics of their play and by aiding in concept formation. Language play is often absent in the speech of handicapped children. For example, Rom and Bliss (1981) compared a group of language-impaired children with normal children of similar overall language level (but younger in age). The language-impaired children spontaneously described objects and actions less often as they played. Geoffrion (in press) found that the hearing-impaired teenagers who had the poorest English language skills were also the ones who were most hesitant to use English spontaneously. This absence of language play may partially cause the severe English language deficits commonly found in the hearing-impaired (Athey, 1980).

Finally, the fourth key principle is the importance of fostering autonomy in severely handicapped individuals. Such individuals are too often defined in terms of their inadequacies rather than their abilities. The learning process is faster when students can use their emerging communication skills to control or manipulate their surroundings. Autonomy may be particularly important for autistic children (Weir and Emanuel, 1976).

This perspective on language development differs from traditional approaches to the remediation of language handicaps. Many programs* emphasize the mastery of specific syntactic structures, often presented in individual sentences with minimal contextual support for their meaning. Popular programs like APPLE TREE (Caniglia *et al*, 1972) emphasize surface structures despite the obvious fact that grammar cannot be reduced to a finite set of independent surface structure rules. Critics have recently argued that some of the language deviations characteristic of communication handicaps may actually be caused by placing greater emphasis on surface structure grammar than on meaning (Wilbur, 1977; Gormley and Franzen, 1978).

Computer implementations

Edison responsive environment

The oldest and most radical implementation of holistic, child-centred instruction is the Edison Responsive Environment Project, commonly known as the 'Talking Typewriter'. The fundamental philosophical differences between this approach and more traditional approaches to computer-assisted instruction* are best summarized by its creator, O K Moore:

> The Talking Typewriter is a *responsive device* . . . An early example of a simple responsive device is the lyre. One does not ask how efficient a lyre is, as if it were a lever or a pulley; one does not ask about a lyre's fidelity as if it were a reproducer, say a phonograph. Instead, the kinds of questions one should ask

about a lyre and the Talking Typewriter, too, are: 'Do they foster emotional-cognitive growth?' 'Are they fun to "play" with?' What I am suggesting is that whereas most of those concerned with computers two decades ago conceived of them as highly efficient and faithful master clerks, we were trying to show their potential for enhancing human growth, especially the kind of growth that arises out of playfulness. (Moore, 1980)

The Talking Typewriter uses four stages to introduce reading. At the simplest level, the child presses any key and the computer pronounces the letter name while displaying a magnified image of it. Children are free to explore any letter or combination of letters they desire. At the second level, the computer reverses roles, asking the child to find a letter. Because the computer picks the target letter, only the correct one elicits a computer response, although children are free to try different letters while searching for the correct one. The third level introduces words by guiding students through the spelling of that word, while the last level involves reading computer-displayed stories. The stories draw heavily from folk literature and other similar materials not commonly used with beginning readers.

Although the Talking Typewriter was designed originally for normal children, many have found it helpful for handicapped students also. Moore (1966) presented case studies of three mentally-retarded children who participated in early tests. In each case the child had been excluded from pre-school classes because of low readiness and inability to adjust to the classroom setting. After using the Talking Typewriter, all of them had learned to read and write and had improved enough socially to attend school. One child even started first grade with better reading skills than her non-handicapped classmates.

The Goodwins (Goodwin and Goodwin, 1969) report that the Talking Typewriter is highly beneficial for autistic children. They present case studies of several children who had scored in the profoundly-retarded range and had been prevented from attending school because of severely deviant behaviours. After using the Talking Typewriter, they read well and their deviant behaviour had diminished enough to allow them to return to school. Interestingly enough, speech skills improved in several students even though speech is not directly taught in the Talking Typewriter's curriculum. It is possible that learning to read may facilitate speech acquisition in severely handicapped individuals (Norden, 1981).

Colby (1973) designed a speech-training system for autistic children which is very similar to the Talking Typewriter. He devised a series of eight computer games, in the simplest of which the computer says the name of any letter pressed. More advanced forms generate a complete sentence for each letter pressed by the student. Furthermore, the computer was programmed to omit a word occasionally in order to encourage the student to pronounce that word. Seventeen autistic children participated in evaluation tests of the system. All were either mute or showed only echolalic speech. By the end of the study, 76 per cent had begun to use speech for social communication, a promising recovery rate compared to other forms of therapy (Colby and Smith, 1971).

CARIS

Geoffrion and Bergeron (1977) developed the Computer Animated Reading Instruction System (CARIS) as an alternative approach to initial reading for children with poor English language skills. The program uses brief computer-animated cartoons to reinforce the meaning of simple noun-verb sentences generated by the students. The cartoons eliminate the need for prior oral vocabulary while the computer controls syntactic sequence. Within the limited vocabulary of words the computer can recognize, children are free to experiment with varied combinations of nouns and verbs. Typing is introduced by gradually giving the student more responsibility for entering the words.

The original prototype was developed on a PDP11-40 computer, which limited student access to occasional field trips to the university computer centre. Nevertheless, the children who used it were full of enthusiasm and demonstrated reading skills previously thought to be beyond their potential (Geoffrion and Goldenberg, 1981).

Recently, CARIS has been rewritten for the APPLE II microcomputer* and is undergoing more extensive field trials with mentally-retarded, hearing-impaired, and autistic children. Initial observations suggest that most handicapped children greatly enjoy the activity and are gradually learning the vocabulary. The responses of autistic students have been especially interesting. They were highly enthusiastic and worked with sustained concentration, although each chose to interact with the computer in ways different from that intended when designing the computer program. For example, one boy was fascinated with numbers and was delighted when given a special vocabulary of number nouns which he could use in sentences. Another boy is showing good typing and reading skills.

Spontaneous speech often accompanies the child's use of CARIS even though the program does not require any oral production from the students. Children often vocalize the words selected and converse with others about the actions taking place. This behaviour has been particularly noticeable among the hearing-impaired students. Thus the CARIS sessions provide a good opportunity to practise speech skills informally.

LOGO

LOGO* is a general purpose computer language* designed primarily for exploratory-learning environments. It is characterized by simple, yet powerful, graphics* and list manipulating operations. LOGO itself contains no explicit curriculum, but instead seeks to develop cognitive and linguistic skills as children use the computer to draw pictures, solve puzzles, play games, or compose music (Papert and Solomon, 1972).

Goldenberg's (1979) book provides the most exciting examples of adapting LOGO to the needs of severely handicapped individuals. The language was used to devise a series of learning environments individually adapted to the specific needs of each handicapped person tested. For example, a non-vocal cerebral-palsied teenager was provided with a picture-drawing procedure accessible through simple motor commands. Special input* interfaces* allowed him to enter these commands with a rod attached to a helmet on his head. In his first session using the computer, he generated drawings of remarkable sophistication (Figure 1), thereby demonstrating an understanding of the principles of sub-routines and recursion. This feat is even more astounding when one realizes that this was his first known encounter with computers. In another experiment, an autistic boy spoke his first clear words while operating the computer. Other students composed music, solved puzzles, or used the computer to write stories.

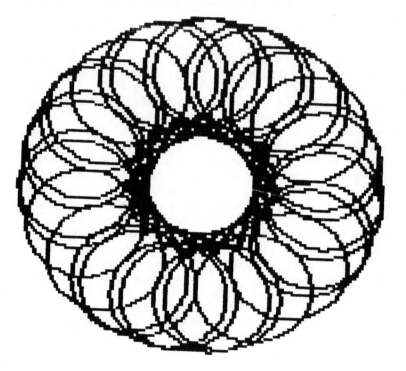

Figure 1 *Example of pictures drawn by cerebral-palsied teenager using LOGO system*

Weir and Emanuel (1976) followed the progress of one autistic boy using LOGO for several sessions. His learning environment was a computer-controlled robot in the shape of a turtle which can be moved around the room by LOGO commands. The autistic boy demonstrated a good understanding of how to operate the turtle when using it for his own purposes, but was unable, or unwilling, to move the turtle appropriately at the request of others. In his case, the ability to control the computer's operation for personal purposes was an essential component.

More recently, Weir (1979; 1981) has shifted her attention to cerebral-palsied children. The students participating in her study have met with more limited success than that found by Goldenberg (1979). Several of them demonstrated problems in spatial perception which limited their ability to understand the graphics features of the LOGO language. Nevertheless, she remains enthusiastic about the potential of this computer language for cerebral-palsied children. She reports that several of the students are considering computer careers and one of the older students is presently studying at a local college.

Writing

Writing is another important communication skill. In addition to being a socially-valued skill, it provides handicapped students with the opportunity to experiment with language without the time constraints inherent in conversation. Thus students are free to revise at their leisure and attempt different rhetorical forms without the pressure of a listener waiting for a response.

The Process Approach to Writing (Graves, 1978) provides an excellent application of the holistic principle to developmental writing instruction. This approach holds that quality writing evolves as a result of an ongoing process of revision and rewriting. In the Process Approach, the teacher's role becomes that of helping the student to discover more mature forms of expression as they revise and develop their papers.

A computer, programmed to serve as a word processor, can be a valuable adjunct to this Process Approach. A word processor acts as a highly sophisticated typewriter. It can store and retrieve texts, change words and phrases rapidly, and even insert material without disturbing the rest of the text. A further benefit for novices is the computer's speed, which permits immediate viewing of the effect of each change on the overall manuscript. Word processors have become popular in business and professional settings because they increase writing productivity. In the classroom, they provide a stimulating writing medium for students.

Geoffrion (in press) describes an experiment using a word processor with deaf teenagers. He showed that even students with poor English language skills had little difficulty in learning to operate the computer and in using it effectively to revise their work. The students who participated needed more exposure to the process approach because, in general, they viewed revision solely as correction rather than development – a misperception common among naive writers (Sommers, 1979).

Weir (1981) adapted LOGO to word processing* for use by a cerebral-palsied teenager who, prior to this intervention, wrote only by dictating his thoughts to a teacher or aide. Figure 2 shows examples of this student's rapid growth after three years of remedial instruction with the LOGO word processor.

'I ment Dr. Sileva Where, Jose Valente and Gary Drescher on October 5,
1978 at 9:32:47 AM. which the compuer I was so excized it like being it a waitting
& maternace room at a hospiltal whiting to fine if oot's a boy or a grail.

We had a and we whont you to do it fist for us I am LOGO number '1' ginny
pig. When they get a new idse they say to hel, michalel we had a and we whont
you to do it fist for us like a nice guy I do if I wont to or not. I do and then I give
my por and con on the idse. I tell them why I came up for a allturative. Why you
mite ask? Becose I know how the person on the arther end feel. Becose I am the
middle man betwee M.I.T. and handcap people.

I also teach five stundts. No tow lean at rate. Some ask then I know they are
intered in leaning about logo. Then the one that take for granted. I can tell.

When I teach I lean form my standt. as well or bedter then form a book. I call
that on the job training.

My fist and every day experreance with the compuer when it cash and it lost
but it keep on losting all that I have tort it but keep no teaching it overy and
overy agian when I bring back to live.'

107 Second Street
Medford, Mass. 02155
February 6, 1981

Mr. Neville Anderson
Bush Farm
2400 Acacia Rd.
Greenfield, N.C. 27405

Dear Nick,

My name is Michael Murphy. I am the person whom your mother saw on
'PM Magazine'. I attend the Cotting School in Boston mass. I have been
work with the compuers for about two and a half years. The name of the system
is 'LOGO'. It has open many new doors for me. Now I can draw picture on a
cheen ane write letter like this one.

I was the first C.P. person in the U.S. to tired the 'LOGO' system.
Inclose I will send some of my work.

Sincerely Yours,

Michael J. Murphy Jr.

P.S. I would be greatful if you could send me a piece of your art.

Figure 2 *Writing samples produced by a cerebal-palsied boy showing
improvement over 2½ years of word processor experience*

Curriculum developers have begun to create additional computer activities
to help students improve their composition, although most of this research has
not involved handicapped children. Some of the more innovative interventions
have been the use of dialogue systems. In these, the computer converses by
asking the student questions designed to help develop a clear writing focus
(Burns, 1979), or a logical sequence (Woodruff, Bereiter and Scardamalia,
1982). The latter researchers found that students enjoyed such dialogues and
believed that they changed their writing habits.

DAVID

The DAVID system currently under development at the National Technical Institute for the Deaf in Rochester, New York (Sims, Vonfelt, Dowaliby, Hutchinson and Myers, 1979) provides useful examples of how drill can be combined with holistic approaches. DAVID teaches speechreading (lip-reading) to hearing-impaired college students through the use of computer-controlled videotape. Typically, the videotape contains conversational fragments, all centring on a single topic such as, for example, searching for a new apartment. The computer displays a segment of videotape for the student to speechread. Beginners respond by a multiple-choice selection. More experienced students must type the correct message, but can request clues from the computer. The computer may provide the key words in the message, word length cues, or other information. This approach is holistic in the sense that the vocabulary is studied within context and the individual messages are arranged in a plausible conversational sequence. Initial evaluation studies showed it to be an effective and enjoyable means of improving speechreading skills (Sims *et al*, 1979). A more complete evaluation of system effectiveness is presently under way.

Cronin (1979) describes an even more dramatic example of the versatility of the DAVID system. In this demonstration, a computer-controlled videotape simulates an employment interview. The videotape segments were filmed as seen through the eyes of the person being interviewed. The lesson starts with entering the personnel manager's office. The student speechreads the manager's greeting and initial question, and responds by typing the answer. Depending on the answer given, the computer branches to a different video segment, thus providing a realistic conversational flow. One hundred video segments were prepared, thereby allowing a wide variety of conversations. At present no formal evaluation of the effectiveness of this simulation has been reported.

Communication aids

Communication aids for cerebral-palsied individuals represent another holistic implementation of computer technology for language remediation. These are special-purpose computers designed to provide an alternative communication mode to those who lack the motor co-ordination to speak, write, or type fluently (Vanderheiden and Grilley, 1977). Computer-based communication aids offer several advantages over other designs. Dynamic displays permit a wider variety of messages by changing the aid's vocabulary upon command. Some aids allow the person to use brief codes* to represent longer message units, thereby reducing the motor demands (Tallman, 1976). Editing* and storage operations allow longer messages to be composed for later use, and both printers* and synthetic speech devices exist for conversing with others.

These devices are used not exclusively in instructional programs but also as general-purpose communicators for the cerebral-palsied. Severely handicapped individuals who have used these aids prefer them to other simpler aids.

They facilitate education by fostering more complex messages and by providing an incentive for improving English language skills. For example, one user reported the following reactions:

> I was so excited about this new machine that I couldn't believe it. My thoughts could quickly and accurately be transcribed on a television screen for all to see! I would be able to communicate with anyone, not just the few who have a lot of contact with me.
>   I had to learn to spell, but this came quickly with the motivation of being able to communicate with others. . . . Without the use of the Autocom, I doubt very much that I would be able to [succeed] in 'regular' classes, as I am presently doing. (Geoffrion and Eshel, in press)

Only one study analysing the effect of such communication aids has appeared in print. Harris (1978) used ethnographic research methods to examine the classroom interactions of five non-vocal students. Despite the presence of electronic communication aids for each student, classroom interaction was overwhelmingly dominated by the teachers. The students seldom initiated interactions or conversed with one another, or spontaneously commented about events – even during free play periods. The communication aids were used less often than head nodding and gestures, but more frequently than vocalizations. She concludes that special educators need further training in the proper instructional use of communication aids.

Communication networks

In a broader sense, advocates of the holistic approach believe that language development comes mainly from its frequent use in everyday situations. Thus any technological innovation which provides increased opportunity for communication should also result in improved language skills. Several such innovations are becoming available to handicapped individuals. Two of the most promising new developments are closed-captioned television and telecommunication networks. In the United States, more than 20 hours per week of popular television shows are now captioned using an available portion of the video signal (Cronin, 1980). Because the captions are visible only with a special decoder*, non-handicapped viewers are unaffected. These should provide a pleasant informal medium for practising reading skills. No studies have been published which examine the effect on reading skills of viewing captioned television.

Telecommunication devices provide the other very promising technological innovation. Until recently, hearing-impaired individuals had no effective means of conducting long-distance conversation and were forced to rely on others using the telephone for them. Teletype* networks are now emerging to permit conversation through print instead of speech over conventional telephone lines (Bellefleur, 1976). These networks were initially developed to provide emergency services for the handicapped, but their potential social and educational benefits are also considerable. Even more advanced is the DEAFNET system in operation in the Boston area. This system uses a central computer as the communication centre. Individuals can converse with other network members, and also leave messages for absent persons or send announcements to several people at once. The computer mail capability within DEAFNET may provide a particularly important writing aid. Using a smaller network, Rubenstein and Rollins (1979) found that it greatly increased the volume of writing produced by hearing-impaired children. They studied a sample of 40 elementary school children who had been described as hating to write. In the first year of the computer mail's operation, these children spontaneously generated over 1500 letters to each other. Informal analysis of the conversations showed that their letters grew more sophisticated during that year, even though there had been no classroom instruction in letter-writing.

Promises and problems

Microcomputers are one of the few areas in education where costs are steadily declining. Advances in integrated circuitry have decreased the cost of computers to about the level of a high-quality home entertainment centre. Journals abound with accounts of newer, more powerful personal computers* which will soon be on the market.

The high cost of the early computers forced educators to limit their use to brief student involvement in a time-shared* situation. Hence, most adopted drills were compatible with inexpensive teletype terminals*. The low cost of personal computers now makes possible nearly unlimited student access to computers. Indeed, many families are now purchasing computers for home use. The problem is no longer that of computer access but of developing enough educationally-valid activities.

At present, the educational software* sold for microcomputers has been dominated by the rote drill of isolated skills. For example, in a recent directory of 500 commercial products (Dresden Associates, 1980), 77 per cent of the language arts material was classified as rote drills or skill practice lessons. Only three of the 105 language arts programs involved language units larger than individual words in a setting other than drills. This overwhelming dominance by isolated drills is unfortunate because it ignores the opportunities available with other approaches, such as those described herein.

Exploratory-learning activities may be especially important for children with communication handicaps. They provide a stimulating environment which handicapped children can manipulate to their own purposes. This environment contains a valuable balance between predictability and flexibility. Predictability is important because many exceptional children need repetition for successful learning even though repetition is an unpleasant activity to most adults. When they encounter a child repeating the same act, they become impatient, interpret it in negative terms (perseveration), and try to induce the child to modify the behaviour. The activities described herein adopt an approach which permits unlimited repetition if the student so desires. Indeed, an unexpected discovery has been that repetition is not always a mechanistic perseveration but a deliberate learning strategy used when attempting to understand a complex system. The following, taken from the author's field notes, is an example of the logic underlying seemingly perseverative patterns:

> Tony, an autistic teenager, was uninterested in the animations within CARIS.
> After the first animation, he reached to the rear of the computer, turned it off
> and then on again. This reinitializes the program, causing the computer to ask
> for the date. He typed 'YDEC71981GHJKFFF'. When the computer asked for
> the student's name, he typed: 'DOITLYPRAYSSSSSSSSSSSSSSSSSSSSTONY'.
> Thinking that he might want to type randomly, I stopped the CARIS program
> and set the computer into a mode which displays whatever is typed. He quickly
> turned the computer off and on again, causing the CARIS program to restart.
> For the next several minutes he repeated the program's start-up cycle,
> experimenting with different forms of the date and with the names of different
> students in the class. He never confused the date and name requests.
>
> I had the chance to observe him again one month later. He started the
> program without a single error or wasted move. He laughed to himself while
> starting it and glanced toward me with a playfully show-off expression. He
> started the program three times, each time using the name of a different student.

Tony's experiences also illustrate the importance of flexibility. He chose to
use the computer in ways markedly different from those originally designed
into the curriculum. In so doing he demonstrated an understanding of how to
type a complex series of commands – skills more advanced than those in the
original CARIS activities. Weir and Emanuel (1976) have also found that
autistic children perform much more successfully when they are allowed to
control their own activities. Case studies of exceptional children using
computer-based exploratory-learning systems commonly describe students
using them in unexpected ways. These unexpected uses have often led to
breakthroughs in program planning for those children.

Another important element of exploratory-learning activities is that they
seek to accommodate the child's limitations. Handicaps can be perceived as a
mismatch between a child's abilities and society's expectations. Special
education has long been dominated by attempts to change the child to
conform to the expectations. An alternative approach consists of changing the
setting to accommodate the child. Instead of waiting for the non-vocal child to
develop adequate speech for classroom instruction, activities like CARIS
provide ways to develop reading skills without speech. Communication aids
and word processors can circumvent motor handicaps by providing special
interfaces.

Finally, computer technology provides novel forms of feedback not usually
available to handicapped children. Animation*, picture drawing, and synthetic speech are all powerful motivators. More importantly, they help to
make abstract ideas more accessible to the child. Papert (1980) argues that the
'turtle geometry' intrinsic to LOGO helps a child to experience important mathematical and geometric concepts. Likewise, the animations within
CARIS help language-impaired children to learn the meaning of common
verbs by observing their effects.

Despite the exciting potential of exploratory learning, it has not been
widely adopted within special education programs. A major cause of this is the
lack of adequate descriptive and evaluative tools beyond the case study
approach. Few studies provide evidence of program effectiveness beyond

testimonials of severely handicapped children who have prospered through the use of computers. While some accounts are very dramatic, more authoritative evaluation methods are clearly needed. Recent adaptations of ethnographic and sociolinguistic techniques show good promise for providing systematic descriptive methods (Harris, 1978; Geoffrion, in press).

Conclusions

It is no longer unreasonable to consider the prospect of providing each severely handicapped student with a personal computer which can serve as the child's educational and communication aid. Nearly all the computer programs described in this chapter can be accommodated in computers no larger than a businessman's attaché case. Likewise, inputs need not be limited to typing. Devices or programs already exist to recognize speech, or detect a child's gross motor movement. Output devices include graphics, music and speech synthesizers, and environmental controllers which can operate nearly any electrically-powered device. The missing link is the development of appropriate instructional uses for the computer.

Computer-based exploratory-learning activities offer great potential for developing communication skills. These activities seek to develop language by creating environments where children can experiment with language and use it functionally. Exceptional children who have used such systems often show dramatic cognitive growth.

Many educators fear that computers may represent a dehumanizing influence, particularly for those who have difficulties relating to others. Observations taken from exploratory-learning environments tell a different story. Social behaviours often improve after participation in these programs, without any explicit attempt at behaviour modification. Spontaneous speech often increases as students become involved in the computer activities. Contrary to the popular myth of the student staring glassy-eyed at a terminal, oblivious to all else, the computer activities described herein frequently become the springboard for social interaction between students and teachers, and among students as they share newly-acquired skills.

References

Athey, I (1980) Language, reading and the deaf *in* Reynolds, H N and Williams, C *eds Proceedings of the Gallaudet Conference on Reading in Relation to Deafness* Gallaudet College Press: Washington

Bellefleur, P A (1976) TTY communication: its history and future *The Volta Review* **78** 107-12

Bloom, L (1970) *Language Development: Form and Function in Emerging Grammars* MIT Press: Cambridge, Mass

Burns, H L (1979) *Stimulating Rhetorical Invention in English Composition through Computer-Assisted Instruction.* Unpublished doctoral dissertation, University of Texas: El Paso

Caniglia, J, Cole, N J, Howard, W, Krohn, E, and Rice, M (1972) *APPLE TREE. A Patterned Program of Linguistic Expansion through Reinforced Experiences and Evaluations* Dormac Publishing: Lake Oswego, Oregon

Colby, K M (1973) The rationale for computer-based treatment of language difficulties in non-speaking autistic children *Journal of Autism and Childhood Schizophrenia* **3**: 254-60

Colby, K M and Smith, D C (1971) Computers in the treatment of nonspeaking autistic children *in* Masserman, J H *ed Current Psychiatric Therapies* (Vol 11) Grune and Stratton: New York

Cronin, B (1979) The DAVID system: the development of an interactive video system at the National Technical Institute for the Deaf *American Annals of the Deaf* **124**: 616-18

Cronin, B (1980) Closed caption television: today and tomorrow *American Annals of the Deaf* **125**: 726-8

Dresden Associates (1980) *School Microware: A Directory of Educational Software* Dresden Associates: Dresden, ME

Ervin-Tripp, S M (1971) An overview of theories of grammatical development *in* Slobin, D I *ed, The Ontogenesis of Grammar: A Theoretical Symposium* Academic Press: New York

Fourcin, A J (1975) Language development in the absence of expressive speech *in* Lenneberg, E H and Lenneberg, E *eds Foundations of Language Development: A Multidisciplinary Approach* Academic Press: New York

Furth, H G (1966) *Thinking Without Language. Psychological Implications of Deafness* Free Press: New York

Furth, H G (1971) Linguistic deficiency and thinking: research with deaf subjects 1964-1969 *Psychological Bulletin* **74**: 58-72

Geoffrion, L D (1982) An analysis of teletype conversation *American Annals of the Deaf* in press

Geoffrion, L D *The Feasibility of Word Processing for Students with Writing Handicaps* Submitted for publication 1981

Geoffrion, L D and Bergeron, R D (1977) *Initial Reading through Computer Animation* Occasional Papers in Education No 1 University of New Hampshire (ERIC Document Reproduction Service No ED 138 329)

Geoffrion, L D and Eshel, R (1982) An autobiographical perspective on severe communication handicaps *Journal of Rehabilitation* in press

Geoffrion, L D and Goldenberg, E P (1981) Computer-based exploratory learning systems for communication-handicapped children *Journal of Special Education* **15**: 325-31

Goldenberg, E P (1979) *Special Technology for Special Children: Computers to Serve Communication and Autonomy in the Education of the Handicapped* University Park Press: Baltimore

Goodwin, M S and Goodwin, T C (1969) In a dark mirror *Mental Hygiene* **53**: 550-63

Gormley, K A and Franzen, A M (1978) Why can't the deaf read? Comments on asking the wrong question *American Annals of the Deaf* **123**: 542-7

Graves, D H (1978) *Balance the Basics: Let Them Write* Ford Foundation: New York

Hammermeister, F K (1971) Reading achievement in deaf adults *American Annals of the Deaf* **116**: 25-8

Harris, D (1978) Descriptive analysis of communicative interaction processes involving non-vocal severely handicapped children. Doctoral dissertation, University of Wisconsin: Madison *Dissertation Abstracts International* **39**: 5446a (Xerox Microfilms No 78-23066)

Kiser, B (1974) *New Light of Hope* Keats Publishing: New Canaan, Conn

Kyle, J G, Conrad, R, McKenzie, M G, Morris, A J M, and Weiskrantz, B C (1978) Language abilities in deaf school leavers *Journal of the British Association of Teachers of the Deaf* **2**: 38-42

Moore, O K (1966) Autotelic responsive environments and exceptional children *in* Harvey, O J *ed Experience, Structure, and Adaptability* Springer: New York

Moore, O K (1980) About talking typewriters, folk models, and discontinuities: a progress report on twenty years of research, development, and application *Educational Technology* **20** 2: 15-27

Norden, K (1981) Learning processes and personality development in deaf children *American Annals of the Deaf* **126**: 404-10

Papert, S (1980) *Mindstorms: Children, Computers and Powerful Ideas* Basic Books: New York

Papert, S and Solomon, C (1972) Twenty things to do with a computer *Educational Technology* **12** 4: 9-18

Rom, A and Bliss, L S (1981) A comparison of verbal communicative skills of language impaired and normal speaking children *Journal of Communication Disorders* **14**: 133-40

Rubenstein, R and Rollins, A (1978) *Demonstration of the Use of Computer Assisted Instruction with Handicapped Children: Final Report* Bolt Beranek and Newman Inc: Cambridge, Mass

Sims, D, VonFelt, J, Dowaliby, F, Hutchinson, K and Myers, T (1979) A pilot experiment in computer-assisted speechreading instruction utilizing the Data Analysis Video Interactive Device (DAVID) *American Annals of the Deaf* **124**: 616, 618-23

Slobin, D I (1975) On the nature of talk to children *in* Lenneberg, E H and Lenneberg, E *eds Foundations of Language Development: a Multidisciplinary Approach* Academic Press: New York

Sommers, N (1979) Revision experiences of student writers and experienced adult writers *College Composition and Communication* **30**: 46-9

Tallman, T M (1976) Computer-assisted communication system *in* Foulds, R and Lund, B *eds Proceedings of the 1976 Conference on Systems and Devices for the Disabled* Tufts-New England Medical Center: Boston

Todd, P H (1972) Learning to talk with delayed exposure to speech. Unpublished doctoral dissertation, University of California, Berkeley: CA

Trybus, R J and Karchmer, M A (1977) School achievement scores of hearing impaired children: national data on achievement, status and growth patterns *American Annals of the Deaf* **122**: 62-9

Vanderheiden, G C and Grilley, K (1977) *Nonvocal Communication Techniques and Aids for the Severely Physically Handicapped* University Park Press: Baltimore

Vernon, M (1968) Fifty years research *Journal of Rehabilitation of the Deaf* **1**: 1-12

Vygotsky, L S (1962) *Thought and Language* MIT Press: Cambridge, Mass

Weir, S (1979) *The Evaluation and Cultivation of Spatial and Linguistic Abilities in Individuals with Cerebral Palsy* LOGO Memo No 55, Massachusetts Institute of Technology: Boston, Mass

Weir, S (1981) *LOGO as an Information Prosthetic for the Handicapped* DSRE Working Paper No WP-9, Massachusetts Institute of Technology: Boston, Mass

Weir, S and Emanuel, R (1976) *Using LOGO to Catalyze Communication in an Autistic Child* Research Report No 15, Department of Artificial Intelligence, University of Edinburgh

Wilbur, R B (1977) An explanation of deaf children's difficulty with certain syntactic structures of English *The Volta Review* **79**: 85-92

Woodruff, E, Bereiter, C and Scardamalia, M (1982) On the road to computer assisted compositions *Journal of Educational Technology Systems* **10**: 133-48

22. The BBC initiative in computer literacy for adults

David Allen

Summary: The British Broadcasting Corporation launched their Computer Literacy Project in 1982 as part of their Continuing Education Programme aimed at adult citizens without any experience of computers. The Project takes a multi-faceted approach to computer literacy, involving a specially designed set of television programmes, a flexible study support scheme through the National Extension College (who published a correspondence text linked to local groups), a comprehensive referral service, a book designed to complement and extend the television coverage, and an advanced personal microcomputer commissioned especially for the purpose, with full telesoftware capabilities through both teletext and viewdata.

The next stage of the Project is aimed more explicitly at owners and potential owners of personal computers. The primary intention remains the demystification of computers and the new telecommunications technology.

In January 1982 the British Broadcasting Corporation's Continuing Education Department launched one of the most complex projects in the history of educational broadcasting. The BBC Computer Literacy Project developed as a result of an increasing awareness over a number of years of the growing importance of information technology* in the lives of ordinary people in industry, commerce, education and in the home. The role of the Continuing Education Department is to respond to and anticipate the needs and interests of learning adults in a wide range of subject areas – from cooking to current affairs, from gardening to engineering. Our series are not labelled 'educational' but their aims are to stimulate activity and promote understanding, so they are usually supported in a variety of ways – by books, courses and so on, which help to take viewers further into a subject.

As a result of what we perceived as educational imperatives, the computer project ended up as a multi-media endeavour. It drew the BBC into a controversial commercial arena, giving its name to a microcomputer*, commissioning and selling computer software* and pioneering the exciting new world of telesoftware*.

It is probably true to say that, as with all innovation, if we had known then what we know now about the difficulties of achieving some of our aims we would maybe have hesitated or gone about things differently. However, the success of the Project so far has sufficiently justified the immense amount of effort poured into it by BBC staff from many different corners of the Corporation.

Origins

Before 1978, few people in Britain talked about the 'microelectronics revolution' – a term which came into vogue in this country after a singularly influential television programme was transmitted in April 1978. 'Now the Chips are Down' drew Britain's attention to the relentless miniaturization of electronic integrated circuitry and to the relative inactivity of British industry at grasping the implications of this. It also helped to galvanize government; James Callaghan, then Prime Minister, by pure chance happened to see the programme. The result – whether direct or indirect – was the Department of Industry's Microelectronics Awareness Programme and the beginning of an active debate in the groves of academe about the social impact of computers. Late in 1978, personal computing in Britain was still the province of a few enthusiasts; today's thriving glossy magazines were but a twinkle in their publishers' eyes and the name Sinclair was still associated with calculators, miniature televisions and the new digital watches.

In the Continuing Education Department, microelectronics was seen as something which needed more systematic explanation to the general public. Early in 1979 a colleague and I took on the task of making three documentary programmes for mid-evening transmission which were called 'The Silicon Factor'. Starting from a position of relative ignorance we began to build up a picture of what was going on and of what the various pundits were saying – particularly about the effects of new technology on jobs. It soon became clear that here was a subject which could be looked at in different ways: there was the technology itself and what it could do, there was the challenge to industry which, by all accounts, was complacent or ignorant of the opportunities which other countries were grasping, and there was the whole area of social impact and the importance of the speed of change. The three 'Silicon Factor' programmes reflected these three areas, achieved a large audience and have subsequently been sold world-wide – including to China.

At the same time as making these programmes we were thinking of the future. Where should the department deploy its limited resources and how much relative importance should it give to information technology? A timely grant from the Manpower Services Commission helped us to look at what other countries were doing and, after visits to the USA, France, Germany, the Netherlands, Sweden, Norway and Japan, a report was produced and presented to the Commission. It reported on what others were saying about the displacement effects on employment, on the new skills required by tomorrow's work-force, on the potential for change both in the methodology and the content of education. We concluded that as broadcasters we should concentrate on two areas: first, explaining the changes which were likely to affect jobs by producing a television series for those in industry and commerce, and second, to concentrate on encouraging popular public

understanding of computers and their effects by encouraging direct contact
with the technology through hands-on* experience.

In early 1980 we began work on both areas. First to be produced was a
series of five programmes called 'Managing the Micro' (presented by Brian
Redhead and later transmitted in the spring of 1981). These were aimed at
industry and looked a little at how 'micros' (we use the term loosely to mean
dedicated* or general-purpose microcomputers) can be incorporated into new
products, at flexible manufacturing techniques and at the flexible working
practices these require, at distributed processing in the retail trade and at the
electronic office*. The series was accompanied by notes drawn up by the
Confederation of British Industry and the Trades Union Congress and it
produced a very large post-bag of enquiries from people who wanted to use
micros but did not know how to go about it, as well as from people who just
wanted the notes. Simultaneously, we began to plan for a long-term Computer
Literacy Project.

Computer literacy

The term computer literacy* is easy to use but more difficult to define. We
believe that it is not synonymous with programming but does imply an
understanding of the range of things that computers can do and some
understanding of how they do it – the understanding coming preferably from
practical exposure to the computer itself in a variety of ways ranging from the
use of applications programs* and high-level languages*, including some
programming. It also means understanding the effects of the use of the
technology on the way information is handled, and of the role of the computer
in a changing society. In a democracy, a powerful technology such as this
needs to be understood by its citizens and its politicians so that it can be
exploited and controlled in positive ways for the benefit of society as a whole.
If indeed profound change is coming, it needs to be anticipated and not just
passively accepted. Brutal exploitation by management or mindless Luddism
by the work-force are less likely if people are informed.

However, as our research showed, many people are frightened and
ignorant of the technology and its effects. Unfortunately, the media do not
help – short articles or items on television are likely to paint a simplistic
picture not only of the 'cleverness' of computers but also of their social
impact. Although no one can really say what the future will be like, it is
important that individuals understand the nature of the debate going on. Most
important of all, as with a lot of areas in education, true understanding comes
with real, rather than vicarious, experience. People need to use computers in
unthreatening situations to lose their awe of them. This is why the growing
personal computer* market is so important in making this practical,
unthreatening experience possible for a wide range of people, and why the
BBC Project aims to provide such a wide range of learning materials.

The Continuing Education Department normally produces a range of
back-up materials to support its television series, though the programmes also

need to stand on their own (unlike those of the Open University). The Department is also used to close liaison with the educational world through a team of education officers. It was natural, therefore, for the Computer Literacy Project to be conceived as more than just a television series. We wanted to make a range of learning materials available to viewers who became intrigued by the subject as a result of watching the series, and who then wanted to develop their interest practically. We were also concerned that there would be a continuing provision, over a number of years, of programmes which would look at various aspects of the subject.

How the Project developed

In the early days in 1980 we intended that the main element of the project would be the television series and that this would concentrate on practical 'how to do it' information, largely concerned with hardware* and programming the microcomputer, encouraging people to gain hands-on experience of the machine(s). Later the philosophy changed so that the series eventually looked much more broadly at the general principles of computer science, very much for a lay audience, and the hands-on element became less central, though still important. We also aimed to commission a book which would reinforce the principles shown in the television series but which would also stand independently of the series as a general introduction to the world of computers and computing.

There was plenty of evidence from the earlier series that people were hungry for information about computers but that they did not know where to go for advice. So, right from the start, we considered it vital to provide some kind of information service for viewers – not to answer their problems or queries directly (this would have been too time-consuming and costly), but to put them in touch with other people in their area who could. This kind of referral service had been pioneered a few years earlier by the Department's Adult Literacy Project, which aimed to put those who could not read in touch with those who were prepared to tutor them. One hundred thousand adults were helped in this way. Computer literacy now seemed to offer a new role for the Referral Service, by this time established as an independent charitable trust, set up to support a range of broadcasting needs.

Interest in computer literacy was also being shown by the National Extension College in Cambridge, an organization with whom we had happily collaborated in the past. They planned a course in programming in BASIC* for beginners and, as this offered another useful dimension to what we were doing, we decided to associate the course with the Project. BBC Audience Research was asked to assess the attitudes of the general public towards computers, towards ideas of learning about them and even of owning them. The results of a large survey were most encouraging. They showed that the majority of ordinary people thought that knowing about computers was important and that they would be interested in watching a series on the subject. Although, predictably, much greater interest was shown by young, middle-class men, the differences in class, sex and age were not so very great.

A pilot television programme was made just before Christmas 1980 and this was shown to groups of people who had shown some interest in the subject to judge their reactions to various kinds of item and to styles of presentation.

The BBC Microcomputer

The most controversial element of the Project has been the decision to commission the BBC Microcomputer. Early in 1980 nearly all the machines on the market which were suitable for personal use were American. All of them had different dialects* of BASIC, none of which was compatible. Short of an association with one manufacturer, how could we systematically show how the machine could be used? We needed a machine we could call our own. Other reasons then reinforced this idea. First, the whole new era of the publishing of software lay ahead and the BBC wanted to participate (BBC Publications is a major publishing house). Yet the prospect of having to produce versions of software for every machine under the sun was daunting. Second, a new kind of software was being talked about: telesoftware. The BBC's teletext* service CEEFAX seemed the ideal medium for the transmission of consumer and educational software, provided that there was suitable hardware available to receive it. The idea of being able to transmit material related to broadcasts which could 'interact' with the viewer is as attractive to us as it is to educational broadcasters. Yet the development of this kind of service required a special technical relationship with the manufacturer of the commercial decoder* which was essential. The BBC's Engineering Research Department was enthusiastic at the idea of extending the teletext service in this new direction, and helped to endorse the need for us to push forward with a BBC machine, provided that the machine had an associated decoder which could not only receive telesoftware but also normal teletext pages.

We wanted a machine which had the following fundamental characteristics:

1. British in design and manufacture;
2. relatively cheap in terms of its performance;
3. easily expandable and, if possible, 'future-proof' – a machine whose owner would not easily outgrow it;
4. having a good, professional quality keyboard*, suitable, for example, for word processing*;
5. capable of sound and of displaying high resolution graphics* and colour
6. with a resident dialect of BASIC which combined maximum compatibility with other dialects on other machines, and the capability to support powerful extensions.

Discussions with users of microcomputers – especially with their largest grouping in Britain, Microcomputer Users in Education (MUSE) – showed that there was a great need to improve on the dialects of BASIC being used on personal microcomputers to bring them in line with modern, more 'structured' approaches to programming.

A promising association with Newbury Laboratories, a company backed by the National Enterprise Board and the National Research and Development Council, developed and then foundered when the company failed to produce a satisfactory prototype before the end of 1980. At this point we approached all the British microcomputer manufacturers who had recently sprung up, to ask to what extent they could meet our requirements with a machine they either produced or were developing.

A technically competent group consisting of BBC engineers and outside consultants weighed the advantages and disadvantages of each company's proposal and eventually decided on a machine designed by Acorn Computers of Cambridge. The basic design more than met our requirements and an early prototype was already running. One major problem was the dialect of BASIC which Acorn were proposing to use; it was out of line with most others in certain areas. Endless discussions led to an agreed technical specification of the language being drawn up and then published by the BBC Engineering Designs Department, who had by this time taken over responsibility for agreeing the design of the machine with the company.

In mid-1981, as the television programmes were being devised, the accompanying book was being edited and the Referral Service was creating its data base* of local contacts, the computer moved towards its final stages of design. The BBC undertook to provide with the machine a 'Welcome' software pack consisting of 16 programs which demonstrated a range of things a computer could do – in this case from producing graphics, playing music, 'writing' a poem, running simulations* and playing games, to creating a data base. This set a good standard for consistency in the screen presentation and in trapping* errors, and also gave us experience in software commissioning and development – an area which was new to us but which requires a great deal of expertise. Slowly we formulated guidelines for software writers and published a booklet setting them out. BBC Publications is now publishing and commissioning a range of software relevant to the Project, which will soon also relate to other areas of broadcasting.

Of crucial importance is the quality of the written material which accompanies software – the documentation*. Anyone who has looked at the technical manuals which accompany most pieces of hardware and software knows how impenetrable and inappropriate these can be to the naive user – they always seem to be written for those who are already in the know. With all our written material we have tried to keep things as simple as possible.

The BBC's CEEFAX service began test transmissions of telesoftware in the autumn of 1981, and in Cambridge these were received and decoded on the prototype teletext decoder, the design of which has been a joint effort between Acorn Computers and BBC Engineering.

The launch of the Project

In January 1982 the television series was transmitted for the first time. Immense press interest had been generated by the existence of the computer and the news that the production of a particularly crucial chip* had caused delays in delivering machines to the many thousands who had ordered in advance. The programmes were transmitted in the mid-afternoon (for schools and colleges), repeated on Sunday mornings and again late on Monday evenings. The combined viewing audiences were relatively large.

The series proved very popular with those who had no previous knowledge of computing. It made use of a technically naive presenter (Chris Serle) who investigated the world of computer science as a journalist in search of enlightenment. Assisting him was Ian McNaught Davies, managing director of a large computer consultancy. The series made extensive use of analogy in putting over ideas, and each programme contained at least one hands-on session where Chris Serle learned some technique at the keyboard. The programmes looked at what the computer is, at what makes it different from other machines, at computer languages, at information storage and retrieval, at the use of computers in communications and in control applications, at modelling and simulation and at artificial intelligence*. The series was well-received, although owners of machines with some technical knowledge found the content too simple but nonetheless enjoyed the style of the programmes. Some critics thought that (as with earlier series) it gave too rosy a view of the reliability of the microcomputer, for example. *The Computer Book*, published at the same time, rapidly became a best seller and the BBC Referral Service answered well over 80,000 enquiries.

However, there were problems with supplying the computer, orders for which had been pouring in since mid-1981. The delays were initially due to poor yields in one of the 'uncommitted logic array' chips specially designed for the machine and later because of the problems in testing the machines reliably.

Fortunately the television series was not designed in such a way that viewers needed a machine to benefit from it. Although our promotional material constantly emphasized this point, a good deal of misconception remained. One thing is certain, however – as a design, the machine has more than exceeded our expectations and has been favourably reviewed for its expandability, its sophisticated graphics and sound facility, its well-structured BASIC and extensive operating system*. At the time of writing, the extensions to the system – disc* storage, the teletext and Prestel decoders, the network interface* and the second processor* are approaching production and should be ready later in 1982.

The next stage of the Project

The machine now takes it place as part of our continuing provision in the area of Computer Literacy and will be a vital foundation for the second series – provisionally called 'Making the Most of the Micro' and due for transmission early in 1983. Further series on information technology will follow in subsequent years. Whereas 'The Computer Programme' provided an introduction to the world of computers and computing for a general audience, especially those with no previous knowledge or experience, the new series will be aimed more at the owners of machines or those about to take a serious plunge into the world of personal computing.

The content of the second series is being influenced by the results of the follow-up audience research survey which was carried out after the transmission of the first one. This showed that the interest is in how to program and how to use the machines for a range of purposes, with particular interest in the use of graphics and business uses/applications. Controversy still rages about the value of teaching programming *per se*. However, there is now growing evidence that, providing that the nitty gritty of coding is seen as the last stage in a process of 'problem-solving', *the* route to computer literacy and the removal of fear of the computer is through hands-on experience. Some of this may be through the use of ready-made programs obtained from outside, some through do-it-yourself programming. The new series will look at both these routes. Now that machines like the BBC Microcomputer are capable of running in full colour, with high quality graphics and multi-channel sound and even *speech*, the rewards for those who are prepared to learn the comparatively few basic principles to enable them to write their own programs are enormous.

The next series will show a range of machines being used for different purposes and will use the BBC Microcomputer to explore the principles of problem-solving. But it will not be uncritical of micros – they do go wrong, they are capable of being over-sold, they can be more trouble than they are worth and people can expect too much of them. Nevertheless, we were encouraged by the impeccably typed letter we received recently from a severely handicapped postgraduate student to explain how he has used his microcomputer not only to run the word processing program which produced the letter, but also to control seven mains relays (attached to fires, bells, television, etc) from a single push button which he operates in the only way he can, using a rod attached to his head. He has written his own programs and they work. He is immeasurably more independent as a result.

So the next series will look into 'how to' in more detail but more critically than the earlier one. It will also be backed up by a range of course material and software, directly related to the BBC Microcomputer, which will help users to develop skills in particular areas of interest, such as control applications, music, speech, structured programming techniques and so forth.

When we first proposed the Computer Literacy Project in 1980, we little imagined the way it would grow. We have made mistakes; we have learned a great deal and, as we have learned, we have reassessed what we have been doing. The important thing is that we have created public interest. We hope that we have helped to dispel some of the mystique surrounding the subject of computers and we have certainly established a range of learning materials from which individuals can learn about a technology which will affect us all.

Part 5:
Bibliography and biographical notes

Bibliography

Agnes McMahon and Jacquetta Megarry

The bibliography is divided into four sections. The first covers published chapters and articles in books, including whole books and booklets, by individual authors, the second lists publications (books and documents) issued by official and corporate bodies, and the third includes articles, periodicals and working papers. These three sections include nearly all of the references cited in individual chapters; unpublished manuscripts and a few specialized references have been omitted.

In section IV a number of key references from sections I, II and III and some other important recent publications have been annotated. An asterisk (*) beside a particular entry in the first three parts of the bibliography indicates that it is among those annotated in section IV.

Section I: Books and pamphlets

Allison, G T (1971) *Essence of Decision: Explaining the Cuban Missile Crisis* Little and Brown: Boston, Mass

Athey, I (1980) Language, reading and the deaf *in* Reynolds, H N and Williams, C (1980)

Baker, K (1980) Planning school policies for INSET: the SITE project *in* Hoyle, E and Megarry, J (1980)

Benjamin, H (1939) Foreword *in The Sabre-tooth Curriculum* McGraw-Hill Inc: New York

Bidwell, C E (1965) The school as a formal organisation *in* March, C G (1965)

Bloom, L (1970) *Language Development: Form and Function in Emerging Grammars* MIT Press: Cambridge, Mass

Boyd, G M (1975) The importance and feasibility of transparent universities *in* Evans, L and Leedham, J

Burns, H L (1979) *Stimulating Rhetorical Invention in English Composition through Computer-assisted Instruction* Unpublished doctoral dissertation, University of Texas: El Paso

Caniglia, J, Cole, N J, Howard, W, Krohn, E and Rice, M (1972) *APPLE TREE. A Patterned Program of Linguistic Expansion through Reinforced Experiences and Evaluations* Dormac Publishing: Lake Oswego, Oregon

Carlson, R O (1965) *Adoption of Educational Innovations* Centre for the Advanced Study of Educational Administration: Eugene, Oregon

Cherry, C (1971) *World Communication: Threat or Promise* John Wiley: London

* Coburn, P, Kelman, P, Roberts, N, Snyder, T F F, Watt, D H and Weiner, C (1982) *Practical Guide to Computers in Education* Addison-Wesley: Reading, Mass

Colby, K M and Smith, D C (1971) Computers in the treatment of non-speaking autistic children *in* Masserman, J H *ed* (1971)

Cox, M J (1981) Developing computer-assisted learning for a vibrations and waves course *in* Wildenberg, D *ed* (1981)

Duckmanton, N (1979) Computers in the classroom *in* Forer, P G *ed* (1979)

Dunn, W R (1980) *The Development of a Computer Assisted Learning Programme on Classroom Management in the Primary School* Department of Education, University of Glasgow

Dwyer, T A and Critchfield, M (1981) Multi-computer systems for the support of innovative learning *in* Smith, P R *ed* (1981)

Edwards, J, Ellis, A, Richardson, D E, Holtznagel, D and Klassen, D (1978) *Computer Applications in Instruction* Houghton Mifflin: Hanover, North Holland

Eichholz, G and Rogers, E M (1964) Resistance to the adoption of audio-visual aids by elementary school teachers *in* Miles, M B (1964)

Emanuel, R and Weir, S (1976) Catalysing communication in an autistic child in a LOGO-like learning environment *in* *Proceedings of Summer Conference on Artificial Intelligence and Simulation of Behaviour* Department of Artificial Intelligence, University of Edinburgh

Ervin-Tripp, S M (1971) An overview of theories of grammatical development *in* Slobin, D I *ed* (1971)

Etzioni, A (1969) *The Semi Professions and their Organisation* Free Press: New York

* Evans, C (1979) *The Mighty Micro* Hodder and Stoughton: Sevenoaks, Kent (Coronet edition)

Evans, L and Leedham, J *eds* (1975) *Aspects of Educational Technology IX* Kogan Page: London

Eysenck, H J, Nias, D K B (1978) *Sex, Violence and the Media* Granada Publishing Company: London

Fenwick, I (1976) *The Comprehensive School 1944-1970* Methuen: London

Fielden, J and Pearson P K (1978) *The Cost of Learning with Computers: Report of the Financial Evaluation of the National Development Programme in Computer Assisted Learning* Council for Educational Technology: London

Fielding, G and Rumage, K W *eds* (1972) *Computerised Instruction in Undergraduate Geography* Technical Paper No 6, Association of American Geographers

Forer, P C (1977) Gaming the space economy: a teaching simulation and its context *in* *Proceedings, 9th New Zealand Geographical Society Conference* (1977)

Forer, P C *ed* (1979) *Geography, Simulation and the Computer in Schools* Canterbury Branch, New Zealand Geographical Society: Christchurch, NZ

Forer, P C (1982) *Report on Computer Assisted Learning in the United Kingdom with Particular Reference to the CAL81 Symposium at Leeds* New Zealand Department of Education: Wellington, NZ

* Forester, T (1980) *The Microelectronics Revolution* Basil Blackwell: Oxford

Foulds, R and Lund, B *eds* (1976) *Proceedings of the 1976 Conference on Systems and Devices for the Disabled* Tufts New England Medical Centre: Boston, Mass

Fourcin, A J (1975) Language development in the absence of expressive speech *in* Lenneberg, E H and Lenneberg, E *eds* (1975)

Fraser, R, Wells, C and Burkill, S (1982) Eureka, Jane-plus and Trans-pots: designing material for the microcomputer and teacher partnership in the classroom *in* Lewis, R and Tagg, E D (1982)

Furth, H G (1966) *Thinking without Language. Psychological Implications of Deafness* Free Press: New York

Geoffrion, L D and Bergeron, R D (1977) *Initial Reading through Computer Animation* Occasional papers in education No 1, University of New Hampshire: NH

Gladstones, W H ed (1981) *Ergonomics and the Disabled Person* Australian Government Printer: Canberra

Goldenberg, E P (1979) *Special Technology for Special Children: Computers to Serve Communication and Autonomy in the Education of the Handicapped* University Park Press: Baltimore

Graves, D H (1978) *Balance the Basics: Let Them Write* Ford Foundation: New York

Gray, L (1980) Education finance *in* Waitt (1980)

Gray, L (1982) *The Management of Resources in Primary Schools* Sheffield Papers in Education Management: Sheffield

Grocke, M A (1981) Computer-assisted reading instruction for intellectually handicapped children *in* Gladstones, W H (1981)

Gross, N, Giaquinta, J and Bernstein, M (1971) *Implementing Organizational Innovations* Harper Row: New York

Hall, E T (1976) *Beyond Culture* Doubleday: New York

Harman, G (1980) How to fight the new technology *in* Forester (1980)

Harris, D (1978) *Descriptive Analysis of Communicative Interaction Processes involving Non-Vocal Severely Handicapped Children* Doctoral dissertation, University of Wisconsin: Madison

Harvey, O J ed (1966) *Experience, Structure and Adaptability* Springer: New York

Hebenstreit, J (1977) Basic Concepts in Information Processing *in* Johnson, D C and Tinsley, J D eds (1977)

Hebenstreit, J (1982) Opening Address *in* Lewis, R and Tagg, E D (1982)

Heydeman, M T and McCormick, S (1982) *Enzyme Kinetic – Chelsea Science Simulations* Edward Arnold: London

Hofstadter, D R (1979) *Godel, Escher, Bach: an Eternal Golden Braid* Penguin: Harmondsworth

Hooper, R (1977) *The National Development Programme in Computer Assisted Learning: the Final Report of the Director* Council for Educational Technology: London

Hooper, R and Toye, I (1975) *Computer Assisted Learning in the United Kingdom: some Case Studies* NDPCAL/Council for Educational Technology: London

Howe, J A M (1981) Teaching handicapped children to read: a computer-based approach *in* Lewis, R and Tagg, E D (1981)

Howe, J A M and du Boulay, B (1981) Microprocessor-assisted learning: turning the clock back *in* Rushby, N ed (1981)

*Howe, J A M and Ross, P M (1981) *Microcomputers in Secondary Education* Kogan Page: London

Hoyle, E (1976) *Strategies of Curriculum Innovation* Unit 28 Open University Course Curriculum Design and Development. Open University Press: Milton Keynes

Hoyle, E and Megarry, J (1980) *World Yearbook of Education 1980: Professional Development of Teachers* Kogan Page: London

Illich, I (1979) *Deschooling Society* Calder and Boyers: London

Ingle, R and Jennings, A (1981) *Science in Schools: Which Way Now? Studies in Education 8* Institute of Education: University of London

Jackson, P W (1968a) *The Teacher and the Machine* University of Pittsburgh Press: Pittsburgh

Jackson, P W (1968b) *Life in Classrooms* Holt, Rinehart and Winston: New York

Jacoby, R (1975) *Social Amnesia* Beacon Press: Boston, Mass

Johnson, D C and Tinsley, J D eds (1977) *Information and Mathematics in Secondary Schools* Amsterdam, North Holland

*Jones, R (1980) *Microcomputers: Their Uses in Primary Schools* Council for Educational Technology: London

Jongsma, E A (1971) *The Cloze Procedure as a Teaching Technique* International Reading Association: Newark, Delaware

Kay, H, Dodd, B and Sime, M (1968) *Teaching Machines and Programmed Instruction* Penguin Books: Harmondsworth

Kemmis, S, Atkin, R and Wright, E (no date) *How do Students Learn?* *Occasional Publication 5* Centre for Applied Research in Education, University of East Anglia: Norwich

Kiser, B (1974) *New Light of Hope* Keats Publishing: New Canaan, Conn

Klapp, O E (1978) *Opening and Closing: Strategies of Information Adaptation in Society* Cambridge University Press. ASA Rose Monograph: London

Knapman, J (1974) *Programs that Write Programs and know what they are doing Bionics Research Reports No 18* School of Artificial Intelligence: Edinburgh

Lally, M R (1981a) Computer-assisted handwriting instruction for intellectually handicapped children and the role of visual and kinaesthetic feedback processes *in* Gladstones, W H (1981)

Lally, M R and Macleod, I D G (1982) Computer-based management and delivery of special education services *in* Sale, A H and Hawthorn, G (1982)

Laurillard, D M (1978) Evolution and evaluation *in* McKenzie, J *et al* (1978)

Laurillard, D M (1981) The promotion of student learning using CAL *in* Wildenberg *ed* (1981)

Lavington, S H *ed* (1980) *Information Processing 80* Amsterdam, North Holland

Lenneberg, E H and Lenneberg, E *eds* (1975) *Foundations of Language Development. A Multidisciplinary Approach* Academic Press: New York

Lewis, R (1981) Mechanism for CAL origination *in* Smith, C H *ed* (1981)

Lewis and Murphy (1978) Product design and development *in* Mckenzie *et al*

*Lewis, R and Tagg, E D *eds* (1980) *Proceedings of the Third IFIP World Conference on Computer Education: Computers in Education* Amsterdam, North Holland

Lewis, R and Tagg, E D *eds* (1982) *Proceedings of the IFIP Working Conference Involving Micros in Education* Amsterdam, North Holland

Litwak, E and Meyer, H J (1974) *Family, School and Neighbourhood* Columbia University Press: New York

Lortie, D (1964) The teacher and team teaching: suggestions for long term research *in* Shaplin, J T and Olds, H *eds* (1964)

Lortie, D (1969) The balance between autonomy and control in elementary school teaching *in* Etzioni, A (1969)

Macdonald, B, Atkin, R, Jenkins, D and Kemmis, S (1977) Computer assisted learning: its educational potential *in* Hooper, R (1977)

Macleod, I D G, Jackson, J J and Eulenberg, J B (1980) A multisensory electronic system for developing handwriting skills with blind trainees *in* Lavington, S H (1980)

Macleod, I D G and Lally, M R (1981) The effectiveness of computer controlled feedback in handwriting instruction *in* Lewis, R and Tagg, E D *eds* (1981)

Marante, G M (1980) Cognitive activities related to student learning through computers *in* Winterburn, R and Evans, L *eds* (1980)

March, C G (1965) *Handbook of Organizations* Rand McNally: Chicago

March, J G and Olsen, J (1976) *Ambiguity and Choice in Organizations* Universitetsforlaget: Bergen

Mason, G E and Blanchard, J S (1979) *Computer Applications in Reading* International Reading Association: Newark, Delaware

Masserman, J H *ed* (1971) *Current Psychiatric Therapies Vol II* Grune and Stratton: New York

McCullough, L (1978) *Basic Interactive Computer Models in Population Dynamics* Department of Geography, University of Queensland: Queensland

*McKenzie, J, Elton, L R B and Lewis, R (1978) *Interactive Computer Graphics in Science Teaching* Ellis Harwood: New York

Megarry, J (1980) Selected innovations in methods of education *in* Hoyle and Megarry *eds* (1980)

Miles, M B (1964) *Innovation in Education* Bureau of Publications, Teachers' College, Columbia University: New York

Moore, O K (1966) Autotelic responsive environments and exceptional children *in* Harvey *ed* (1966)

Nelson, T (1981) *Literary Machines* Ted Nelson Pub Co: Box 128, Swarthmore, PA 19081 USA

Osin, L (1981) Computer-assisted instruction in arithmetic in Israeli disadvantaged elementary schools *in* Lewis, R and Tagg, E D (1981)

*Papert, S (1980) *Mindstorms: Children, Computers and Powerful Ideas* Harvester Press: Brighton

Parlett, M R and Hamilton, D (1972) *Evaluation as Illumination: a New Approach to the Study of Innovatory Programs* (Occasional Paper 9). Centre for Research in the Educational Sciences: University of Edinburgh

*Peters, H J and Johnson, J W (1978) *Author's Guide: Design Development Style Packaging Review* Conduit: University of Iowa, Iowa

Piaget, J (1928) *Judgment and Reasoning in the Child* Routledge and Kegan Paul: London

Poore, J H Jr, Qualls, J E and Brown, B L (1979) *FSU PLATO Project: Basic Skills in Math for Florida High Schools (Final Report)* Computing Center, Florida State University: Florida

Reynolds, H N and Williams, C *eds* (1980) *Proceedings of the Gallaudet Conference on Reading in Relation to Deafness* Gallaudet College Press: Washington

Rockhart, J F and Scott Morton, M S (1975) *Computers and the Learning Process in Higher Education* A report prepared for the Carnegie Commission on Higher Education. McGraw Hill: New York

Rogers, E and Shoemaker, A (1971) *The Communication of Innovations* Free Press: New York

Rubenstein, R and Rollins, A (1978) *Demonstration of the Use of Computer Assisted Instruction with Handicapped Children: Final Report* Bolt Berenek and Newman Inc: Cambridge, Mass

*Rushby, N J *ed* (1981) *Selected Readings in Computer-Based Learning* Kogan Page: London

Sale, A H and Hawthorn, G (1982) *Proceedings of the 9th Australian Computer Conference* Australian Computer Society: Hobart

Satir, V (1972) *Peoplemaking* Science and Behaviour Books: Palo Alto, CA

Shaplin, J I and Olds, H *eds* (1964) *Team Teaching* Harper and Row: New York

Shepherd, I D H, Cooper, Z A and Walker, D R F (1980) *Computer Assisted Learning in Geography* Council for Educational Technology: London

Slobin, D I *ed* (1971) *The Ontogenesis of Grammar: a Theoretical Symposium* Academic Press: New York

Slobin, D I (1975) On the nature of talk to children *in* Lenneberg, E H and Lenneberg, E *eds* (1975)

Smith, C H *ed* (1981) *Microcomputers in Education* Ellis Harwood: New York

Smith, L and Keith, P (1971) *Anatomy of Educational Innovation: an Organizational Analysis of an Elementary School* John Wiley: New York

*Smith, P R (1981) *Computer Assisted Learning* Pergamon: Oxford

Smith, P W *et al* (1981) *A CAL Software Library Manual* Schools Council/Chelsea College: London

Stodolsky, D (1981) Automatic mediation of group communication skill training *in* *Proceedings of the 25th Annual Meeting of the Society for General Systems Research* Louisville, Kentucky

Tagg, W (1981) *A Standard for CAL Dialogue* AUCBE Hertfordshire County Council: Hertfordshire

Tallman, T M (1976) Computer assisted communication system *in* Foulds, R and Lund, B *eds* (1976)

Tedd, L A (1979) *Case Studies in Computer-Based Bibliographic Information Services*

British Library Research and Development Reports, The British Library: London

Todd, P H (1972) Learning to talk with delayed exposure to speech. Unpublished doctoral dissertation, University of California, Berkeley: CA

* Toffler, A (1980) *The Third Wave* Collins: London

Townley, H M (1978) *Systems Analysis for Information Retrieval* Andre Deutsch: London

Turoff, M (1975) *The Delphi Method: Technique and Applications* Addison Wesley Co: Reading, Mass

Vanderheiden, G C and Grilley, K (1977) *Nonvocal Communication Techniques and Aids for the Severely Physically Handicapped* University Park Press: Baltimore

Virgo, P (1981) *Learning for Change* Bow Publications: London

Vygotsky, L S (1962) *Thought and Language* MIT Press: Cambridge, Mass

Waitt, I ed (1980) *College Administration* NATFHE: London

Want, D L (1982) Keyword driven interaction in computer assisted learning *in* Lewis, R and Tagg, E D (1982)

Watson, D (1979) *Computers in the Curriculum Project: Geography* Edward Arnold: London

Watson, D (1982) Some implications of micros on curriculum developments *in* Lewis, R and Tagg, E D (1982)

Wearing, A J, Cass, B W and Fitzgerald, D (1976) *Computers and Teaching in Australia* Australian Advisory Committee on Research and Development in Education Report No 6, Australian Government Publishing Service: Canberra

Weir, S (1979) *The Evaluation and Cultivation of Spatial and Linguistic Abilities in Individuals with Cerebral Palsy* LOGO Memo No 55, Massachusetts Institute of Technology: Boston, Mass

Weir, S (1981) *LOGO as an Information Prosthetic for the Handicapped* DSRE Working Paper No WP-9 Massachusetts Institute of Technology: Boston, Mass

Weir, S and Emanuel, R (1976) *Using LOGO to Catalyze Communication in an Autistic Child* Research Report No 15, Department of Artificial Intelligence, University of Edinburgh

Welford, A T (1976) *Skilled Performance: Perceptual and Motor Skills* Scott, Foresman and Co: Glenview, Illinois

Wildenberg, D ed (1981) *Computer Simulations in University Teaching* Amsterdam, North Holland

Winterburn, R and Evans, L eds (1980) *Aspects of Educational Technology XIV* Kogan Page: London

Youngmann, C (1980) *CAC-Apple: A Mapping and Data Management Utility for the Apple II* Morgan-Fairchild Group: Seattle

Secton II: Official and corporate publications

Assistant Masters and Mistresses Association (1981) *New Information and Communication Technologies and Secondary Education* AMMA: London

Cockcroft Committee (1982) *Mathematics Counts: Report of the Committee of Inquiry into the Teaching of Mathematics in Schools* HMSO: London

DEC (1975) *101 BASIC Computer Games* Digital Equipment Games, Digital Equipment Corporation: Maynard, Mass

Dresden Associates (1980) *School Microware: A Directory of Educational Software* Dresden Associates: Dresden, ME

H M Inspectors of Schools (1978) *The Education of Pupils with Learning Difficulties in Primary and Secondary Schools in Scotland* HMSO: Edinburgh

H M Inspectors of Schools (1982) *Learning and Teaching in Scottish Secondary Schools: the Contribution of Educational Technology* HMSO: Edinburgh

Maths Newsletter (1980) Proposals for computer education in New Zealand high schools *Maths Newsletter* Department of Education, Wellington

Minnesota Educational Computing Consortium (1978) *Brochure* Minnesota

McCann Committee (1975) *The Secondary Education of Physically Handicapped Children in Scotland* HMSO: Edinburgh

Open University (1982) *Micros in Schools – an Awareness Pack for Teachers* Centre for Continuing Education/Open University: Milton Keynes

National Association of Teachers in Further and Higher Education (1982) *Draft Association Policy Statement on Microelectronics and Further Education* NATFHE: London

Schools Council (1979) *Computers in the Curriculum: Geography* Edward Arnold: London

Trades Union Congress (1979) *Employment and Technology* TUC: London

World Confederation of Organizations of the Teaching Profession (1981) *Implications of New Technology for Society and the Impact on Educational Policy and Provision* WCOTP: Morges, Switzerland

Section III: Articles, periodicals and working papers

Alderman, D L, Appel, L R and Murphy, R T (1978) PLATO and TICCIT: an evaluation of CAI in the community college *Educational Technology* 18 4: 40-5

Bellefleur, P A (1976) TTY communication: its history and future *The Volta Review* 78: 107-12

Bork, A M (1975) Effective computer use in physics education *American Journal of Physics* 43 81

Boyd, G M (1982) Four ways of providing computer assisted learning and their probable impacts *Computers and Education* 6: 305-10

Bradbeer, R (1981a) How I plan to spend the money: an interview with Richard Fothergill *Educational Computing* 2 3: 22-6

Bradbeer, R (1981b) Exciting prospects for networks *Educational Computing* 2 6: 27-31

Brown, J S and Burton, R R (1978) Diagnostic models for procedural bugs in basic mathematical skills *Cognitive Science* 2: 155-92

Burton, R R and Brown, J S (1979) An investigation of computer coaching for informal learning activities *International Journal of Man-Machine Studies* 11 1: 5-24

Chalmers, A, Thompson, W and Keown, P (1980) The use of a computer-based simulation model in the geography classroom *New Zealand Journal of Geography* 67: 6-9

Colby, K M (1973) The rationale for computer-based treatment of language difficulties in non-speaking autistic children *Journal of Autism and Childhood Schizophrenia* 3: 254-60

Cooper, Z A (1975) Computers in secondary school geography *Computer Education* 19: 8-14

Costa, B (1981) Microcomputers in Colorado – it's elementary! *Wilson Library Bulletin* May 1981: 676-8, 717

Cronin, B (1979) The DAVID system: the development of an interactive video system at the National Technical Institute for the Deaf *American Annals of the Deaf* 124: 616-8

Cronin, B (1980) Closed caption television: today and tomorrow *American Annals of the Deaf* 125: 726-8 du Boulay, J B H (1980) Teaching teachers mathematics through programming. Mathematical Education in Science and Technology *International Journal of Mathematical Education in Science and Technology* **11** 3: 347-60

du Boulay, J B H and Howe, J A M (1982) LOGO building blocks: student teachers using computer-based mathematics apparatus *Computers and Education* **6** 1: 93-8

Dwyer, T (1974) The significance of Solo Mode computing for curriculum design *EDU*: Sept 1974

Dwyer, T (1981) Multi-micro learning environments: a preliminary report on the SOLO/NET/works Project *Byte* January 1981: 104-14

Fletcher, S G (1982) Seeing speech in real time *Institute of Electronic and Electrical Engineering Spectrum* **19** 4: 42-5

Forer, P and Owens, I (1979) Frontiers of geography in the 1980s *New Zealand Journal of Geography* **67**: 2-5

Furth, H G (1971) Linguistic deficiency and thinking: research with deaf subjects 1964-1969 *Psychological Bulletin* **74**: 58-72

Geoffrion, L D (1982) An analysis of teletype conversation *American Annals of the Deaf* in press

Geoffrion, L D and Bergeron, R D (1977) *Initial Reading through Computer Animation* Occasional Papers in Education No 1, University of New Hampshire: New Hampshire

Geoffrion, L D and Eshel, R (1982) An autobiographical perspective on severe communication handicaps *Journal of Rehabilitation* in press

Geoffrion, L D and Goldenberg, E P (1981) Computer-based exploratory learning systems for communication-handicapped children *Journal of Special Education* **15**: 325-31

Goodwin, M S and Goodwin, T C (1969) In a dark mirror *Mental Hygiene* **53**: 550-63

Gormley, K A and Franzen, A M (1978) Why can't the deaf read? Comments on asking the wrong question *American Annals of the Deaf* **123**: 542-7

Gunn, V P and Elkins, J (1979) Clozing the reading gap *Australian Journal of Reading* **2**: 144-51

Hammermeister, F K (1971) Reading achievement in deaf adults *American Annals of the Deaf* **116**: 25-8

Hartley, R J and Lewis, R (1982) A computer language system for model building and experimentation *International Journal of Mathematical Education in Science and Technology* in press

Holroyd, M (1982) *Seeing in the dark* Observer: 10.1.82

Howe, J A M (1982) The microelectronic revolution: a challenge to education *Scottish Educational Review* **2**: 3-13

Howe, J A M and du Boulay, B (1979) Microprocessor assisted learning: turning the clock back? *Programmed Learning and Educational Technology* **16** 3: 240-6

Hoyle, E (1974) Professionality, professionalism and control in teaching *London Educational Review* **3** 2: 13-19

Hoyle, E (1982) The micropolitics of educational organizations *British Journal of Educational Management and Administration* **10** 2: 87-9

Kyle, J G, Conrad, R, McKenzie, M G, Morris, A J M and Weiskrantz, B C (1978) Language abilities in deaf school leavers *Journal of the British Association of Teachers of the Deaf* **2**: 38-42

Lally, M R (1980) Computer assisted development of number conservation in mentally retarded school children *Australian Journal of Developmental Disabilities* **6**: 131-6

Lally, M R (1981) Computer assisted teaching of sight word recognition to retarded school children *American Journal of Mental Deficiency* **85**: 383-8

Lally, M R (1982) Computer assisted handwriting instruction and visual/kinaesthetic feedback processes *Applied Research in Mental Retardation* **3** (in press)

Macleod, I D G and Procter, P S (1979) A dynamic approach to teaching handwriting skills *Visible Language* **13** 1: 29-42

Moore, O K (1980) About Talking Typewriters, folk models, and discontinuities: a progress report on twenty years of research, development and application *Educational Technology* **20** 2: 15-27

Moore, W (1981) Catching up in the computer race *Education News* **17** 7: 16-19

Norden, K (1981) Learning processes and personality development in deaf children *American Annals of the Deaf* **126**: 404-10

O'Shea, T (1979) A self-improving quadratic tutor *International Journal of Man-Machine Studies* **11** 1: 97-124

Papert, S (1972) Teaching children thinking *Mathematics Teaching* **58** Spring

Papert, S and Solomon, C (1972) Twenty things to do with a computer *Educational Technology* **12** 4: 9-18

Papert, S (1982) Tomorrow's classrooms? *Times Educational Supplement* 5.3.82: 31-41

Parslow, R D (1981) Computerized destruction of Western Civilisation *Computers and Society II* **2**: 16-21

Payne, A (1981) On-line information retrieval in schools *CAL News* **16** March 1981: 11

Reynaud, B (1982) No cause for people concern *Management Today* April 1982: 37-40

Rom, A and Bliss, L S (1981) A comparison of verbal communicative skills of language impaired and normal speaking children *Journal of Communication Disorders* **14**: 133-40

Sims, D, VonFelt, J, Dowaliby, F, Hutchinson, K and Myers, T (1979) A pilot experiment in computer assisted speechreading instruction utilizing the Data Analysis Video Interactive Device (DAVID) *American Annals of the Deaf* **124**: 616, 618-23

Smart, N and Jennings, R (1982) Microelectronics technology and geography in the Scottish secondary school *Scottish Educational Review* Special Issue **2**: 23-33

Sommers, N (1979) Revision experiences of student writers and experienced adult writers *College Composition and Communication* **30**: 46-9

Stenning, R (1979) The changing nature of employment relations in secondary schools *Educational Administration* **7** 2: 99-121

Trybus, R J and Karchmer, M A (1977) School achievement scores of hearing impaired children: national data on achievement, status and growth patterns *American Annals of the Deaf* **122**: 62-9

Turing, A M (1950) Computing machinery and intelligence *Mind* **59**: 433-60

Urban, G (1981) The perils of foreign policy: a conversation with Dr Zbigniew Brzezinski *Encounter* May 1981

Vernon, M (1968) Fifty years research *Journal of Rehabilitation of the Deaf* **1**: 1-12

Walker, D and Graham, L (1979) Simulation games and the microcomputer *Simulation/Games for Learning* **9** 4: 151-8

Wilbur, R B (1977) An explanation of deaf children's difficulty with certain syntactic structures of English *The Volta Review* **79**: 85-92

Wilson, R (1979) Looking towards the 1990s *British Journal of Educational Technology* **10** 1: 45-91

Woodruff, E, Bereiter, C, and Scardamalia, M (1982) On the road to computer assisted compositions *Journal of Educational Technology Systems* **10**: 133-48

Section IV

Baker, F B (1978) *Computer Managed Instruction: Theory and Practice* Educational Technology Publications: Englewood Cliffs, New Jersey

This substantial book (417pp) presents a comprehensive analysis of the field of computer-managed instruction in the USA. The concept of CMI is explored in detail, representative systems are described, a detailed case study presented and the underlying technical and educational issues explored in depth.

Bradbeer, R, De Bono, P and Laurie, P (1982) *The Computer Book: An Introduction to Computers and Computing* BBC Publications: London
Published in conjunction with the first transmission of the BBC's series *The Computer Programme*, this book is an important part of the BBC's Computer Literacy Project (see Chapter 22). It is lucidly written and well laid out with profuse illustrations (appealing cartoons as well as photographs and diagrams). It makes no unrealistic assumptions about the layman's level of knowledge and starts from an interesting group of computer applications. It proceeds logically from problem-solving through flow-charting to programming and debugging before going into the details of hardware and coding. Personal computers (especially the BBC Micro!) are considered with a view to future possibilities including networks, robotics and electronic offices and publishing. There is an excellent unstuffy glossary and a full index.

Coburn, P, Kelman, P, Roberts, N, Snyder, T F F, Watt, D H and Weiner, C (1982) *Practical Guide to Computers in Education* Addison-Wesley: Reading, Mass
A well-written and practical handbook for teachers who are getting interested in the potential of computers. It is extremely well illustrated with anecdote, case study and photographs, and refreshingly free of jargon. It recognizes and introduces the subculture of educational computing, illustrates varieties of CAI and CAL with dialogue, introduces programming, CPU, memory and peripherals. Good appendix with computer comparison charts, (mostly American), an excellent classified bibliography and a comprehensive resources section which covers indexes, on-line information retrieval, research and development projects, user groups, computer clubs, hardware and software, associations, periodicals and funding. The book finishes with a good glossary and index.

Curnow, R and Curran, S (1979) *The Silicon Factor: Living with the Microprocessor* National Extension College: Cambridge
This book was originally designed as stimulus material for discussion groups viewing the BBC TV series of the same name (see Chapter 22), but is independently useful. It provides a chapter and discussion sheet for seven sessions, covering microelectronics and the second industrial revolution; the possible effects of microelectronics on education and training, learning at home, home life, work and the way we live; and the age of information and control. It encourages students to question the inevitability of the new technology and to make them aware of our capacity to choose how we apply it. It is attractively illustrated with photographs and cartoons and the style is accessible to the general reader.

Day, C and Alcock, D (1982) *Illustrating Computers (Without Much Jargon)* Pan Books: London and Sydney
Claiming to be a beginners' guide to how computers work, this slim paperback rewards the serious reader with a clear notion of the principles underlying the internal mechanics of a computer. It is written, as it claims, with a minimum of jargon but curiously is entirely reproduced from handwriting. This makes it less legible than it might be, though some may find it adds to the charm of little diagrams and cartoons. A useful source of explanation for those who *really* want to know 'Yes, but *how* does the computer do it?'

Dwyer, T and Critchfield, M (1978) *BASIC and the Personal Computer* Addison-Wesley: Reading, Mass
This book is a helpful introduction to BASIC for personal computing. It demonstrates various applications including games, business, art and simulations, and draws on the experience of Project SOLO.

Evans, C (1979) *The Mighty Micro* Victor Gollancz and Hodder & Stoughton Coronet
    Paperback: Sevenoaks, Kent
A popular best-seller on the future impact of the microelectronics revolution by the late
psychologist, computer scientist, and presenter of the eponymous television series. It is
readable, stimulating, and well-informed if sometimes slightly idiosyncratic. Many of
his short-term forecasts have already come true, and the middle and long-term ones are
always provocative, sometimes all too plausible. His section on intelligent machines is
excellent, and his exploration of 'bizarre issues' thought-provoking.

Forester, T (1980) *The Microelectronics Revolution* Basil Blackwell: Oxford
A massive (589 pp) and contributed tome which nevertheless contains a refreshing
element of dialogue in the shape of reactions and commentary on some of the chapters.
However, this is a reference collection rather than a book to read through. It covers all
aspects of the impact of the new technology and its applications. There are good
sections on the likely effects on industry and offices (including industrial relations) and
its social impact (eg town planning). Edited by a former industrial correspondent for
New Society, this book is wide-ranging, mostly readable, and in places well-illustrated.

Gosling, W (1981) *The Kingdom of Sand* (CET Occasional Paper 9) Council for
    Educational Technology: London
Subtitled 'Essays to salute a world in process of being born', this collection comprises
five lectures given between 1978 and 1981 by the technical director of Plessey Electronic
Systems to a remarkably diverse collection of audiences. 'In the Age of the Thinking
Machines' was given to the Institute of Craft Education; 'Augusta Ada and the
Religious Education Problem' was to the Convent of La Sainte Union. The well-known
'Kingdom of Sand' essay is reprinted here, too, and its halftone photographs and line
diagrams help to make this an attractive little volume as well as an important one. In
'Invention, too, has a Natural History' he analyses the distinctive marketing and
investment implications of the new technology. 'Some Possible Futures for the
Developed World' is an informed and level-headed look into the future which avoids
both Utopian over-optimism and Orwellian gloom.
    The origin of these essays in the spoken word leaves its welcome footprint. Professor
Gosling writes with style and elegance and has a regard for the chiselled edge of
meaning. He is also – as Geoffrey Hubbard remarks in his Foreword – a man of
remarkable vision, and an engineer with catholic interests and eclectic thinking whose
ideas are always interesting and thought-provoking.

Hills, P *ed* (1980) *The Future of the Printed Word* Frances Pinter: London
An early collection of papers which examine the impact and implications of the new
communications technology in publishing, librarianship, information science,
computing and education. The authors are mostly British but there are a couple from
the USA and a notable chapter from Luxembourg on Euronet Diane, the on-line
'intelligent' network of the European Community for scientific and socio-economic
information. For a book about the future of books, the absence of an index or even a
collected bibliography is a surprising omission, which seriously limits its usefulness for
reference purposes.

Howe, J A M and Ross, P M (1981) *Microcomputers in Secondary Education: Issues
    and Techniques* Kogan Page: London
An edited collection of 13 papers by contributors to the British Educational Research
Association's 1980 symposia on microcomputers in secondary education. They range
from rather general reviews (eg by Rushby on microcomputers in Europe) to a specific
and detailed exploration of the role of microcomputers in creative writing by Sharples,
extensively illustrated by a fictional and actual 'language workshop' with dialogue.
Although the pages are clearly reproduced directly from the output of a word processor,
there is no index or bibliography.

Jenkins, C and Sherman, B (1981) *The Leisure Shock* Eyre Methuen: London
This book takes up the argument where *The Collapse of Work* (by the same authors,

1979) left off. How should society prepare for five million unemployed in Britain to benefit from life in the 1990s? The General Secretary and Director of Research of the Association of Scientific, Technical and Managerial Staff (ASTMS) offer a wide-ranging review of changing patterns of life, death, work and leisure and examine the implications for education, social services, recreation and the media. Of interest outside the British trade union circles from which its authors come.

Jones, R (1980) *Microcomputers: Their Uses in Primary Schools* Council for Educational Technology: London
This is the first comprehensive analysis of the use of microcomputers in British primary schools. A survey of schools and software is included, and the author analyses the special problems posed for microcomputer users in the primary school. The enormous potential is charted, especially for the development of games and simulation software. It has a useful glossary and six Appendices contain valuable material for practitioners and teachers.

Jones, R (1982) *Five of the Best: Computer Programs for Primary School Children* (Microelectronics Education Programme Case Study 2) Council for Educational Technology (on behalf of MEP): London
This is one of four booklets prepared by the Micros and Primary Education group for MEP (the others, from the same publishers, are a *Before-you-buy Guide*, *Managing the Microcomputer in the Classroom* and *The Core Subjects*). The book contains five unedited pen-portraits, written by six practising teachers, depicting the use of five well-known programs (SUBTRACT, HANGMAN UK, ANIMAL, HUNT THE THIMBLE and SPANISH MAIN) in their own classrooms, in their own words. They are inter-spersed with editorial 'teach-in' commentaries and apart from the introduction have otherwise been allowed to speak for themselves. A vivid 'slice-of-life' approach which will find a variety of uses for discussion groups, in-service courses and private study.

Jones, T ed (1980) *Microelectronics and Society* Open University Press: Milton Keynes
This collection contains seven essays on different aspects of its theme by a mixture of British academics, consultants and journalists. Donald Michie's essay on social aspects of artificial intelligence is of particular interest, and laymen will appreciate Malcolm Peltu's informed and intelligible introduction to information technology.

Lafferty, P (1981) *Personal Computing* Butterworth/Newnes Technical Books: London
An economical, concise and thorough set of questions and answers for relative beginners. It explains technical terms like hex, ASCII, floppy disc simply, and is organized into eight chapters with a glossary, further reading, list of addresses and index. Useful for dipping into but compact enough to read straight through. It is reliable and up-to-date on most topics but chapter 7 ('Some personal computers') reviews a slightly eccentric collection – no mention of the RML 380Z or BBC Micro, for example.

Large, P (1980) *The Micro Revolution* Fontana Paperbacks: London
This is a readable account by the technology correspondent of the *Guardian* of how the microchip is already changing our lives. One chapter provides a stimulating future scenario which is both thought-provoking and well-informed. It is good on economic and political consequences as well as technological mechanisms. Although there is little material specifically about education, this is one of the best attempts to render the technology intelligible to the general reader. It has a useful index and a brief bibliography.

Lewis, R and Tagg, E D eds (1980) Computer Assisted Learning: Scope, Progress and Limits North Holland: Amsterdam (hardback) and Heinemann: London (1981 paperback)
These are the printed proceedings of the International Federation for Information Processing (IFIP) Working Group on Education's conference of the same name, which was held at Roehampton, England, in September 1979. It contains 17 papers from South Africa, France, the Netherlands, Denmark, Sweden, Italy, Canada and the

United States – the latter group including Alfred Bork, Lud Braun and Sylvia Charp. There are also reports of seven discussion sessions on topics such as design, implementation, evaluation and the future. Apart from a contents list and a list of contributors, there is no assistance to a reader who wants to access a particular topic.

Luehrmann, A, Peckham, H and Ramirez, M (1982) *A First Course in Computing* McGraw-Hill: New York
This activity-oriented introduction to BASIC is aimed at early secondary students and up. It includes both theory and practical applications in BASIC programming and is an excellent introduction for use with any microcomputer.

McKenzie, J, Elton, L R B and Lewis R (1978) *Interactive Computer Graphics in Science Teaching* Ellis Horwood: Chichester
This is an important pioneering book on the use of graphics as an aid to learning in science-based subjects. Most of the work described is based on the Computers in the Undergraduate Science Curriculum project and the use of computer graphics is set within the broad field of computer-assisted learning with sound coverage of the design, evaluation, implementation and integration into the curriculum of CAL packages.
There have been major changes in the technology of computer graphics since the book was written but they only render obsolete the sections in which the authors describe how they overcame the problems posed by the machinery available at the time. The book is strongly influenced by the need to produce practical materials that can be used by students, and it describes one of their major achievements: the writing of a series of program modules that allowed graphic images to be incorporated into programs easily. The team then went on to develop around 40 packages for use in the undergraduate level teaching of physics, chemistry and biology and they were used by up to 1000 students. The book concludes with a good glossary and reference section.

McMahon, H F (1978) Progress and prospects in computer-managed learning in the United Kingdom. *Programmed Learning & Educational Technology* **15**: 2 and reprinted in Rushby (1981)
This article is a review of the then current situation in computer-managed learning in the United Kingdom written by a practitioner from the practitioner's point of view. The major CML systems then extant in the UK are examined in turn and references are given to resource material available for further study of these systems. Some of the key issues and problems facing developers and users of CML are identified and analysed under the headings of testing, routing and record-keeping. The article ends with a speculative look at the future of CML in the UK.

Maddison, A (1982) *Microcomputers in the Classroom* Hodder & Stoughton Educational: Sevenoaks, Kent
A practical and informed introduction to the subject for teachers and others who are new to the field. It introduces microcomputer hardware and software, various kinds of classroom applications and uses in school administration. The Appendices contain a useful check-list to help in the choice and assessment of programs, a brief list of (British) sources of software and information, a rather sketchy table of hardware systems available and a minimally annotated bibliography. This book will be valued more for its lucid text than as a work of reference.

Megarry, J (in press) *Computer World* (A Piccolo Factbook) Piper Books: London
Although intended for junior readers, this simply written paperback gives an accessible and compact introduction to computers and microelectronics which may be valuable to adults, too. It covers computers and thought, the advent of the chip, hardware and software, flow charts and programming, everyday applications and also looks at the future. There are lots of colour illustrations and diagrams and also a black and white reference section with glossary and index.

Papert, S (1980) *Mindstorms: Children, Computers and Powerful Ideas* Harvester Press: Brighton and Basic Books: New York
Humane, imaginative and profound, Papert has drawn not only on his pioneering work

with LOGO and Turtles but also on a lifetime of thought about human learning. He challenges flat-earth convergent thinking about computers and helps to break mental habits. He explains novel ways in which computers can help children to develop powerful ideas. Child-centred, rather than teacher-centred, it raises profound questions about conventional wisdom and practice. Following Piaget, whom Papert knew, he analyses how children learn from experience, and illustrates how programming helps them to grasp the structure of new knowledge. Beautifully illustrated and written, this is arguably one of the most important recent books to have been published on computer-assisted learning.

Payne, A, Hutchings, B and Ayre, P (1980) *Computer Software for Schools* Pitman Education Ltd: London
This book demonstrates the process of working from a topic to producing actual software. It contains 11 classroom-tested exercises drawn from a range of disciplines – history, French, home economics, geography, information retrieval and library monitoring as well as the expected subjects like maths and physics. By following how to work out flow charts and derive lines of coding from them, the reader picks up a certain amount of knowledge of BASIC, the programming language used. The provision of extensive commentary on technique and full listings of the programs means that readers could try out the programs.

Peters, H J and Johnson, J W (1978) *Author's Guide: Design Development Style Packaging Review* Conduit: University of Iowa, Iowa
This is a well-known reference work that has proved useful in establishing guidelines for developing and evaluating software. Some of it is addressed to specific applications for microcomputer software, but the ideas are easily adapted to other areas. The sample review forms are particularly useful. The authors assume some computer background in their readers.

Poirot, J L (1980) *Computers and Education* Sterling Swift: Texas
This is a practical and unpretentious little book aimed clearly at classroom teachers. It is full of workable classroom suggestions for using computers effectively, including details like furniture arrangements, wall charts, etc. It has a useful section on computer-based educational administration (applicable mainly to the USA) and includes a variety of educational games. One of these, 'Hands-up', is an effective way for a group of pupils to demonstrate binary addition and subtraction.

Rushby, N J ed (1981) *Selected Readings in Computer-Based Learning* Kogan Page: London
This is an Occasional Publication of the Association for Educational and Training Technology which, in association with Kogan Page, publishes the well-known serials *Programmed Learning and Educational Technology* (a quarterly periodical) and *Aspects of Educational Technology* (the annual proceedings of the Educational Technology International Conference series). It is a selective anthology of papers published in the last five years in either publication, some of them updated for the purpose. They have been arranged into three somewhat arbitrary sections, given a foreword and cumulative bibliography. It is thus a convenient source of key papers, including some by *WYBE* authors like McMahon, Howe, Boyd and du Boulay. There are also some overview papers, eg of CAL in Europe by Rushby and in the USA by Zinn. A convenient and compact reference source.

Sheingold, K and Billings, K (1981) *Issues Relating to the Implementation of Computer Technology in Schools: A Cross-Sectional Study* Children's Electronic Laboratory Memo No 1, Bank Street College of Education, USA
This is the report of a study funded by the National Institute of Education of the US Department of Health Education and Welfare which discusses three case studies of communities that have implemented the use of microcomputers into their schools. The study documented the innovation process in these towns through interviews and observations. At the end, the authors raise a series of questions about the impact of microcomputers on education as a result of their preliminary work.

Shelley, J (1981) *Microfuture* Pitman Education: London
Misleadingly titled, this brief account is aimed at students and non-specialists and tries to cover silicon chips, microcomputers, and their implications; it is, not surprisingly, only partially successful. However, this little book will be valued by many for its large clear photographs and diagrams of the manufacture and applications both of chips and assembled microcomputers. It is an attractively laid out book and useful for those who have no mental picture of some of the devices.

Shepherd, I D H, Cooper, Z A and Walker, D R F (1980) *Computer Assisted Learning in Geography* Council for Educational Technology: London
Although aimed principally at geographers, this book deserves a wider readership. It gives a lucid analysis of current trends and future prospects, with emphasis always on *appropriate* use of technology to serve curriculum ends. After basic explanation of the computer, how it works and how it can be used, a number of well-illustrated case studies are provided, and excellent sections are devoted to practical issues in classroom use of CAL and the issue of student-centred versus teacher-centred CAL. After a look to the future, there is a useful Yellow Pages section which includes details of software packages for geography teaching, further reading and a list of helpful organizations, a comprehensive set of references and bibliography and a nine-page glossary.

Sledge, D (1980) *Microcomputers in Education* Council for Educational Technology: London
This is a collection of articles assembled and reprinted especially to help teachers who are considering using or buying a microcomputer. They cover the management and use of a micro as well as the various types of equipment and their compatibility or otherwise. Purchase and running costs are considered, as well as the different programming languages and the acquisition of software.

Smith, P R (1981) *Computer Assisted Learning: Selected Papers from the CAL 81 Symposium* Pergamon Press: Oxford, New York, Toronto, Sydney
Twenty-seven papers selected from the hundreds presented at the biennial international conference of the CAL community held at Leeds in April 1981. They reflect the diversity and main themes well, though some omissions are regrettable; the principle of selective publishing is justified here, and the workmanlike editing welcome.

Taylor, R P (1980) *The Computer in the School: Tutor, Tool, Tutee* Teachers College Press: Columbia University, New York
This book provides both an introduction to and an anthology of the writings of five key American pioneers in computer-assisted learning: Al Bork, Tom Dwyer, Art Luehrmann, Seymour Papert, and Patrick Suppes. Each section contains a biographical sketch and three or four key articles which convey the flavour of their thinking. Taylor's introduction sets out the framework which associates Bork and Suppes particularly with the computer-as-tutor model, and Dwyer, Luehrmann and Papert especially with the computer-as-tutee: all five put forward the case for the computer-as-tool, although they conceptualize it differently.

Thomas, J L ed (1981) *Microcomputers in the Schools* The Onyx Press: Phoenix, Arizona
This book contains over 30 articles grouped under the following headings: selection considerations, hardware and software development, curriculum applications, and trends and issues. Articles are written by distinguished educators and educational technologists. Annotated bibliography and appendices add to its usefulness for teachers interested in classroom computer use.

Toffler, A (1980) *The Third Wave* Collins: London, Sydney, Toronto, Johannesburg
A decade after *Future Shock*, Alvin Toffler provides an analysis of the great tidal forces which have transformed Western society. After the agricultural revolution, and the industrial revolution, the third and mightiest is already colliding with and overtaking the second, and the microelectronic and communications technologies are at the centre of its origins. Toffler follows his analysis with a major synthesis of the impact of these

changes on industry, transport, home and family life, communications media, national and international politics, mental health and the future of the human race. Vivid prose makes the book highly readable, and Toffler is always thought-provoking.

Willis, J and Donley, W Jr (1981) *Nailing Jelly to a Tree* Dilithium Press: Beaverton, Oregon
Introduces the reader to the basics of computing, to the various types of software in common use, and to the essentials of programming in machine, assembly, and BASIC languages. While not intended to produce skilled programmers, the book simply and clearly provides the information to enable the user to modify, enhance and experiment with software already published.

Biographical notes
on contributors and editors

David Allen (Chapter 22) was educated at Harrow Weald Grammar School, where he gained a State Scholarship, going on to Balliol College, Oxford, to read for a degree in chemistry and the science of metals. On leaving Oxford in 1962 he became the head of the science department at Beaumont College, Windsor, and then subsequently head of chemistry at Stonyhurst College, Lancashire, before joining the BBC as a production assistant in 1969. Since then he has worked in educational broadcasting, producing series on medicine, education, child care, consumer affairs and a series for the deaf. In 1976 he became senior producer in the BBC Continuing Education Department and is now responsible editorially for the BBC's Computer Literacy Project, which he helped to create. Recent series include Managing the Micro and The Silicon Factor. He has edited various books including *Early Years at School, Measurement in Education, Other People's Children, It's a Great Life* and the recent best-selling *Computer Book*.

Benedict du Boulay (Chapter 17) is a lecturer in the Department of Computing Science, University of Aberdeen. His interests are artificial intelligence, in particular intelligent teaching systems, the more general use of computers in education and problems of man-computer communication, particularly the difficulties faced by novices learning programming. Having graduated with a degree in physics from Imperial College, London, he spent several years as a secondary school teacher before joining the Department of Artificial Intelligence, Edinburgh. There he worked on the problem of helping student teachers whose mathematics was weak to explore their difficulties through computer programming.

Gary M Boyd (Chapter 4) has been active in the field of computer-assisted learning since 1968. He helped to develop the Canadian CAL language NATAL, and spent a period of leave with the UK National Development Program in CAL. His original studies were in radio-physics, English and philosophy. He now teaches educational cybernetics as professor, Graduate Programme in Educational Technology, Concordia University, Montreal, Quebec.

Louise Dubuc (Chapter 15) was born in Montreal, Quebec. She studied anthropology at the University of Montreal, and linguistics at the Ecole des Hautes Etudes en Sciences Sociales (EHESS) in Paris before turning to the field of education where she obtained her PhD in 1980. Her research experience lies mostly in an experiment with a teaching machine in Paris, where, under the direction of Jacques Perriault, she was in charge of the production and validation of courseware in computer science (from 1973 to 1977). She taught computer science at the Université de Paris V and EHESS from 1970 to 1972 and she was a visiting assistant professor at Concordia University, Montreal in 1977-8 in the Educational Technology programme. From 1970 to 1973, she was consultant to the OECD working group on the introduction of informatics in the secondary school. Since 1979 she has been in charge of the dossier 'pedagogical use of computers' in the Service Général des Moyens d'Enseignement (SGME) of Quebec's Ministry of Education and she is co-editor of its periodical *BIP – BIP*. She has also been the co-ordinator of the team 'Orientations et développement' in the Service de Développement de la Technologie Educative since 1980.

Donald P Ely (Chapter 11) is professor of education (instructional design, development, and evaluation) and director of the ERIC Clearing-house on Information Resources at Syracuse University in the USA. He has been a consultant to universities in Australia, Canada, the Netherlands, Peru, and Venezuela. He is a past president of the Association for Educational Communications and Technology (AECT) in the USA and serves on the editorial boards of *The British Journal of Educational Technology* and *Technologia Educativa*. He is co-author of *Teaching and Media: A Systematic Approach* and *Media Personnel in Education: A Competency Approach*.

Derek Esterson (Chapter 18), previously trained as a mathematician, has been involved in developing educational computing since 1960. First in the county of Kent, and for the last ten years in Inner London, he has been responsible for stimulating politicians, administrators and teachers to provide the necessary resources, facilities and training so that computers could take on their essential role in education, particularly as an object of study and as a powerful aid to teaching. His activities in the British Computer Society, of which he was made an honorary fellow in 1977, has brought his work to the notice of a wide audience.

Pip Forer (Chapter 16) has an academic career spanning the Universities of Oxford, Bristol, Edinburgh and finally Canterbury (New Zealand) where he is now a senior lecturer in human geography. From an early research interest in mainframe computers his interests switched to teaching and microcomputers with the arrival of a Wang 2200 in 1976. He now works mainly with Apple and Poly-I machines. He has been active in promoting geography CAL in New Zealand through dissemination and writing programs. In addition to program suites for gaming, interactive mapping and use of graphics, he has written several papers in the area of CAL in geography and has edited a collection of papers. In 1978 he co-convened the New Zealand Geographical Society's Working Group on Computers in Education and has been active in promoting CAL through seminars and workshops.

Richard Fothergill (Chapter 13) taught biology for nine years in a secondary school in East London. He then moved into research with the Council for Educational Technology where he examined the organization of resources in higher education. In 1972, he joined Newcastle Polytechnic where he started PETRAS, the educational development unit which organized the production of non-book resources for the institution, and stimulated course and curriculum development. He was appointed director of the Microelectronics Education Programme in November 1980.

Leo D Geoffrion (Chapter 21) received his PhD in psychology from the Johns Hopkins University in Maryland and has held faculty positions in education at the University of New Hampshire and the State University of New York. His current position is assistant director for academic computing at Skidmore College, where he is responsible for co-ordinating student and faculty use of computer facilities. His research interests focus on communication problems in handicapped children and the role of computers in language remediation. He is the principal developer of the Computer Animated Reading System (CARIS) described in his chapter.

Lynton Gray (Chapter 2) taught for eight years in schools, then became a senior lecturer in geography and subsequently in educational technology at a college of education. He is currently senior lecturer in charge of education management at the Anglian Regional Management Centre's London base at Stratford, where he is also the union branch chairman for NATFHE. The Anglian Regional Management Centre is the management faculty for the North-East Polytechnic, where active trade unionism has involved him in staving off three attempts to introduce the first compulsory redundancies in higher education. Experience as co-founder of an organization set up to serve the needs of colleges of education faced with closure has proved valuable here. He was a major contributor to the reference text *College Administration*, edited by Ian Waitt and published by NATFHE in 1980, and co-editor (with Ian Waitt) of *Simulation in Management and Business Education* (Kogan Page, 1982). He is currently involved in research into aspects of the professional development of teachers. He has been visiting professor at the University of Utah, and has undertaken education management consultancies in India, Egypt and Korea.

Ivan Gregory (Chapter 14) taught in secondary schools in Britain, South Africa, Zambia and Zimbabwe, before joining the staff of a college of education in Zimbabwe. Subsequently, he lectured in education at the University of Zimbabwe, where he later headed an educational technology unit. He is presently course leader for the Higher Diploma in Education (Postgraduate) at the University of the Witwatersrand and teaches educational technology at the postgraduate level. His interests and publications are concerned principally with the education of teachers, for all levels of education, and with educational technology, whilst his research has focussed mainly on microteaching and educational technology.

Jacques Hebenstreit (Chapter 12) trained as an electrical engineer at the Ecole Supérieure d'Eléctricité and obtained his PhD in mathematics from the University of Paris. Since then he has taught at the Ecole Supérieure d'Electricité where he is now head of the Department of Computer Science. He is also a lecturer in computer science in the University of Paris. He is a member of the Informatics Commission at the French Ministry of Universities and a member of the National Pedagogical Committee for Informatics in Secondary Education at the French Ministry of Education. He is chairman of the Technical Committee for Education of the International Federation for Information Processing and was a member of the Programme Committee of its Third World Conference on Computers in Education held in Lausanne in 1981. He has given many papers at international congresses and conferences and has written numerous articles in scientific journals. He is a member of the editorial board of the British Journal *Digital Processes* and a member of the scientific committee of the French journal *Education et Informatique*. In 1980 he received the annual award in computer science of the French Academy of Sciences and he is a senior member of the Institute of Electrical and Electronic Engineers. He is a consultant in CAI for Unesco, OECD and the European Communities.

Richard Hooper (Chapter 9) took a first class honours degree in modern languages at Oxford in 1963. From there he went to the BBC, working as a television and radio producer. In 1967-8 he was awarded a Harkness Fellowship in the USA. In 1968-9 he served as special staff consultant to President Johnson's Commission on Instructional Technology. From 1970-2 he was senior BBC producer in the Faculty of Educational Studies at the Open University.

From 1973-7 he was director of the UK government-sponsored £2.6 million National Development Programme in Computer-Assisted Learning (NDPCAL). In 1978-9 he was managing director of Mills & Allen Communications Ltd, one of the first major information providers on Prestel. Whilst at Mills & Allen, he pioneered the concept of the 'umbrella information provider' which has become a major feature of Prestel's growth. He joined British Telecom as director of Prestel in 1980 and in 1981 was appointed chief executive (information services) within British Telecom Enterprises, with responsibility for Prestel and Yellow Pages.

Jim Howe (Chapter 6) took his first degree at St Andrew's and a PhD at Cambridge where he also conducted research in experimental psychology. In 1966 he moved to Edinburgh University as a founder member of the Department of Machine Intelligence and Perception (now the Department of Artificial Intelligence). He became a senior lecturer there in 1973 and has specialized in the application of computer-based techniques to helping children to learn. He has been involved in the design of special computer peripherals for input/output and the 'turtle' miniature robot (similar to Papert's MIT turtles). He has been a central figure in the exploitation of the LOGO programming language and also in its adaptation to microcomputers such as the Research Machines 380Z. He has published, travelled and lectured on his work extensively, in Scotland and abroad. Recent publications include the May 1982 special issue of *Scottish Educational Review* on microelectronics in education and (with P M Ross) he edited *Microcomputers in Secondary Education* (Kogan Page 1981).

Eric Hoyle (Consultant Editor and Chapter 5) has been professor of education at the University of Bristol since 1971. His previous posts included teaching in two secondary schools, a college of education and a university. His interests and published works are in the areas of educational administration, the process of innovation, the professional development of teachers and the relationship between research and policy.

He is also interested in the sociology of knowledge and the sociological study of organizations and of the professions. He was founding co-editor of *Research in Education* and is on the editorial boards of a number of other journals including the *British Journal of Teacher Education*. He was research consultant to the Donnison Commission on direct grant schools, vice-chairman of the Educational Research Board of the Social Science Research Council and is currently a member of the Executive Committee of the Universities Council for the Education of Teachers and a co-opted member of Avon Education Committee. He has lectured in various colleges and universities in Africa, Australia, North America and Malaysia.

Mike Lally (Chapter 19) completed his PhD in the psychology department at the University of Adelaide in 1978. Research for this degree, started in 1974, was directed toward the problem of intellectual handicap and speed of information processing. Since late 1978, he has been associated with a project on computer-aided teaching based in the Department of Engineering Physics at the Australian National University but largely carried out at The Woden School and the City Educational Clinic in Canberra. Since 1978 this project has been supported by research grants from the Australian Education Research and Development Committee and the Schools Commission.

Diana Laurillard (Chapter 20) was formerly a lecturer in mathematics at the Polytechnic of the South Bank, London and lecturer in computer-assisted learning at the University of Surrey's Institute of Educational Technology. She is currently a lecturer in the audio-visual media Research Group at the Open University's Institute of Educational Technology. Her research interests continue work begun in her PhD thesis on descriptions of student learning, applying these to how students learn from a range of media, such as CAL and television. Her experience includes research in, development of, evaluation of and teaching the design of educational materials.

Bob Lewis (Chapter 7) was originally a physicist who dabbled in geophysics before becoming a physics teacher. He was involved in curriculum research and development at the Centre for Science and Mathematics Education, Chelsea College in the University of London for 13 years, where he finally held the title of reader in computer-assisted education and was head of educational computing. During that time he was director of a number of curriculum development projects including the Chelsea Science Simulation Project and the Computers in the Curriculum Project. He is now director of the Institute for Educational Computing at St Martin's College, Lancaster. He is a member of the Institute of Physics and the British Computer Society and fellow of the Royal Society of Arts. He is also chairman of the Working Group on the Educational Uses of Computers for the International Federation for Information Processing. He has been a visiting reader at the Centre for Multi-disciplinary Studies in the University of Belgrade and an honorary research fellow at Chelsea College.

Harry McMahon (Chapter 8) is senior lecturer in education at the New University of Ulster. A graduate in physics and education, he is an experienced teacher, educational technologist and curriculum developer, with special expertise in computer-based education. His research and development efforts have concentrated on the use of CML in education and training, and a highlight in this work was his establishment of the first implementation of ICL CAMOL in the UK. Currently his two major projects are directing a Regional Information Centre under the Microelectronics Education Programme (Chapter 13) in Northern Ireland and co-designing and developing a new microcomputer-based CML system called CAMELOT on behalf of a consortium of British, American and Canadian colleges.

Iain Macleod (Chapter 19) gained his PhD from the department of engineering physics at the Australian National University in 1970 as a result of research into computer processing of visual information. His current research interests lie in the field of man/machine interaction, with particular reference to interactive image analysis and computer-aided teaching. He was responsible for initiation of The Woden School project in late 1974 and performed most of the research in that project prior to Mike Lally's appointment in 1978. Since that time he has been examining wider aspects of computer-aided teaching of students with both physical and intellectual handicaps.

Jacquetta Megarry (Series Editor and Chapter 1) is a freelance author and educational consultant. She trained and practised as a teacher in schools in and around Glasgow and was a lecturer in education at Glasgow University and Jordanhill College of Education (1973-80), where she later also worked in the department of audio-visual media and helped to pioneer the teaching of educational technology including the use of computers in education.

Her interest in computers dates back to school holidays when she programmed and operated mainframe computers for Distillers Company Ltd, and London University, both in Autocode and machine code. She studied computing among other subjects at Cambridge University and taught programming as part of mathematics lessons in secondary school. However, her chief interest in computers is from the educational standpoint. She spent a year on leave of absence from Jordanhill as Research Fellow at IBM's UK Scientific Centre, designing courseware for geography, health education and physics. She has also recently worked for government-sponsored microelectronics education programmes in the UK, writing and editing software, documentation, and teacher education materials.

She has been closely identified with the Society for the Advancement of Gaming and Simulation in Education and Training (SAGSET), and the development of educational gaming and simulation with and without computers. She has founded and edited three periodicals, and published extensively on educational technology, innovative methods, distance learning, and teacher education. She has also had a long-standing interest in sex-typing in education and she conducted research and produced teacher education materials in this area for the Equal Opportunities Commission.

Stanley Nisbet (Associate Editor) retired from the Chair of Education at the University of Glasgow in 1978. Starting his professional life as a classics teacher he was caught up in the vigorous psychometric activity at Moray House in Edinburgh under Godfrey Thomson, and his early work was in this field. After five years of war-time service in the RAF, part of the time in its Training Research Branch, and a short spell in the University of Manchester, he became professor of education in Queen's University, Belfast and was involved in some of the post-war educational developments in Northern Ireland. From 1951 to 1978 he was professor of education in the University of Glasgow, holding various administrative posts in the University (eg Dean of the Faculty of Arts, 1965-7) and serving on many bodies outside the University (eg the Scottish Council for Research in Education). His teaching was mainly on educational theory, curriculum study (in 1957 he wrote one of the earliest books in this field) and comparative education (with a special interest in Germany and the USSR). Much of his writing has consisted of contributions to official publications. Since his retirement he has participated in projects on a number of subjects, including home-school co-operation in the EEC countries and the monitoring of in-service courses for primary school teachers.

Bill Tagg (Chapter 10) started life as a mathematics teacher, but since 1968 he has been employed full-time in computer education, a subject on which he has published extensively.

As director of the Microelectronics Education Programme's Chiltern Region, he is continuing the work he started in Hertfordshire in 1973 when the Advisory Unit for Computer-Based Education was set up as part of the county advisory service. He sees that role as being a co-ordinating one, encouraging and supporting other people. However, he still sometimes writes programs himself.

As director of the Advisory Unit for Computer-Based Education, he is also county adviser for computer education. In addition, he is examiner for two postgraduate courses in computer education, a GCE Advanced level moderator and member of a panel of the Council for National Academic Awards.

David R F Walker (Chapter 3) is a senior lecturer in geography at Loughborough University. After a first degree at Oxford and a teaching qualification at Cambridge he taught in secondary schools for seven years, followed by a further seven years in teacher training colleges. His first contact with computer-assisted learning was in 1973 when he undertook a survey on behalf of the Geographical Association on the potential uses of the computer for geography teaching. Since then he has directed the Geographical Association's Package Exchange (GAPE), and has been secretary and then chairman of the Association's Educational Computing Working Party. For several years he has directed research and development projects that have produced computer-assisted learning materials for use in schools. His other interests include educational simulations and games with and without computers. He has been secretary and chairman of the Society for the Advancement of Games and Simulation in Education and Training. His publications include articles on simulations and games, CAL and geography and he co-authored *Computer Assisted Learning in Geography* (CET 1980).

Part 6:
Glossary

Glossary

David Walker, Jacquetta Megarry and Howard Midgley

Note: Words in block capitals indicate principal cross references to further glossary items.

ACOUSTIC COUPLER A gadget which translates the audible sounds carried by a telephone into the digital signals used by a computer (and *vice versa*). By these means a computer can be linked to another computer through the telephone system. A similar job is performed by a MODEM.

ALGORITHM A clearly defined series of steps which will provide a solution to the problem for which it has been designed. Computer PROGRAMS employ algorithms to enable the computer to solve problems.

ANALOGUE A quantity which varies continuously like time or temperature, not discretely like the number of books in a library or fingers on a hand (which are DIGITAL). We can measure an analogue quantity like time by the movement of hands across a conventional clock face (analogue) or by digits on a modern electronic watch (digital).

ANIMATION The process whereby the computer repeatedly plots a picture on the screen so that the impression of movement of the picture is given.

ARTIFICIAL INTELLIGENCE Some computer programs perform tasks in such a way that if a human were to do the same thing, their behaviour would be described as intelligent. For example, programs can 'learn' from experience, play championship chess, converse in 'natural-sounding' English, prove theorems in geometry. See also the Turing Test for machine intelligence (page 17 in Megarry).

ASSEMBLER (or ASSEMBLY) LANGUAGE or CODE A low-level computer language which uses simple mnemonics instead of ordinary words to make the computer execute simple tasks. It is harder to write in than a high-level language, and is mostly used to control INPUT, OUTPUT and DISC operations and to perform animated GRAPHICS.

AUTHOR LANGUAGE A very high-level programming language designed to enable people without much experience or skill to write programs of a particular kind. Some writers use it to refer only to specialized CAI languages like PILOT, PLATO and COURSEWRITER which tend to encourage a specific style of programming. Others use it more generally to include advanced and conversational languages like LOGO.

BAR CODING A code consisting of vertical bars of varying width and spacing which can be read by a LIGHT PEN attached to a computer. They are also known as Zebra codes because of their appearance. Bar coded labels are now used on most grocery products for use with automated check-outs. Computer PROGRAMS can be turned into bar codes and distributed in the form of 'books' which can be 'read' into the computer using a light pen.

BASIC Beginners All-purpose Symbolic Instruction Code. A language which converts the instructions contained in the PROGRAM to a form which the computer can read and obey. It is the most widely used language for MICROCOMPUTERS.

BATCH PROCESSING A system of computer operation where no interaction with the user is required. This allows the computer to concentrate all its power on one PROGRAM until it is completed. Hence it is fast for the machine and useful in survey and research work but of limited value in the practice of education where INTERACTIVE use is generally preferable.

BINARY In general a binary choice offers only two alternatives: 1 or 0, 'on' or 'off', black or white. Binary numbers are expressed as powers of 2, unlike our usual counting system which is based on 10's. For example, 9 would be represented as 1001 in binary code. Deep down all computers work in binary.

BIT Short for BINARY digit. Represented in the computer as a 1 or 0 ('on' or 'off').

BUG An error in a PROGRAM or, more generally, in the logical processes leading to it.

BYTE A unit of MEMORY in which the computer can store one character, or piece of information. Thus a computer with 32K bytes of memory can store 32,000 characters, which is about five pages of this book. (See also K.)

CAI (See COMPUTER-AIDED INSTRUCTION)

CAL (See COMPUTER-ASSISTED LEARNING)

CHIP A small piece of silicon on which has been printed an integrated electrical circuit capable of processing and/or storing information. Its small size has enabled MICROCOMPUTERS to be developed. (See MICROPROCESSOR.)

CML (See COMPUTER-MANAGED LEARNING)

CODE The actual instructions which comprise the PROGRAM. The terms 'programming' and 'coding' are often used interchangeably.

COMPILER A PROGRAM inside the computer which converts a complete program written in HIGH-LEVEL LANGUAGE into the MACHINE CODE version which the computer can execute.

COMPUTER A machine which processes information electronically. See also MAINFRAME, MINICOMPUTER and MICROCOMPUTER.

COMPUTER-AIDED (or ASSISTED) INSTRUCTION (CAI) Where computers are used to guide the user through a prescribed course of learning and testing. The computer assumes the role of teacher, asking questions and assessing the user's responses.

COMPUTER-ASSISTED (or AIDED) LEARNING (CAL) Where teaching and learning in any part of the curriculum are aided by some application of the computer. The role of the computer can be as a teaching aid, or it can be more student-centred. The latter approach is becoming more significant with the spread of MICROCOMPUTERS.

COMPUTER-BASED LEARNING (CBL) See COMPUTER-ASSISTED LEARN-ING above.

COMPUTER LITERACY Often used generally to indicate awareness of computers and appreciation of their power and limitations. By analogy with book literacy it may denote skills like KEYBOARD familiarity, screen reading and information retrieval. Some writers use the term to mean the ability to use or even to program a computer. There is controversy over whether such skills are needed for computer literacy.

COMPUTER-MANAGED LEARNING (CML) The use of the computer to monitor, analyse and report on student's learning in an individualized curriculum.

COMPUTER-MANAGED INSTRUCTION The American equivalent of CML.

CONTENT-FREE CML A CML system which can be used with any subject matter.

CONTEXT-FREE CML A CML system which can be used in some way to support any method of learning.

COURSEWARE Educational material comprising SOFTWARE and DOCUMEN-TATION. Some writers use the term more specifically to mean COMPUTER-AIDED INSTRUCTION (CAI) materials.

CURSOR A symbol (sometimes flashing) which appears on the screen to show where the next character put in to the KEYBOARD will appear.

DATA Information; especially information that can be processed by the computer.

DATA BANK This is a collection of DATA in various forms, usually collected for use in education.

DATA BASE An organized collection of DATA, usually for analysis by a computer.

DATA BASE MANAGEMENT SYSTEM A set of PROGRAMS to allow the estab-lishment, sorting and searching of a DATA BASE stored in the computer. It usually also provides a procedure for producing reports and may have calculating facilities.

DATA PROCESSING One of the major roles performed by a computer. It makes use of the computer's power to handle and compare information and is educationally most useful in information retrieval.

DEBUG The process of removing BUGS (errors) from PROGRAMS. Seymour Papert and others have drawn attention to the heuristic value of debugging as a process which helps in problem solving.

DECISION RULES The rules, written by a CML system designer or a CML user, which govern the generation of individualized feedback in a CML system.

DECODER A gadget which translates the code used to transmit data (eg as broadcast television) into the code used by the computer.

DEDICATED Describes a computer which is designed for only one application, such as those that are found in washing machines.

DIALECT A variant of a computer LANGUAGE. All too often different manufac-turers offer slightly different versions of a language, which leads to a lack of PORT-ABILITY. This is a particularly serious problem with BASIC.

DIGITAL Relating to numbers (see ANALOGUE). Modern electronic devices usually operate on digital principles. Computers basically depend on representing information and instruction as a series of 1's and 0's (see BIT).

DIGITIZER A device connected to the computer which can detect and record the position of a pointer as a digital code. This facility can be used to record map outlines and engineering drawings for subsequent use by a computer PROGRAM.

DISC See FLOPPY DISC and HARD DISC.

DISC DRIVE A device which enables the computer to store and retrieve information on DISC. Disc drives may be single-sided or double-sided and can 'read' and 'write' information in varying densities (usually either 'single' or 'double' density).

DOCUMENTATION The written materials which accompany the computer PROGRAM, which instruct the user in its use, and provide additional information such as background details and ways in which the use of the program can be extended.

DOWNLOAD The process of transferring PROGRAMS or DATA from one computer directly into the MEMORY of another, usually smaller, computer. It can be done by telephone (using an ACOUSTIC COUPLER) or by TELESOFTWARE (using appropriate DECODERS).

EDITING The process of altering text, DATA or PROGRAMS by the insertion and deletion of characters from the KEYBOARD. Editing programs are useful for WORD PROCESSING, for revising and debugging programs and for DATA BASE MANAGEMENT.

ELECTRONIC OFFICE The use of computers and microelectronic devices to perform office functions such as WORD PROCESSING, DATA BASE MANAGEMENT and accounting and copying. It also includes the transfer of documents between offices by telecommunications.

ERROR MESSAGE A message produced by the computer system when it detects an error made by the user. They are often cryptic and can be discouraging to the novice user.

FIRMWARE Intermediate between HARDWARE and SOFTWARE. It is the name given to the connections that can be made on a semi-permanent basis within the computer. The term is also used for PROGRAMS that are distributed as a plug-in memory unit.

FLOPPY DISC A thin flexible disc, coated with magnetic particles, used to store DATA and PROGRAMS. It is contained within a protective paper sleeve within which it revolves. 'Standard' discs are 8 inches in diameter and the more common 'mini' disc is 5¼ inches. A mini disc could hold around 15 to 20 pages of this book.

FORTRAN The earliest HIGH-LEVEL LANGUAGE, FORmula TRANslation is still widely used on MAINFRAME computers for scientific and graphic applications.

FRAME GRABBER A PROGRAM which 'grabs' information from a television camera and turns it into a form which can be displayed and analysed by a computer.

GAMES PADDLE A rotating knob, similar to a volume control on a radio. It is used instead of the KEYBOARD to feed information into the computer. For example the paddles can be used like joysticks to draw pictures or to control the movement of objects on the screen – for example a Space Invader or a droplet of oil in a simulated physics experiment.

GATE One of the fundamental units of the microprocessor; when it carries a charge it will prevent a current passing, and when the charge has been released the current is able to flow. The use of this device is fundamental to all the processes in the computer.

GOTO A statement used freely in BASIC programming which sends control to another part of the PROGRAM. It is considered by purists to indicate a lack of structure in the design of the program and is used as an argument for replacing BASIC with more structured languages.

GRAPHICS Computers can draw pictures and diagrams as well as text on the screen. RESOLUTION varies according to the MEMORY available. MICROCOMPUTERS usually offer LOW or MEDIUM RESOLUTION GRAPHICS.

HANDS-ON The direct interaction with the computer by the user, normally by means of the KEYBOARD.

HARD DISC External computer MEMORY with much greater capacity than a FLOPPY DISC (50 to 5000 times as much). Hard disc units are more expensive than FLOPPY DISC drives and the discs cannot usually be removed. WINCHESTER hard discs are small sealed units often used with MICROCOMPUTERS.

HARDWARE The computer equipment and its associated PERIPHERALS which comprise a computer system (as opposed to the SOFTWARE which tells it what to do).

HIGH-LEVEL LANGUAGE See PROGRAMMING LANGUAGE.

HIGH RESOLUTION GRAPHICS GRAPHICS which are resolved to individual picture cells of about 500 down by 500 across so that the individual cells are difficult to distinguish. This gives really convincing curves and lines, and can produce a crude 'photographic' image. They use a lot of MEMORY and processing power.

INFORMATICS A term that is used to describe all aspects of the processing of information by machine. It is thought to be a more precise definition than computing which refers back to the times when the major use of the computer was for mathematical computation.

INFORMATION TECHNOLOGY The technology which surrounds the storage and retrieval of information (see DATA BASE, VIDEOTEX, WORD PROCESSING).

INTERACTIVE A style of computing in which the user and the program interact with each other as opposed to BATCH PROCESSING. The difference is like that between a telephone and correspondence by mail. Most CAL is now interactive, though batch processing is still used for administrative applications like timetabling and marks processing.

INTERFACE A piece of equipment which enables computers and/or PERIPHERALS to be connected to each other.

K short for Kilo, but in computer circles actually just over a thousand ($2^{10} = 1024$). When used to describe a computer's memory (as in '32K RAM') it means a kilobyte (see also BYTE).

KEYBOARD A set of keys, similar to those on an electric typewriter, which enables the user to communicate directly with the computer.

KEYPAD A set of keys, similar to those on a calculator.

LANDSAT A series of survey satellites capable of transmitting digital data about radiation from the earth in four different wavebands. It is possible to process this data by computer to produce simulated photographs of quite high resolution.

LANGUAGE See PROGRAMMING LANGUAGE.

LEARNING CYCLE The cycle of learning frequently encountered in CML. Successive steps are to select a learning task, study the task, take a test, receive feedback from the computer including a prescription or recommendation for the next task.

LIGHT PEN A pen-like device which can be pressed against the screen to provide INPUT without using the KEYBOARD. The computer can detect what the pen is pointed at so the user can choose an option from a list or enter a shape (eg a map).

LINE-PRINTER See PRINTER.

LOGO A powerful and easily learned PROGRAMMING LANGUAGE which has been developed by Seymour Papert at the Massachusetts Institute of Technology and used to develop learning through programming and debugging. It has recently been implemented on MICROCOMPUTERS. For examples of its applications see Chapters 6 and 17 and Papert, 1980.

LOW-LEVEL LANGUAGE See PROGRAMMING LANGUAGE.

LOW-RESOLUTION GRAPHICS GRAPHICS which any computer can produce resolved to individual picture cells of about 40 across to 20 down, suitable for blocks, bar charts and crude diagrams.

LSE Langage Symbolique d'Enseignement (literally: a symbolic teaching language). Developed by Hebenstreit (see Chapter 12) to facilitate the easy transfer of educational COURSEWARE from one MICROCOMPUTER to another. More structured than BASIC, it is the standard CAL language used in France.

MACHINE CODE The sequence of BINARY numbers which the computer can understand. All PROGRAMS written in computer languages have to be converted into machine code at some stage.

MAINFRAME A large multi-purpose computer, usually serving the needs of a large community of both local and remote users. Each user communicates with the computer either through a TIME-SHARING TERMINAL or through a BATCH PROCESSING system.

MEDIUM RESOLUTION GRAPHICS GRAPHICS which are resolved to individual picture cells of about 200 down by 300 across, suitable for fairly fine lines and recognizable circles.

MEGABYTE Measure used for the MEMORY capacity of a computer. One megabyte represents approximately one million stored alphabetic characters. This is much more than current MICROCOMPUTERS, or even large computers, can hold in internal memory. But external memory capacities of several megabytes are now becoming available for microcomputers and can be provided on WINCHESTER disc drives. The cost of these is now low enough for them to be purchased for educational use.

MEMORY Computers store some PROGRAMS and DATA inside them for immediate use while they are switched on. This is internal memory which is limited but quickly accessed. Computers can also store programs and data permanently in external memory, which can be much more extensive though it takes longer to retrieve from DISCS and *much* longer from cassettes. (See RAM and ROM.)

MICROCOMPUTER A compact portable computer based on MICROPROCESSORS and silicon chips. It can be operated wherever there is electric power, or even by battery, and is often used by just one person or for a single purpose. Microcomputers have become fairly cheap – from £50 to £500 – though the PERIPHERALS needed to use them (eg DISC DRIVES, PRINTERS) may cost more.

MICROELECTRONICS The branch of electronics which deals with very small voltages and currents. Usually in connection with silicon chip technology. (See MICROPROCESSOR, RAM AND ROM.)

MICROFICHE A photographic representation of text or graphic data in microscopic form, needing a special machine to examine it. It is now both possible and convenient for computers to produce their results directly in this form and the advantages of reduced storage needs are thought to outweigh the need for special microfiche readers. They are widely used in connection with the production of reports from major information retrieval systems.

MICROPROCESSOR A silicon chip containing the components needed to perform the operations determined by a PROGRAM. Microprocessors are now used in all computers and in control applications in industry and in the house (eg robot welding machines, washing machines and cameras).

MINICOMPUTER A computer which is smaller than a MAINFRAME, but which has similar facilities, such as TIME-SHARING. A minicomputer may be part of a larger system.

MODEM Performs the same functions as an ACOUSTIC COUPLER, but is directly wired to the telephone system instead of using the handset.

MULTI-USER SYSTEMS Enable many users from different TERMINALS to use the same computer. Common on MAINFRAMES, but much less on MICROCOM-PUTERS which mostly do not have enough power to handle more than one user at a time.

NETWORK A system which allows computers (and their PERIPHERALS) to communicate with each other using wires, fibres or broadcasting.

NETWORK INTERFACE A device which allows computers and PERIPHERALS to link into a NETWORK.

ON-LINE Now a rather dated concept but once used to distinguish active connection to a computer through a TERMINAL as opposed to the then conventional way of preparing punched cards off-line and then entering them directly into the computer.

OPERATING SYSTEM The PROGRAM used by a computer to enable it to load a HIGH-LEVEL LANGUAGE and to control its communication with the user and with PERIPHERALS like DISC DRIVES and PRINTERS.

OUTPUT A general term for any result produced by the computer. Output can be in the form of voice, printed paper (print-out), magnetic tape, etc.

PAPER TAPE A continuous narrow strip of paper with punched holes used as a means of storing information and PROGRAMS. This can be 'read' by the computer. It used to be a widespread method for sending programs from one computer to another.

PERIPHERALS The 'plug-in' components which enable a computer to receive, store and transmit information. The more common peripherals are a VISUAL DISPLAY UNIT, PRINTER and DISC DRIVE.

PERSONAL COMPUTER See MICROCOMPUTER.

PLATO (Programmed Learning At a Terminal On-line). A CAI system and AUTHOR LANGUAGE developed at the University of Urbana-Champaign, Illinois and by Control Data Corporation. It is very powerful but has so far only been available on expensive hardware.

PORTABILITY The extent to which a PROGRAM can be run on different computer systems. This term essentially refers to the program itself, and not to the means of storage (eg DISC) in which it is contained. A highly portable program will run successfully on many computer systems. Unfortunately a disc can only be 'read' by the type of computer on which it was 'written'.

PRINTER A piece of equipment which, when connected to a computer, enables its OUTPUT to be printed on paper. Some printers are capable of printing characters only, while others are also capable of printing GRAPHICS.

PRINT-OUT The results produced by the computer on paper.

PROGRAM A set of instructions, written in a computer language, eg BASIC, FORTRAN. It is these instructions which instruct the computer to perform the specified tasks. A computer without a program is like a gramophone without a record (see SOFTWARE).

PROGRAMMING LANGUAGE The language in which the PROGRAM is written. There are many such languages, of which BASIC is the most common in domestic and educational use. Others include FORTRAN, COBOL, ALGOL and Pascal. HIGH-LEVEL LANGUAGES resemble natural language or mathematical notation whereas LOW-LEVEL LANGUAGES are closer to MACHINE CODE.

PUNCHED CARD Thin cards, on which combinations of small holes have been punched as a means of storing and entering information and PROGRAMS. The standard punched card can hold up to 80 characters. Now only found on a few MAIN-FRAME installations.

QUERY An information retrieval program produced by Hertfordshire Advisory Unit for Computer Based Learning.

RAM (RANDOM ACCESS MEMORY) That part of the computer's memory which stores PROGRAMS and DATA temporarily. The information is erased when the power is switched off.

RESIDENT A PROGRAM which is always present in the computer, usually stored in ROM.

RESOLUTION A measure of the fineness with which lines can be drawn on the screen. A colour transparency is high resolution, a TV picture is medium resolution and a newspaper photograph is lower resolution still. By computer standards, however, all are high – see LOW, MEDIUM AND HIGH RESOLUTION GRAPHICS.

ROM (READ ONLY MEMORY) Memory which can only be 'read' not 'written on' (see RAM). It is used to store PROGRAMS which are used frequently, or which are needed before other programs can be implemented. ROM can be plugged into a computer and is sometimes used as a way of distributing programs (especially games).

ROUTING The process of steering an individual student on a unique course through modularized curriculum.

SCREEN DIGITIZING A technique for turning a shape placed over the VDU screen into DIGITAL form suitable for processing by the computer. This can be done by directing the CURSOR around a transparency of the shape either with GAME PADDLES or with the KEYBOARD.

SECOND PROCESSOR An additional processor which can handle the computation while the first handles transfers of information from the KEYBOARD and to the PERIPHERALS. It enables the computer to work much faster.

SIMULATION The process of representing the real world in some easily manageable form. Educational simulations simplify the real world to some extent to assist learning. Simulated experiments allow students to interpret the results of an experiment that would be too difficult, dangerous, expensive, or time-consuming to carry out 'for real'. Computer simulations may produce graphic or mathematical models, and for research purposes are often quite complex.

16-BIT PROCESSOR This processes 16 BITS at once. Most MICROPROCESSORS in use handle only eight bits simultaneously and are slower and can directly access much less internal MEMORY than a 16-bit processor.

SOFTWARE Computer PROGRAMS and DATA.

STORAGE DEVICES Covers both internal RAM and ROM and external DISC and cassette MEMORY.

STRUCTURED PROGRAMMING A method of programming whereby the computer PROGRAM consists of clearly labelled and defined sections, each of which performs a specific task. A standard structure enables quite complex programs to be read and understood.

STUDENT PROFILE The computer-stored record of information about each individual student registered on a CML system.

SUM CHECK A procedure to check that the total number of digits transmitted in each block is correct. When using a telephone link it allows the automatic re-transmission of a block if an error is detected.

TELEPRINTER Similar to a TELETYPE, but only able to receive information.

TELESOFTWARE A new development which allows SOFTWARE to be transmitted directly into a computer's MEMORY over a distance by telephone (using VIEWDATA) or television (using TELETEXT). The computer receiving the PROGRAM needs a suitable DECODER.

TELETEXT An information system which is broadcast as part of a television transmission. A suitable DECODER enables the information to be displayed on a domestic television screen. Unlike VIEWDATA services, telesoftware is basically a one-way transmission of information.

TELETYPE A rather crude electric typewriter that can be connected to a computer and used for INTERACTIVE computing. Both the users' entries and the responses made by the computer are typed on a continuous roll of paper.

TERMINAL A piece of equipment containing a KEYBOARD with a PRINTER and/or a VDU, which enables the user to communicate with a computer (usually a MAINFRAME or MINICOMPUTER). The terminal may be distant from the computer (see TIME-SHARING).

TIME-SHARING A system which lets a number of people have INTERACTIVE use of a single computer at the same time. Each user should have the illusion of sole use of the computer, though if the system is overloaded or inefficient there may be delays in response.

TOUCH-(SENSITIVE) SCREEN A VDU screen which is able to detect the position of the user's finger. This can be used to enable users who are not familiar with the use of the KEYBOARD to pick selections from a menu of choices.

TRANSFERABILITY The extent to which a PROGRAM will be run on another computer. This implies PORTABILITY, but it also involves the ease of use by a novice and depends on good DOCUMENTATION.

TRAP Part of a computer PROGRAM which prevents the user from entering information which is irrelevant or wrong, and which prevents the computer from giving one of its own ERROR MESSAGES, which are not usually easy for the user to understand. A trap will usually inform the user of his mistake and invite him to make another attempt at typing in the information.

USER-FRIENDLY Describes an interactive PROGRAM which gives helpful and informative messages to guide the user. More generally used to describe any computer SOFTWARE, system or environment which is friendly and accessible to the user.

VDU See VISUAL DISPLAY UNIT.

VIDEODISC A device which stores digital information on a DISC about the size of a gramophone record. The initial application is for replaying television quality material through a domestic television set. The fact that enough information for one hour of video can be stored on a disc indicates the enormous storage potential if used for text, DATA or PROGRAMS. Access to sections of the disc can be under the control of computer program also contained on the disc so it has great potential for the development of educational materials.

VIDEOTEX A method of receiving electronic digital information at a distance and displaying it on a screen. Videotex can be transmitted by telephone lines (VIEWDATA) or broadcasting (TELETEXT).

VIEWDATA The transmission of digital information by the use of the telephone system, linking DATA BASES on large MAINFRAME systems to local users. VIEWDATA systems may be public (like Prestel and Antiope) or private (like the Open University's Optel). Unlike the TELETEXT services, Viewdata is INTERACTIVE, and the user can make choices, answer questions and order information or goods using a KEYPAD.

VISUAL DISPLAY UNIT (VDU) A television-like screen, (black and white or colour), which displays the output of the computer.

WEIGHTING The multiplication of a test score by some factor before it is added to an item, sub-total or total score.

WINCHESTER A type of HARD DISC which packs DATA very tightly and has to be sealed against the entry of dust.

WORD PROCESSING A powerful technique for EDITING, storing and rearranging text. The text is stored magnetically (on a DISC or in MEMORY) until it is ready for the final PRINT-OUT. Word processing can be performed either by a dedicated word processor (purpose built) or by general-purpose computers. Although MICROCOMPUTERS can be used for word processing, a disc-based system is almost essential.

Index